Essential Business Letters:

1500 Ways to Say it Right

. . . . .

By the Editors of Socrates

SOCRATES™
KNOW HOW TO DO MORE
AND SAVE

Socrates Media, LLC
227 West Monroe, Suite 500
Chicago, IL 60606
www.socrates.com

Special discounts on bulk quantities of Socrates books and products are available to corporations, professional associations and other organizations. For details, contact our Special Sales Department at 800.378.2659.

This publication is designed to provide accurate and authoritative information in regard to the subject matter covered. It is sold with the understanding that the publisher is not engaged in rendering legal, accounting or other professional service. If legal advice or other expert assistance is required, the services of a competent professional person should be sought.

From a Declaration of Principles Jointly Adopted by a Committee of the American Bar Association and a Committee of Publishers and Associations

ISBN 1-59546-241-4

This product is not intended to provide legal or financial advice or substitute for the advice of an attorney or advisor.

Printing number 10 9 8 7 6 5 4 3 2 1

Essential Business Letters:

1500 Ways to Say it Right

· · · · ·

By the Editors of Socrates

Special acknowledgment to the following:

Jane Jerrard, Managing Editor; Michele Freiler, Associate Editor; Matt Gronwold, Editor; Chip Butzko, Encouragement Press, Production; Jeannie Staats, Product Manager; Peri Hughes, Editor; Alison Somilleda, Copy Editor; Kristen Grant, Production Associate; Edgewater Editorial Services, Inc.

Get the most out of Essential Business Letters: 1500 Ways to Say it Right

The enclosed CD contains a read-only version of this book, Microsoft® Word versions of all of the letters in this book, the Socrates Personal Law and Business Law dictionaries as well as instructions to link to the dedicated resource section of Socrates.com:

www.socrates.com/books/BusinessLetters.aspx.

Use the 8-digit registration code provided on the CD to register your purchase at Socrates.com. Once registered, you will have access to more than $100 worth of FREE letters and writing aids.

Your registration also provides you with special discounts on selected Socrates products, designed to save you time and money with your Personal, Business and Real Estate matters.

Table of Contents

· · · · ·

Section One

. . . . .

Letter Perfect:
A General Overview
of Business Letters

Introduction

· · · · · ·

If you are uncomfortable when it comes to drafting formal business communications, have trouble phrasing delicate information or simply lack the time to write every letter from scratch, then this is the book for you.

In addition to finding three different versions of more than 200 business letters, you can start here, with this section, and learn the basics of formatting, writing, proofreading and sending your letters. You will find electronic versions of all of the letters on the enclosed CD.

What Is on the CD?

On the enclosed CD, you will have three different versions of every letter in this book: a long version, a short version and an e-mail version. All can be copied to your computer's hard drive so that you can customize each for your own purposes.

In addition, readers will have full access to the Socrates Personal Law and Business Law Dictionaries written specifically to improve your understanding of key business and legal terms.

What Is on the Resource Page Online?

On the dedicated Resource Page online, you will find a list of abbreviations for addresses; grammar and punctuation tips; a list of frequently misused words; and a list of Web resources for finding people. In addition, more letters are provided for personal and business use: Collection Letters; Poor Service Action Letters; Consumer Demand and Complaint Letters; Essential Airline Letters and more.

In addition to the information in this book and on the accompanying CD, you can visit **Socrates.com** for continually updated information on business letters.

When to Send a Letter

In this day and age, when e-mail and instant messages vie with cell phones and text messages for the fastest, briefest communications, why mail a hard copy business letter? It is obvious that some situations call for more formality or for creating a definite paper trail. When you apply for a job, it is not typically acceptable to send a brief e-mail. You send a complete cover letter with resume, because this not only conveys more information, it is more impressive and follows a business precedent for how such applications are made. Likewise, businesses and their customers, vendors and employees sometimes expect or appreciate certain communications in writing.

All of the letters in this book provide specific examples of such communications. Nearly all of them have e-mail versions, but you will see that these e-mails are more formal and precise than casual ones.

A Word about Paper

All of your business communications should be printed on your company letterhead, including second-sheet letterhead if you have it. Good letterhead should include complete contact information for your company—if not you, specifically—including the

Web site. You should also use matching, pre-printed envelopes with your company name and return address. Ideally, you will use standard #10 envelopes and larger envelopes in case you mail packets of information.

If you are sending a business e-mail, your signature must stand in for letterhead. If your e-mail program allows you to set up a signature, you will end each e-mail message automatically with this signature. Otherwise, you should either type it in each time or cut and paste from a preset document. Your e-mail signature should include:

- your name
- your complete title
- your company name
- your direct phone number
- your e-mail address
- your company Web site

Including this information at the end of each e-mail provides the recipient with vital information he or she might not otherwise have.

Formatting Facts

All of the letters in this book, and on the accompanying CD, use what is called a block-style format. In a block-style format, each line, from the date through the postscript, is flush with the left margin. The paragraphs in the body of the letter are not indented. Leaf through the pages of the book to see what a block-style format looks like.

Alternatively, you can use a modified block-style format. In this format, the date line and the closing and signature lines are deeply indented so that the end of each line is nearly at the right margin. You may want to use this style if your company letterhead provides more blank space at the upper and lower right than it does on the left side. Here is an example of a modified block-style letter:

January 13, 2008

Ricardo Garcia
Director of Finance
Medi-Stock, Inc.
592 Wells St.
Topeka, KS 66921

Dear Mr. Garcia:

This letter is in response to your request for three credit references for Occupational Health, Inc. I have attached a list of four of our current suppliers, along with contact information for our bank. All references have been alerted that you or someone from your company will be contacting them.

Please let me know if you require any additional information in order to provide us with a line of credit from Medi-Stock. Otherwise, I will look forward to hearing from you regarding our new payment arrangements.

Sincerely,

Daniel J. Rak
Chief Financial Officer

Your other option is a semiblock-style format. This format is identical to a modified block-style, but each paragraph in the body of the letter is indented five letter spaces. Here is an example of a semiblock-style format:

January 13, 2008

Ricardo Garcia
Director of Finance
Medi-Stock, Inc.
592 Wells St.
Topeka, KS 66921

Dear Mr. Garcia:

    This letter is in response to your request for three credit references for Occupational Health, Inc. I have attached a list of four of our current suppliers along with contact information for our bank. All references have been alerted that you or someone from your company will be contacting them.

    Please let me know if you require any additional information in order to provide us with a line of credit from Medi-Stock. Otherwise, I will look forward to hearing from you regarding our new payment arrangements.

Sincerely,

Daniel J. Rak
Chief Financial Officer

Tip

If you do not have a specific name for a recipient, using a generic title on your salutation line is best, as in "Dear Customer Service Representative." If this is not appropriate, use "To Whom It May Concern:" or "Dear Sir or Madam:" either of which should cover all contingencies.

Note the spacing of the elements is the same in each format. A formal business letter will use the following line spacing:

- one line space between the date and the recipient's name;
- one line space between the last line of the recipient's address and the salutation line;
- one line space between the salutation line and the body of the letter;
- one line space between the body of the letter and the sign-off;
- four line spaces between the sign-off and the sender's typed name (for a written signature); and
- one or two line spaces between the sender's title and additional information, which may include a postscript, enclosures, references and copy information.

Saying Goodbye

There are many ways to end a business letter. It is best to choose a sign-off that suits your personality and the tone you typically use. Then use that sign-off for all business letters you write in order to provide consistency. Here are some sign-offs to choose from:

- Sincerely,
- Sincerely yours,
- Respectfully,
- Respectfully yours,
- Kindest regards,
- Best regards,
- Cordially,

Watch Your Tone

When you are composing your own letter or e-mail, it is important to read it over carefully and make sure your words or tone will not be misunderstood. This is particularly important in e-mail communications, which are usually quickly typed and sent. A brief message composed on the fly like this can be read as being abrupt and rude when it is not meant to be. Some letters suffer from the same problem. If possible, have a colleague review your letter before you finalize it to make sure your message is getting across.

Tips on Proofreading

Always proofread your letter or e-mail before you send it. You cannot count on your computerized spell-checker program to catch everything. Carefully read over the letter at least twice. If you are too familiar with it to read it word by word, start at the end and read each line backward, checking each word for misspellings. If possible, have another person read it over for typos, misspellings and grammar usage.

How to Send Your Letter

Most letters can be sent through regular postal mail. However, if a letter is urgent, or you want to be 100 percent certain that it is received, you can use U.S. Postal Service Registered Mail™ or a private shipping company like UPS™ or FedEx®—or a messenger service, if the recipient is local.

> **Tip**
>
> Note that Express Mail® from the U.S. Postal Service does not guarantee delivery within a specific time frame and is not guaranteed to arrive like registered mail is.

Consider spending a little more money for Registered Mail, or for shipping a letter, in the following cases:

- when you need to ensure delivery of time-sensitive information by a specific date or time, such as submitting an order for products you need right away;
- when you need to legally prove that the recipient accepted your letter, such as a letter of termination to an employee; or

- when you want to show the recipient how important this communication is, such as an extra-sensitive communication with a dissatisfied customer.

This book is organized into sections to help you find the type of letter you are looking for. You can also use the Table of Contents to look up specific letters. Remember—all letters are on the enclosed CD. Use any or all of the letters as templates to create your own effective business letters.

Section Two
.....
Essential Finance Letters

Inquiry Regarding Loan Application

Purpose

- To request information from a bank or other lending institution about applying for a loan

Alternative Purposes

- To request information from your own bank about loans
- To request information from the Small Business Administration about applying for a loan
- To request information about grants from a nonprofit organization

January 23, 2008

Business Loan Officer
Greater Newark Financial
4921 S. Des Plaines Ave.
Newark, NJ 09358

Dear Business Loan Officer:

My company, Occupational Health Inc., is seeking funding to help us expand our services over the next year. I understand that your institution provides loans for small businesses.

Occupational Health Inc. is a privately owned corporation based in Newark that was founded by the chief executive officer and me in 2005. Last year we had a net profit of more than $92,000. We are seeking a $500,000 to $750,000 loan.

Please send me all applicable information on your loans for companies like ours. Specifically, I would like to know how your loan process works, what information the application requires and, perhaps most important, what your payment terms are.

If you need more details about Occupational Health Inc. in order to provide appropriate information, please do not hesitate to contact me at 555.555.5555.

Thank you and I look forward to hearing from you soon.

Sincerely,

Daniel J. Rak
Chief Financial Officer

If you are requesting information from your current bank:

My company, Occupational Health Inc., has been a customer of yours for the past 4 years. Your bank handles all our accounts, and now we are looking to you as a possible loan source. We are seeking funding to help us expand our services over the next year.

If you are requesting information about grants from a nonprofit organization:

… I understand that your institution provides grants for small businesses.

Occupational Health Inc. is a privately owned corporation based in Newark that was founded by the chief executive officer and me in 2005. Last year we had a net profit of more than $92,000. We are seeking approximately $500,000 to $750,000 in funding to provide physical therapy services to low-income individuals with inadequate health insurance coverage.

Please send me all applicable information on your grants for programs like ours, along with an application.

If you are requesting information from the Small Business Administration:

Please send me all applicable Small Business Administration brochures, forms and other documentation necessary to learn about your loan programs and submit the correct application.

E-Mail

Dear Business Loan Officer:

I am writing to request information on your loans to small businesses. My company, Occupational Health Inc., is seeking funding to help us expand our services over the next year.

Occupational Health Inc. is a privately owned corporation based in Newark that was founded by the chief executive officer and me in 2005. Last year we had a net profit of more than $92,000.

We are seeking a $500,000 to $750,000 loan.

Please send me all applicable information on your loans for companies like ours. Specifically, I would like to know how your loan process works, what information the application requires and, perhaps most important, what your payment terms are.

If you need more details about Occupational Health Inc. in order to provide appropriate information, please do not hesitate to contact me.

Thank you and I look forward to hearing from you soon.

Sincerely,

<e-mail signature, including name, title, company and contact information>

Cover Letter for Loan Application

Purpose

- To highlight the reasons your company should receive a loan

Alternative Purposes

- To request that the lender expedite your loan application
- To notify the lender that your loan application is incomplete
- To highlight the reasons your company should receive a grant from a nonprofit organization

---

If you are submitting an incomplete loan application:

Enclosed please find an application for a loan for the Newark-based Occupational Health Inc. Please note that the application does not include any business references; I will forward this information to you as soon as possible. I have not been able to notify my choices because our industry trade show is taking place right now in Europe. Once our references return to the office and I give them advance notice that you will be contacting them, I will send their information to you directly.

If you are submitting an application for a grant:

Enclosed please find an application for a Community Health Grant for the Newark-based Occupational Health Inc. I believe that we have provided all the information and references you need to confirm that our program is an excellent candidate for your community funding.

If you are asking the lender to expedite your application:

Enclosed please find an application for a loan for the Newark-based Occupational Health Inc. We have already begun our expansion project, and it would be a tremendous help to us if you could expedite the processing of our application by the end of the month.

February 12, 2008

Business Loan Officer
Greater Newark Financial
4921 S. Des Plaines Ave.
Newark, NJ 09358

Dear Business Loan Officer:

Enclosed please find an application for a loan for the Newark-based Occupational Health Inc. I believe that we have provided all the information and references you need to confirm that our company is an excellent candidate for a commercial loan from your bank.

I would like to point out that we own our office building at 392 W. May St. and that our financial history is very sound. I believe in being fiscally conservative both with our continued growth and with our cash reserves.

Once you have looked over our application, please let me know if you need more information. I would be happy to meet with you in person or you can call me at 555.555.5555.

I hope to hear good news about the loan soon.

Sincerely,

Daniel J. Rak
Chief Financial Officer

E-Mail

Dear Business Loan Officer:

Attached please find an application for a loan for the Newark-based Occupational Health Inc. Please confirm that you have received it and can open the attachment.

I believe that we have provided all the information and references you need to confirm that our company is an excellent candidate for a commercial loan from your bank.

I would like to point out that we own our office building at 392 W. May St. and that our financial history is very sound. I believe in being fiscally conservative both with our continued growth and with our cash reserves.

Once you have looked over our application, please let me know if you need more information. I would be happy to meet with you in person or you can respond to this message.

I hope to hear good news about the loan soon.

Sincerely,

<e-mail signature, including name, title, company and contact information>

Inquiry Requesting Commercial Line of Credit

Purpose

- To request a line of credit for your business from a current supplier or vendor

Alternative Purposes

- To request a line of credit from a first-time supplier
- To offer references and an application for a line of credit
- To respond to a cash on delivery (c.o.d.) shipment with a request for a line of credit

---

February 12, 2008

Laura L. Anderson
Director of Sales
Medi-Stock Inc.
592 Wells St.
Topeka, KS 66921

Dear Ms. Anderson:

Occupational Health Inc. has been ordering medical supplies from your company regularly for 6 months now. Since we placed our first order with you for $2,300 in sterilization equipment, we have paid for every shipment either in advance or, on rare occasions, upon delivery, spending a total of $24,750 to date.

From this point forward, we would prefer to be billed for our Medi-Stock orders. Therefore, I am requesting that you open a $10,000 line of credit for Occupational Health Inc., allowing us to move to a payment-on-invoice system.

If you require further information or references on our company, I would be happy to supply anything you need. You can contact me at 555.555.5555 or fax a credit application to my attention at 555.555.5555.

Thank you in advance for your help with this matter.

Sincerely,

Daniel J. Rak
Chief Financial Officer

If you are responding to a c.o.d. shipment:

Today our warehouse received a c.o.d. shipment from your company, and it took us some time and trouble to get a check cut. I would like to request that we use an invoice system for future shipments.

If you are requesting a line of credit from a first-time supplier:

We would like to purchase a large quantity of your sterilization supplies. Your catalog states that you require payment in advance, but I am writing to request that you set up an ongoing line of credit for Occupational Health Inc. with 30-day payment terms.

Occupational Health Inc. is a privately owned corporation based in Newark that was founded by the chief executive officer and me in 2005. Last year we grossed approximately $750,000 and had a net profit of more than $92,000.

If you are offering references and an application:

I have enclosed a document that outlines a brief history of our company, a list of our financial holdings (including bank accounts) and three business references. Please let me know if you need further information to change our payment terms.

E-Mail

Dear Ms. Anderson:

As you are aware, Occupational Health Inc. has been ordering medical supplies from your company regularly for 6 months now and has spent a total of $24,750 to date.

Since we placed our first order with you for $2,300 in sterilization equipment, we have paid for every shipment either in advance or upon delivery.

We would prefer to be billed for our Medi-Stock orders. Therefore, I am requesting that you open a $10,000 line of credit for Occupational Health Inc., allowing us to move to a payment-on-invoice system.

If you require further information or references on our company, I would be happy to supply anything you need. You can respond to this e-mail or fax a credit application to my attention at 555.555.5555.

Thank you in advance for your help with this matter.

<e-mail signature, including name, title, company and contact information>

Inquiry Requesting Extended Line of Credit

Purpose

- To request more credit or better terms for your business from a current supplier

Alternative Purposes

- To request an extended line of credit from a first-time supplier
- To offer references and an application for an extended line of credit
- To ask your bank for an extended line of credit

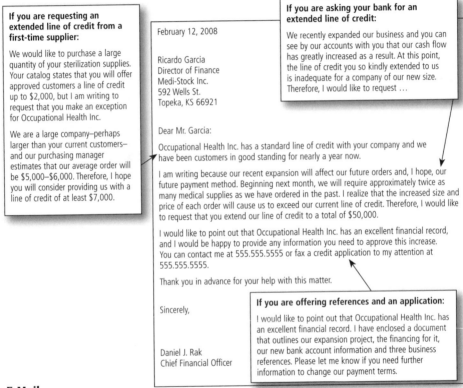

If you are requesting an extended line of credit from a first-time supplier:

We would like to purchase a large quantity of your sterilization supplies. Your catalog states that you will offer approved customers a line of credit up to $2,000, but I am writing to request that you make an exception for Occupational Health Inc.

We are a large company—perhaps larger than your current customers—and our purchasing manager estimates that our average order will be $5,000–$6,000. Therefore, I hope you will consider providing us with a line of credit of at least $7,000.

If you are asking your bank for an extended line of credit:

We recently expanded our business and you can see by our accounts with you that our cash flow has greatly increased as a result. At this point, the line of credit you so kindly extended to us is inadequate for a company of our new size. Therefore, I would like to request …

February 12, 2008

Ricardo Garcia
Director of Finance
Medi-Stock Inc.
592 Wells St.
Topeka, KS 66921

Dear Mr. Garcia:

Occupational Health Inc. has a standard line of credit with your company and we have been customers in good standing for nearly a year now.

I am writing because our recent expansion will affect our future orders and, I hope, our future payment method. Beginning next month, we will require approximately twice as many medical supplies as we have ordered in the past. I realize that the increased size and price of each order will cause us to exceed our current line of credit. Therefore, I would like to request that you extend our line of credit to a total of $50,000.

I would like to point out that Occupational Health Inc. has an excellent financial record, and I would be happy to provide any information you need to approve this increase. You can contact me at 555.555.5555 or fax a credit application to my attention at 555.555.5555.

Thank you in advance for your help with this matter.

Sincerely,

Daniel J. Rak
Chief Financial Officer

If you are offering references and an application:

I would like to point out that Occupational Health Inc. has an excellent financial record. I have enclosed a document that outlines our expansion project, the financing for it, our new bank account information and three business references. Please let me know if you need further information to change our payment terms.

E-Mail

Dear Mr. Garcia:

Occupational Health Inc. has a standard line of credit with your company and we have been customers in good standing for nearly a year now.

I am writing because our recent expansion will affect our future orders and, I hope, our future payment method. Beginning next month, we will require approximately twice as many medical supplies as we have ordered in the past.

I realize that the increased size and price of each order will cause us to exceed our current line of credit. Therefore, I would like to request that you extend our line of credit to a total of $50,000.

I would like to point out that Occupational Health Inc. has an excellent financial record, and I would be happy to provide any information you need to approve this increase. You can respond to this e-mail or fax a credit application to my attention at 555.555.5555.

Thank you in advance for your help with this matter.

Sincerely,

<e-mail signature, including name, title, company and contact information>

Letter to Bank Noting Error

Purpose

- To point out an error in a company bank account in writing and for the record

Alternative Purposes

- To point out a repeated error on the part of the bank
- To point out an error on the part of your company
- To point out poor or incomplete service from the bank

If you are pointing out an error on the part of your company:

Our records indicate that on January 29, we deposited three checks totaling $2,345 in our checking account. However, the statement shows a total of $2,435. Because our accounts receivables department did not log in the individual checks when we received them, we have no record of how much each check was for. Is it possible for you to supply any additional information on each of these checks, such as photocopies?

March 6, 2008

Carla Dinatale
Corporate Customer Representative
Bank of West Allis
8309 Lawrence Ave.
Lincoln, NE 72910

If you are pointing out a repeated error:

We continue to have problems with our account statements from your bank. Several times in the past 2 months, a member of my accounting department has visited your branch in person to sort out discrepancies in our accounts; now, faced with the third such error—and a more expensive one—I am addressing this problem personally. On our last monthly statement ...

Dear Miss Dinatale:

On our last monthly statement from Bank of West Allis, there appears to be an error regarding our corporate checking account (#8291023).

Our records indicate that on January 29, we deposited three checks totaling $2,345 in our checking account. This deposit was made in person at your Lawrence Ave. branch. However, it does not show up on our statement. I have a printed receipt for the deposit and have enclosed a photocopy of it.

Please check your records and verify that this deposit will be credited to our account as soon as possible.

I would like to hear back from you in person on this matter. When you have it resolved, please contact me at 555.555.5555.

Sincerely,

Elliott Rothenberg
Director of Accounting

If you are pointing out poor or incomplete service:

Members of my accounting department have had numerous problems dealing with your bank's tellers and other branch employees who work with the public. All automated functions, such as direct deposit, after-hours deposit and online banking, seem to be efficient and accurate. However, several times—perhaps more than I know of—one of the tellers at your Lawrence Ave. branch has made an error in counting or attributing funds for deposit.

For now, I have asked my staff to avoid depositing funds in person. This seems like a poor solution, but I would like to have the problem resolved before we have to spend more time correcting your errors.

E-Mail

Dear Miss Dinatale:

On our last monthly statement from Bank of West Allis, there appears to be an error regarding our corporate checking account (#8291023).

Our records indicate that on January 29, we deposited three checks totaling $2,345 in our checking account. This deposit was made in person at your Lawrence Ave. branch. However, it does not show up on our statement. I have a printed receipt for the deposit and can send you a copy if you like.

Please check your records and verify that this deposit will be credited to our account as soon as possible.

I would like to hear back from you in person on this matter. When you have it resolved, please call me at 555.555.5555.

Sincerely,

<e-mail signature, including name, title, company and contact information>

Letter to Bank Requesting Change to or Addition of Accounts

Purpose

- To request that your bank make a change to your existing business accounts

Alternative Purposes

- To request one or more additional accounts
- To request a change in authorization
- To make a second request for a change to your accounts

If you are requesting a change in authorization:

Please delete the name of Simon Garrison from all applicable lists of guarantors for Gentry. Mr. Garrison has left our employment, so I would appreciate your prompt action on this. I will come in next week with our new chief executive officer, Renee Wheeler, to have her established as an additional guarantor.

If you are requesting an additional account:

We would like to open a second checking account for petty cash purposes. Please use $2,000 out of our current checking account (#8291023) to create a separate account with the same parameters and authorities. We will need the checks for this account shipped to us no later than April 15.

If you are making a second request for a change:

I spoke with you last month about adding a feature to the current accounts you hold for Gentry Men's Clothing Stores. I have not seen any correspondence from you regarding this change, so I am following up with a request in writing. If you check your records …

March 6, 2008

Carla Dinatale
Corporate Customer Representative
Bank of West Allis
8309 Lawrence Ave.
Lincoln, NE 72910

Dear Miss Dinatale:

Please consider this letter a formal request from Gentry Men's Clothing Stores for a change in our accounts with you. If you will check your records, you will see that I am the authorized contact on all accounts for Gentry.

We would like to have the capability of transferring monies from our lockbox account (#592190) to the money market account that I set up late last year. We would prefer to be able to transfer funds to the account electronically. If your Web technology does not support this, then we would like to be able to transfer funds with a phone call, using proper authorities, of course.

Please send me written confirmation when this change has been implemented.

Thank you in advance for taking care of this. Please do not hesitate to call me at 555.555.5555 if you need any more information or other means of confirmation.

Sincerely,

Elliott Rothenberg
Director of Accounting

E-Mail

Dear Miss Dinatale:

I spoke with you on the phone about changing the capabilities on our accounts.

Please consider this message a formal request from Gentry Men's Clothing Stores for a change in our accounts with you.

We would like to have the capability of transferring monies from our lockbox account (#592190) to the money market account that I set up late last year. We would prefer to be able to transfer funds to the account electronically. If your Web technology does not support this, then we would like to be able to transfer funds with a phone call, using proper authorities, of course.

Please send me confirmation when this change has been implemented.

Thank you in advance for taking care of this. Please do not hesitate to contact me if you need any more information or other means of confirmation.

Sincerely,

<e-mail signature, including name, title, company and contact information>

Letter to Bank Terminating Accounts

Purpose

- To alert your bank that you plan to terminate one or more accounts

Alternative Purposes

- To alert your bank that you are closing all investment accounts
- To alert your bank that you are terminating all accounts
- To alert your bank that you are unhappy with their service and are ending your business relationship

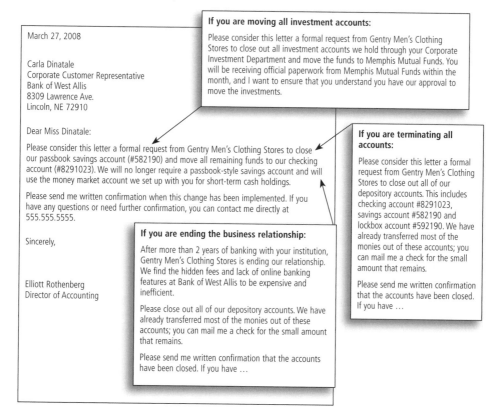

March 27, 2008

Carla Dinatale
Corporate Customer Representative
Bank of West Allis
8309 Lawrence Ave.
Lincoln, NE 72910

Dear Miss Dinatale:

Please consider this letter a formal request from Gentry Men's Clothing Stores to close our passbook savings account (#582190) and move all remaining funds to our checking account (#8291023). We will no longer require a passbook-style savings account and will use the money market account we set up with you for short-term cash holdings.

Please send me written confirmation when this change has been implemented. If you have any questions or need further confirmation, you can contact me directly at 555.555.5555.

Sincerely,

Elliott Rothenberg
Director of Accounting

If you are moving all investment accounts:

Please consider this letter a formal request from Gentry Men's Clothing Stores to close out all investment accounts we hold through your Corporate Investment Department and move the funds to Memphis Mutual Funds. You will be receiving official paperwork from Memphis Mutual Funds within the month, and I want to ensure that you understand you have our approval to move the investments.

If you are terminating all accounts:

Please consider this letter a formal request from Gentry Men's Clothing Stores to close out all of our depository accounts. This includes checking account #8291023, savings account #582190 and lockbox account #592190. We have already transferred most of the monies out of these accounts; you can mail me a check for the small amount that remains.

Please send me written confirmation that the accounts have been closed. If you have …

If you are ending the business relationship:

After more than 2 years of banking with your institution, Gentry Men's Clothing Stores is ending our relationship. We find the hidden fees and lack of online banking features at Bank of West Allis to be expensive and inefficient.

Please close out all of our depository accounts. We have already transferred most of the monies out of these accounts; you can mail me a check for the small amount that remains.

Please send me written confirmation that the accounts have been closed. If you have …

E-Mail

Dear Miss Dinatale:

I spoke with you on the phone about closing our savings account.

Please consider this message a formal request from Gentry Men's Clothing Stores to close our passbook savings account (#582190) and move all remaining funds to our checking account (#8291023).

We will no longer require a passbook-style savings account and will use the money market account we set up with you for short-term cash holdings.

Please send me written confirmation when this change has been implemented. Please contact me directly if you have any questions or need further confirmation.

Sincerely,

<e-mail signature, including name, title, company and contact information>

Letter Providing Credit References

Purpose

- To provide requested credit references for your business and to stress your organization's excellent credit and financial situation

Alternative Purposes

- To provide unsolicited credit references for your business
- To provide updated or additional credit references for your business
- To provide credit references along with a credit application

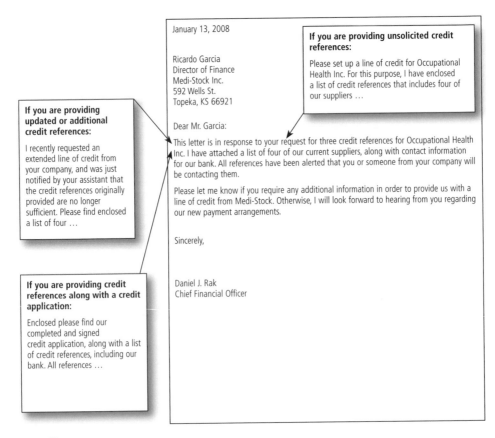

January 13, 2008

If you are providing unsolicited credit references:

Please set up a line of credit for Occupational Health Inc. For this purpose, I have enclosed a list of credit references that includes four of our suppliers ...

Ricardo Garcia
Director of Finance
Medi-Stock Inc.
592 Wells St.
Topeka, KS 66921

If you are providing updated or additional credit references:

I recently requested an extended line of credit from your company, and was just notified by your assistant that the credit references originally provided are no longer sufficient. Please find enclosed a list of four ...

Dear Mr. Garcia:

This letter is in response to your request for three credit references for Occupational Health Inc. I have attached a list of four of our current suppliers, along with contact information for our bank. All references have been alerted that you or someone from your company will be contacting them.

Please let me know if you require any additional information in order to provide us with a line of credit from Medi-Stock. Otherwise, I will look forward to hearing from you regarding our new payment arrangements.

Sincerely,

If you are providing credit references along with a credit application:

Enclosed please find our completed and signed credit application, along with a list of credit references, including our bank. All references ...

Daniel J. Rak
Chief Financial Officer

E-Mail

Dear Mr. Garcia:

This message is in response to your request for credit references for Occupational Health Inc.

I have attached a PDF of a list of four of our current suppliers, along with contact information for our bank. All references have been alerted that you or someone from your company will be contacting them.

Please let me know if you require any additional information in order to provide us with a line of credit from Medi-Stock.

Otherwise, I will look forward to hearing from you regarding our new payment arrangements.

Sincerely,

<e-mail signature, including name, title, company and contact information>

Customer Letter Noting Payment Terms

Purpose

- To explain your company's payment terms to a customer

Alternative Purposes

- To explain your company's payment terms before an order is placed
- To accompany an invoice to be paid before delivery
- To accompany an invoice to be paid within 30 days

March 1, 2008

Tina Edmundsen
Purchasing Agent
Arrowdyne Industries
2817 W. Waveland Ave.
Falls Church, VA 18305

Dear Ms. Edmundsen:

Thank you for your order dated February 23. We are delighted to welcome you as a customer of Recycled Metal Inc.

After you have become an established customer with a solid payment history, we will accept a purchase order from your company. But for now, I will need some payment information from you before we can process your order.

You have two payment options: You can pay by credit card or by check or money order. I have attached a copy of your order form. Please fill in the bottom section with your credit card information, or if you prefer, you can mail this copy along with a check for the full amount to the address at the top of the form.

If you have any questions, please feel free to contact me at 555.555.5555. I am in charge of your company's account and will be happy to guide you through the ordering process.

Sincerely,

Christopher J. Jamison
Customer Service Representative

If you are explaining payment terms before an order is placed:

Thank you for your interest in purchasing recycled aluminum and other metals from our company. I have enclosed a brochure that outlines our products, prices and delivery options.

After you have become an established customer with a solid payment history, we will accept a purchase order from your company. But for your first few orders, I will need some payment information from you.

If you are sending an invoice to be paid before delivery:

After you have become an established customer with a solid payment history, we will accept a purchase order from your company. But for now, I have enclosed an invoice for your order. You have two payment options: You can pay by credit card or by check or money order. As soon as payment is received, we will begin processing your order.

If you are sending an invoice to be paid in 30 days:

Enclosed please find an invoice for your order, payable within 30 days. You have two payment options: You can pay by credit card or by check or money order.

E-Mail

Dear Ms. Edmundsen:

Thank you for your order dated February 23. We are delighted to welcome you as a customer of Recycled Metal Inc.

After you have become an established customer with a solid payment history, we will accept a purchase order from your company. But for now, I will need some payment information from you before we can process your order.

You have two payment options: You can pay by credit card or by check or money order. I have attached a PDF of your order form. Please print it out and fill in the bottom section with your credit card information. If you prefer, you can mail this copy along with a check for the full amount to the address at the top of the form. Either way, for security reasons, please mail a hard copy of the form to my attention rather than responding to this e-mail.

If you have any questions, please feel free to contact me. I am in charge of your company's account and will be happy to guide you through the ordering process.

Sincerely,

<e-mail signature, including name, title, company and contact information>

Letter Stating or Reiterating Policies to Customer

Purpose

- To introduce a new customer to your company's relevant policies

Alternative Purposes

- To restate your policies to an existing customer
- To respond to a customer's question regarding your policies
- To refuse a customer request due to your policies

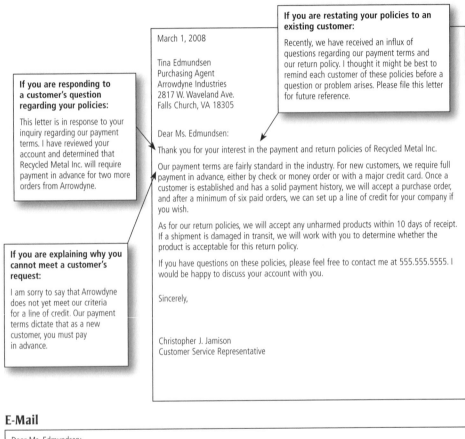

If you are restating your policies to an existing customer:

Recently, we have received an influx of questions regarding our payment terms and our return policy. I thought it might be best to remind each customer of these policies before a question or problem arises. Please file this letter for future reference.

If you are responding to a customer's question regarding your policies:

This letter is in response to your inquiry regarding our payment terms. I have reviewed your account and determined that Recycled Metal Inc. will require payment in advance for two more orders from Arrowdyne.

If you are explaining why you cannot meet a customer's request:

I am sorry to say that Arrowdyne does not yet meet our criteria for a line of credit. Our payment terms dictate that as a new customer, you must pay in advance.

March 1, 2008

Tina Edmundsen
Purchasing Agent
Arrowdyne Industries
2817 W. Waveland Ave.
Falls Church, VA 18305

Dear Ms. Edmundsen:

Thank you for your interest in the payment and return policies of Recycled Metal Inc.

Our payment terms are fairly standard in the industry. For new customers, we require full payment in advance, either by check or money order or with a major credit card. Once a customer is established and has a solid payment history, we will accept a purchase order, and after a minimum of six paid orders, we can set up a line of credit for your company if you wish.

As for our return policies, we will accept any unharmed products within 10 days of receipt. If a shipment is damaged in transit, we will work with you to determine whether the product is acceptable for this return policy.

If you have questions on these policies, please feel free to contact me at 555.555.5555. I would be happy to discuss your account with you.

Sincerely,

Christopher J. Jamison
Customer Service Representative

E-Mail

Dear Ms. Edmundsen:

Thank you for your interest in the payment and return policies of Recycled Metal Inc.

Our payment terms are fairly standard in the industry:

- For new customers, we require full payment in advance, either by check or money order or with a major credit card.
- Once a customer is established and has a solid payment history, we will accept a purchase order.
- After a minimum of six paid orders and a review of the account, we can set up a line of credit for your company.

As for our return policies, we will accept any unharmed products within 10 days of receipt. If a shipment is damaged in transit, we will work with you to determine whether the product is acceptable for this return policy.

If you have questions on these policies, please feel free to contact me.

Sincerely,

<e-mail signature, including name, title, company and contact information>

Reply to Request for Credit—Acceptance

Purpose

- To inform a business customer that he or she has been approved to receive credit from your company

Alternative Purposes

- To inform a customer that you require additional information in order to approve him or her
- To inform a customer that he or she has been approved to receive credit with certain limitations
- To inform an individual that he or she has been approved to receive credit from your company

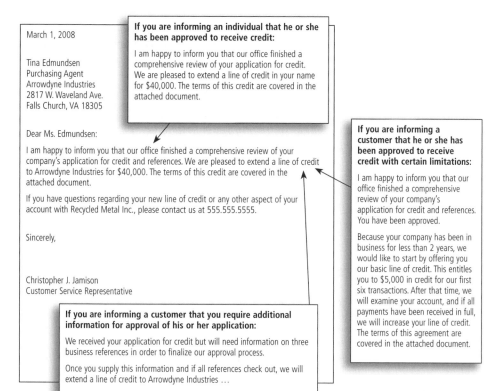

March 1, 2008

Tina Edmundsen
Purchasing Agent
Arrowdyne Industries
2817 W. Waveland Ave.
Falls Church, VA 18305

Dear Ms. Edmundsen:

I am happy to inform you that our office finished a comprehensive review of your company's application for credit and references. We are pleased to extend a line of credit to Arrowdyne Industries for $40,000. The terms of this credit are covered in the attached document.

If you have questions regarding your new line of credit or any other aspect of your account with Recycled Metal Inc., please contact us at 555.555.5555.

Sincerely,

Christopher J. Jamison
Customer Service Representative

If you are informing an individual that he or she has been approved to receive credit:

I am happy to inform you that our office finished a comprehensive review of your application for credit. We are pleased to extend a line of credit in your name for $40,000. The terms of this credit are covered in the attached document.

If you are informing a customer that he or she has been approved to receive credit with certain limitations:

I am happy to inform you that our office finished a comprehensive review of your company's application for credit and references. You have been approved.

Because your company has been in business for less than 2 years, we would like to start by offering you our basic line of credit. This entitles you to $5,000 in credit for our first six transactions. After that time, we will examine your account, and if all payments have been received in full, we will increase your line of credit. The terms of this agreement are covered in the attached document.

If you are informing a customer that you require additional information for approval of his or her application:

We received your application for credit but will need information on three business references in order to finalize our approval process.

Once you supply this information and if all references check out, we will extend a line of credit to Arrowdyne Industries …

E-Mail

Dear Ms. Edmundsen:

I am happy to inform you that our office finished a comprehensive review of your company's application for credit and references. We are pleased to extend a line of credit to Arrowdyne Industries for $40,000. The terms of this credit are covered in the attached PDF.

If you have questions regarding your new line of credit or any other aspect of your account with Recycled Metal Inc., please do not hesitate to contact me.

Sincerely,

<e-mail signature, including name, title, company and contact information>

Reply to Request for Credit—Rejection

Purpose

- To inform a business customer that he or she will not receive credit from your company

Alternative Purposes

- To inform a customer that you do not offer credit
- To inform a customer that you will issue credit with a guarantor
- To inform an individual that he or she will not receive credit from your company

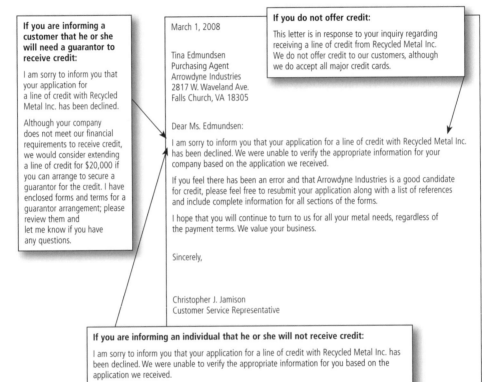

If you are informing a customer that he or she will need a guarantor to receive credit:

I am sorry to inform you that your application for a line of credit with Recycled Metal Inc. has been declined.

Although your company does not meet our financial requirements to receive credit, we would consider extending a line of credit for $20,000 if you can arrange to secure a guarantor for the credit. I have enclosed forms and terms for a guarantor arrangement; please review them and let me know if you have any questions.

March 1, 2008

Tina Edmundsen
Purchasing Agent
Arrowdyne Industries
2817 W. Waveland Ave.
Falls Church, VA 18305

Dear Ms. Edmundsen:

I am sorry to inform you that your application for a line of credit with Recycled Metal Inc. has been declined. We were unable to verify the appropriate information for your company based on the application we received.

If you feel there has been an error and that Arrowdyne Industries is a good candidate for credit, please feel free to resubmit your application along with a list of references and include complete information for all sections of the forms.

I hope that you will continue to turn to us for all your metal needs, regardless of the payment terms. We value your business.

Sincerely,

Christopher J. Jamison
Customer Service Representative

If you do not offer credit:

This letter is in response to your inquiry regarding receiving a line of credit from Recycled Metal Inc. We do not offer credit to our customers, although we do accept all major credit cards.

If you are informing an individual that he or she will not receive credit:

I am sorry to inform you that your application for a line of credit with Recycled Metal Inc. has been declined. We were unable to verify the appropriate information for you based on the application we received.

If you feel there has been an error and that you are a good candidate for credit, please feel free to resubmit your application along with a list of references and include complete information for all sections of the forms.

E-Mail

Dear Ms. Edmundsen:

I am sorry to inform you that Arrowdyne Industries' application for a line of credit with Recycled Metal Inc. has been declined.

We were unable to verify the appropriate information for your company based on the application we received.

If you feel there has been an error and that Arrowdyne Industries is a good candidate for credit, please feel free to resubmit your application along with a list of references and include complete information for all sections of the forms.

I hope that you will continue to turn to us for all your metal needs, regardless of the payment terms. We value your business.

Sincerely,

<e-mail signature, including name, title, company and contact information>

Letter Requesting Additional Financial Information on a Customer

Purpose

- To request that a customer supply missing information on his or her credit application

Alternative Purposes

- To request correct or updated contact information for references
- To request information that is additional to the standard requirements
- To follow up on an initial request for additional information

---

February 23, 2008

Tina Edmundsen
Purchasing Agent
Arrowdyne Industries
2817 W. Waveland Ave.
Falls Church, VA 18305

Dear Ms. Edmundsen:

I received Arrowdyne Industries' application for credit from Recycled Metal Inc. and passed it on to our financial department for processing. I have been told that your application is incomplete and cannot be processed until additional information has been provided.

It seems that there is information missing from section three of the application, which covers your company's bank accounts. I have attached a copy of the original form; please fill in the third section, complete with contact information for your bank(s) and relevant account numbers. You can fax the completed form directly to our financial department to the attention of Credit Application Processing at 555.555.5555.

The sooner you can supply this information, the sooner we can process your application and, I hope, offer you a line of credit sufficient to your purchasing needs with Recycled Metal Inc.

Sincerely,

Christopher J. Jamison
Customer Service Representative

If you are following up on an initial request for additional information:

Nearly 2 weeks ago, I wrote to you to request some missing information on Arrowdyne Industries' application for credit from Recycled Metal Inc. If you are still interested in receiving a line of credit from us, please supply the information below.

If you are requesting information that is additional to the standard requirements

... financial department for processing. It seems that because Arrowdyne's credit history barely meets our requirements for credit, we will need one final piece of information in order to consider extending a basic line of credit.

Please use the attached form to supply us with contact information for your bank(s) ...

If you are requesting correct contact information for references:

It seems that we cannot locate two of your business references using the contact information supplied on the application. Please forward correct telephone numbers and/or e-mail addresses for Sally Winkler at William Mason Manufacturing and for Randolph Russell at Ensign Motors. You can fax that information directly to our financial department to the attention of Credit Application Processing at 555.555.5555.

E-Mail

Dear Ms. Edmundsen:

I received Arrowdyne Industries' application for credit from Recycled Metal Inc. and passed it on to our financial department for processing.

I have been told that your application is incomplete and cannot be processed until additional information has been provided.

It seems that there is information missing from section three of the application, which covers your company's bank accounts. I have attached a PDF of the original form; please fill in the third section, complete with contact information for your bank(s) and relevant account numbers.

You can fax the completed form directly to our financial department to the attention of Credit Application Processing at 555.555.5555.

The sooner you can supply this information the sooner we can process your application and, I hope, offer you a line of credit sufficient to your purchasing needs with Recycled Metal Inc.

Sincerely,

<e-mail signature, including name, title, company and contact information>

Letter Requesting Credit References for a Customer

Purpose

- To formally request business references from a customer as part of your credit check

Alternative Purposes

- To request personal references for a credit check of an individual consumer
- To request correct or updated contact information for references
- To follow up on an initial request for references

If you are requesting correct contact information for references:

It seems that we cannot locate two of the business references you provided us on February 19. Please forward correct telephone numbers and/or e-mail addresses for Sally Winkler at William Mason Manufacturing and for Randolph Russell at Ensign Motors. You can fax that information directly to our financial department to the attention of Credit Application Processing at 555.555.5555.

If you are requesting personal references from an individual customer:

In order to process your request, we will need contact information for three credit references. Please supply all information, including a contact name and title, direct phone number, company name and complete mailing address for three companies or individuals who can verify your financial status. These references may include your bank, a current or recent landlord and your employer.

If you are following up on an initial request for additional information:

Nearly 2 weeks ago, I wrote to you to request business references for Arrowdyne Industries in order to process your request for a line of credit from Recycled Metal Inc. If you are still interested in receiving a line of credit from us, please supply the information below.

February 23, 2008

Tina Edmundsen
Purchasing Agent
Arrowdyne Industries
2817 W. Waveland Ave.
Falls Church, VA 18305

Dear Ms. Edmundsen:

Thank you for your interest in setting up a line of credit from Recycled Metal Inc.

In order to process your request, we will need contact information for three credit references. Please supply all information, including a contact name and title, direct phone number, company name and complete mailing address for three businesses from which Arrowdyne currently purchases materials.

The enclosed form contains instructions and return information.

Our financial department will contact each of these references immediately after receiving the information. Once they have ascertained your good standing, I will notify you of our decision.

Again, I thank you for your interest and would like to remind you that you can now order from us with a check or credit card while you wait for your application for credit to be approved.

Sincerely,

Christopher J. Jamison
Customer Service Representative

E-Mail

Dear Ms. Edmundsen:

Thank you for your interest in setting up a line of credit from Recycled Metal Inc.

In order to process your request, we will need contact information for three credit references. Please supply all information, including a contact name and title, direct phone number, company name and complete mailing address for three businesses from which Arrowdyne currently purchases materials.

The attached PDF form contains instructions and return information.

Our financial department will contact each of these references immediately after receiving the information. Once they have ascertained your good standing, I will notify you of our decision.

Again, I thank you for your interest and would like to remind you that you can now order from us with a check or credit card while you wait for your application for credit to be approved.

Sincerely,

<e-mail signature, including name, title, company and contact information>

Letter to Customer's References Requesting Information

Purpose

- To officially ask a customer's business reference to verify the customer's good standing

Alternative Purposes

- To ask a bank to verify account information as part of your credit check
- To ask a reference who has already responded for additional information
- To ask a reference for a telephone interview

February 27, 2008

Sally Winkler
Accounts Receivable
William Mason Manufacturing
481 N.W. Stockton Dr.
Wilmington, DE 22739

Dear Ms. Winkler:

Tina Edmundsen, the purchasing agent with Arrowdyne Industries in Falls Church, Virginia, listed you as a credit reference for her company.

We would appreciate it if you could provide some information on Arrowdyne. The enclosed form should take only a few minutes to complete, and you can fax it back to us toll-free at 555.555.5555. There is space at the bottom to write in additional information on this customer, and it would be helpful to us if you can take the time to do so.

Thank you in advance for your time in providing this important information. I am sure that your contacts at Arrowdyne will appreciate it, as do we here at Recycled Metals Inc.

Sincerely,

Christopher J. Jamison
Customer Service Representative

If you are asking a bank to verify account information:

Tina Edmundsen, the purchasing agent with Arrowdyne Industries in Falls Church, Virginia, has given her permission on the enclosed Deposit Verification Form for you to release information to us regarding Arrowdyne's accounts.

We would appreciate it if you could fill out the enclosed form and fax it back to us toll-free at 555.555.5555.

If you are asking a reference for additional information:

As you may recall, you recently provided me with some credit information on Arrowdyne Industries in Falls Church, Virginia.

Upon examining the form you returned to us, I find that we are missing some crucial information on Arrowdyne's payment history with you. I have enclosed a copy of the form so that you can provide this history.

If you are requesting a telephone interview:

… some information on Arrowdyne in a brief telephone interview. I will call you next week for a 5- or 10-minute conversation about Arrowdyne's history of transactions with your company. I have just a few short questions and believe it will be most convenient for both of us if we speak on the phone.

E-Mail

Dear Ms. Winkler:

Tina Edmundsen, the purchasing agent with Arrowdyne Industries in Falls Church, Virginia, listed you as a credit reference for her company.

We would appreciate it if you could provide some information on Arrowdyne.

The attached PDF form should take only a few minutes to complete. Please print it out, complete it and fax it back to us toll-free at 555.555.5555.

There is space at the bottom to write in additional information on this customer—it would be helpful to us if you can take the time to do so.

Thank you in advance for your time in providing this important information. I am sure that your contacts at Arrowdyne will appreciate it, as do we here at Recycled Metals Inc.

Sincerely,

<e-mail signature, including name, title, company and contact information>

Letter Notifying Customer That His or Her Credit Card Has Been Declined

Purpose

- To inform a current customer that his or her credit card was declined

Alternative Purposes

- To notify a customer that the credit card you have on file has expired
- To notify a customer that the credit card information he or she provided is incorrect
- To notify a customer that you are canceling his or her order because his or her card was declined

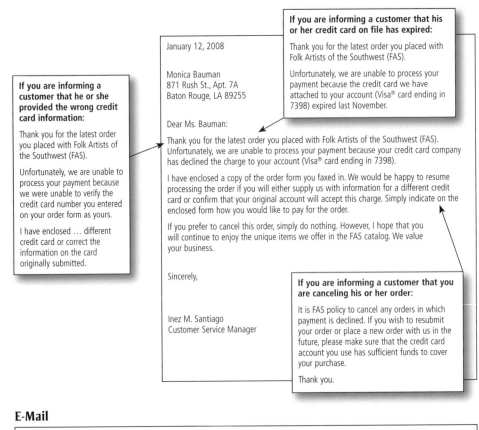

If you are informing a customer that his or her credit card on file has expired:

Thank you for the latest order you placed with Folk Artists of the Southwest (FAS).

Unfortunately, we are unable to process your payment because the credit card we have attached to your account (Visa® card ending in 7398) expired last November.

If you are informing a customer that he or she provided the wrong credit card information:

Thank you for the latest order you placed with Folk Artists of the Southwest (FAS).

Unfortunately, we are unable to process your payment because we were unable to verify the credit card number you entered on your order form as yours.

I have enclosed … different credit card or correct the information on the card originally submitted.

January 12, 2008

Monica Bauman
871 Rush St., Apt. 7A
Baton Rouge, LA 89255

Dear Ms. Bauman:

Thank you for the latest order you placed with Folk Artists of the Southwest (FAS). Unfortunately, we are unable to process your payment because your credit card company has declined the charge to your account (Visa® card ending in 7398).

I have enclosed a copy of the order form you faxed in. We would be happy to resume processing the order if you will either supply us with information for a different credit card or confirm that your original account will accept this charge. Simply indicate on the enclosed form how you would like to pay for the order.

If you prefer to cancel this order, simply do nothing. However, I hope that you will continue to enjoy the unique items we offer in the FAS catalog. We value your business.

Sincerely,

Inez M. Santiago
Customer Service Manager

If you are informing a customer that you are canceling his or her order:

It is FAS policy to cancel any orders in which payment is declined. If you wish to resubmit your order or place a new order with us in the future, please make sure that the credit card account you use has sufficient funds to cover your purchase.

Thank you.

E-Mail

Dear Ms. Bauman:

Thank you for your latest order on the Folk Artists of the Southwest (FAS) Web site. Unfortunately, we are unable to process your payment because your credit card company has declined the charge to your account (Visa® card ending in 7398).

We would be happy to resume processing the order if you will either supply us with information for a different credit card or confirm that your original account will accept this charge. Simply indicate on your saved online order form how you would like to pay for the order.

If you prefer to cancel this order, simply do nothing. However, I hope that you will continue to enjoy the unique items we offer in the FAS catalog. We value your business.

Sincerely,

<e-mail signature, including name, title, company and contact information>

Letter Notifying Customer That His or Her Bank Account Has Insufficient Funds

Purpose

- To inform a current customer that his or her account will not cover a purchase

Alternative Purposes

- To notify a customer that his or her check contained the wrong information
- To notify a customer that you will no longer accept his or her personal checks
- To notify a customer that you are canceling his or her order because of insufficient funds

If you are informing a customer that he or she provided the wrong information on his or her check:

Thank you for the latest order you placed with Folk Artists of the Southwest (FAS). However, we are unable to fulfill your order because the check you enclosed (#00382367464) was made out to the wrong company.

… processing the order if you will supply a new check with the correct information.

January 12, 2008

Monica Bauman
871 Rush St., Apt. 7A
Baton Rouge, LA 89255

Dear Ms. Bauman:

Thank you for the latest order you placed with Folk Artists of the Southwest (FAS). However, we are unable to fulfill your order because the check you enclosed (#00382367464) could not be processed due to insufficient funds.

I have enclosed a copy of the order form you faxed in. We would be happy to resume processing the order if you will either supply us with a money order for the full amount ($385.42) or provide a credit card number. Simply indicate on the enclosed form how you would like to pay for the order.

If you prefer to cancel this order, simply do nothing. However, I hope that you will continue to enjoy the unique items we offer in the FAS catalog. We value your business.

Sincerely,

Inez M. Santiago
Customer Service Manager

If you are informing a customer that you will no longer accept his or her personal checks:

It is FAS policy to stop acceptance of personal checks after a single incident like this. If you would like us to resume processing the order and for all future FAS orders, please supply us with a money order or provide a credit card number.

If you are informing a customer that you are canceling his or her order:

It is FAS policy to cancel any orders for which payment cannot be made immediately. If you wish to resubmit your order or place a new order with us in the future, please make sure that the account you use has sufficient funds to cover your purchase.

E-Mail

Dear Ms. Bauman:

We are unable to fulfill your latest order with FAS because the check you enclosed (#00382367464) with your order form could not be processed due to insufficient funds.

We would be happy to resume processing the order if you will either supply us with a money order for the full amount ($385.42) or provide a credit card number.

If you prefer to cancel this order, simply do nothing. However, I hope that you will continue to enjoy the unique items we offer in the FAS catalog. We value your business.

Sincerely,

<e-mail signature, including name, title, company and contact information>

Letter Notifying Customer That His or Her Payment Is Late or Incomplete

Purpose

- To address the problem of a payment that is incomplete

Alternative Purposes

- To notify a customer that his or her payment is late
- To notify a customer that he or she has paid too much
- To notify a customer that he or she owes money for a cash on delivery (c.o.d.) shipment

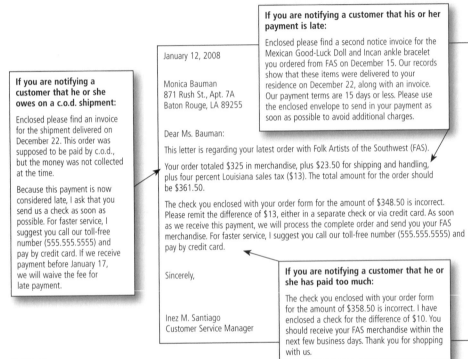

If you are notifying a customer that his or her payment is late:

Enclosed please find a second notice invoice for the Mexican Good-Luck Doll and Incan ankle bracelet you ordered from FAS on December 15. Our records show that these items were delivered to your residence on December 22, along with an invoice. Our payment terms are 15 days or less. Please use the enclosed envelope to send in your payment as soon as possible to avoid additional charges.

If you are notifying a customer that he or she owes on a c.o.d. shipment:

Enclosed please find an invoice for the shipment delivered on December 22. This order was supposed to be paid by c.o.d., but the money was not collected at the time.

Because this payment is now considered late, I ask that you send us a check as soon as possible. For faster service, I suggest you call our toll-free number (555.555.5555) and pay by credit card. If we receive payment before January 17, we will waive the fee for late payment.

January 12, 2008

Monica Bauman
871 Rush St., Apt. 7A
Baton Rouge, LA 89255

Dear Ms. Bauman:

This letter is regarding your latest order with Folk Artists of the Southwest (FAS).

Your order totaled $325 in merchandise, plus $23.50 for shipping and handling, plus four percent Louisiana sales tax ($13). The total amount for the order should be $361.50.

The check you enclosed with your order form for the amount of $348.50 is incorrect. Please remit the difference of $13, either in a separate check or via credit card. As soon as we receive this payment, we will process the complete order and send you your FAS merchandise. For faster service, I suggest you call our toll-free number (555.555.5555) and pay by credit card.

Sincerely,

Inez M. Santiago
Customer Service Manager

If you are notifying a customer that he or she has paid too much:

The check you enclosed with your order form for the amount of $358.50 is incorrect. I have enclosed a check for the difference of $10. You should receive your FAS merchandise within the next few business days. Thank you for shopping with us.

E-Mail

Dear Ms. Bauman:

This message is regarding your latest order from Folk Artists of the Southwest (FAS), for which we received an incorrect payment.

The total cost of your order is $361.50, as broken down here:

$325.00 in merchandise
$ 23.50 for shipping and handling
$ 13.00 in sales tax (four percent in Louisiana)
$361.50

The check you enclosed with your order form was for $348.50.

Please remit the difference of $13 either in a separate check or via credit card.

As soon as we receive this payment, we will process the complete order and send you your FAS merchandise. For faster service, I suggest you call our toll-free number (555.555.5555) and pay by credit card.

Sincerely,

<e-mail signature, including name, title, company and contact information>

Letter of Collection—Initial Friendly Reminder (30 Days Overdue)

Purpose

- To politely notify a customer that his or her payment is overdue

Alternative Purposes

- To notify a first-time customer that payment is overdue
- To notify a long-time customer in good standing that payment is overdue
- To notify a chronically late-paying customer that payment is overdue

If you are notifying a first-time customer that payment is overdue:

On February 1, you received your first completed print job from ASAP Printing. I hope you are satisfied with the quality of the materials and with your service from us. I did notice that payment …

March 4, 2008

Vernon Allen
Accounting Department
Connecticut Construction Co.
4900 N. Federal Pl.
Stamford, CT 28499

Dear Mr. Allen:

You received shipment of 10,000 copies of Connecticut Construction's new Winter 2008 Brochure in early February, and I hope that you are finding them helpful in your marketing efforts. However, I notice that payment for our printing of this brochure is overdue.

I have enclosed a copy of the invoice in case you do not have the original. Please note the payment terms outlined at the bottom of the page; our standard requirement is full payment within 30 days of receipt. The invoice is dated January 28, making your payment due last week.

I am sure that you will take care of this overdue invoice immediately. However, if there are circumstances that prevent you from doing so, I would appreciate it if you would let me know personally. You can reach me at 555.555.5555.

If I do not hear from you, I will expect a check for $5,329.43 by March 10.

Sincerely,

Karen J. Greene
Accounts Receivable Manager

If you are notifying a long-time customer in good standing that payment is overdue:

On February 1, you received the latest in a long line of print jobs from ASAP Printing. In the past, you have been very prompt in paying for our shipments. However, I notice that payment …

If you are notifying a chronically late-paying customer that payment is overdue:

On February 1, you received the latest in a long line of print jobs from ASAP Printing. I know that your accounting department is not always able to process our payments as quickly as we would like, and I notice that payment for this brochure is now overdue.

E-Mail

Dear Mr. Allen:

You received shipment of 10,000 copies of Connecticut Construction's new Winter 2008 Brochure in early February and I hope that you are finding them helpful in your marketing efforts.

However, I notice that payment for our printing of this brochure is overdue.

I have attached a PDF of the invoice in case you do not have the original. Please note the payment terms outlined at the bottom of the page; our standard requirement is full payment within 30 days of receipt. The invoice is dated January 28, making your payment due last week.

I am sure that you will take care of this overdue invoice immediately. However, if there are circumstances that prevent you from doing so, I would appreciate it if you would let me know personally. You can reach me at 555.555.5555.

If I do not hear from you, I will expect a check for $5,329.43 by March 10.

Sincerely,

<e-mail signature, including name, title, company and contact information>

Letter of Collection—Initial Stern Reminder (30 Days Overdue)

Purpose

- To give a customer second notice that his or her payment is overdue

Alternative Purposes

- To notify a first-time customer that payment is overdue
- To notify a long-time customer in good standing that payment is overdue
- To notify a chronically late-paying customer that payment is overdue

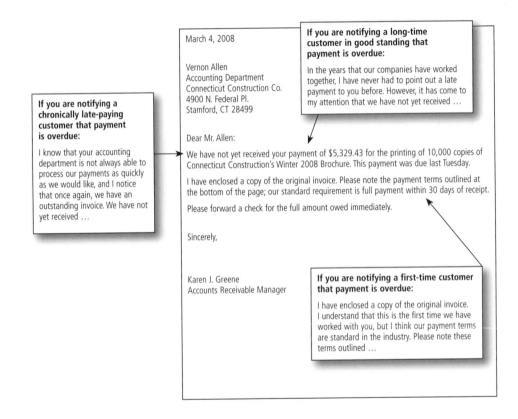

March 4, 2008

Vernon Allen
Accounting Department
Connecticut Construction Co.
4900 N. Federal Pl.
Stamford, CT 28499

Dear Mr. Allen:

We have not yet received your payment of $5,329.43 for the printing of 10,000 copies of Connecticut Construction's Winter 2008 Brochure. This payment was due last Tuesday.

I have enclosed a copy of the original invoice. Please note the payment terms outlined at the bottom of the page; our standard requirement is full payment within 30 days of receipt.

Please forward a check for the full amount owed immediately.

Sincerely,

Karen J. Greene
Accounts Receivable Manager

If you are notifying a long-time customer in good standing that payment is overdue:

In the years that our companies have worked together, I have never had to point out a late payment to you before. However, it has come to my attention that we have not yet received …

If you are notifying a chronically late-paying customer that payment is overdue:

I know that your accounting department is not always able to process our payments as quickly as we would like, and I notice that once again, we have an outstanding invoice. We have not yet received …

If you are notifying a first-time customer that payment is overdue:

I have enclosed a copy of the original invoice. I understand that this is the first time we have worked with you, but I think our payment terms are standard in the industry. Please note these terms outlined …

E-Mail

Dear Mr. Allen:

One of our invoices should have been paid by you last Tuesday.

We have not yet received your payment of $5,329.43 for the printing of 10,000 copies of Connecticut Construction's Winter 2008 Brochure.

I have attached a PDF of the original invoice. Please note the payment terms outlined at the bottom of the page; our standard requirement is full payment within 30 days of receipt.

Please mail a check for the full amount owed immediately.

Sincerely,

<e-mail signature, including name, title, company and contact information>

Second-Notice Letter of Collection (30 Days Overdue)

Purpose

- To notify a customer for the second time that his or her payment is overdue

Alternative Purposes

- To notify a first-time customer that payment is overdue
- To notify a long-time customer in good standing that payment is overdue
- To notify a chronically late-paying customer that payment is overdue

April 4, 2008

Vernon Allen
Accounting Department
Connecticut Construction Co.
4900 N. Federal Pl.
Stamford, CT 28499

Dear Mr. Allen:

This is your second notice that payment of $5,329.43 for the printing of 10,000 copies of Connecticut Construction's Winter 2008 Brochure is overdue.

We have paid for some of the expenses of printing your four-color brochure, including the purchase of expensive paper, and we do not wish to carry that expense any longer.

Please use the enclosed return envelope to send us a check for the full amount immediately. If you have any questions or problems regarding this payment, please contact me directly at 555.555.5555.

Sincerely,

Karen J. Greene
Accounts Receivable Manager

If you are notifying a chronically late-paying customer that payment is overdue:

Your account is now 30 days past due. Please remit $5,329.43 for printing …

If you are notifying a long-time customer in good standing that payment is overdue:

We are concerned that we have not received payment or word from you regarding your Winter 2008 Brochure. We have enjoyed a good business relationship in the past, and now I find myself writing once again to remind you that payment is overdue for this job.

If you are notifying a first-time customer that payment is overdue:

You may not be familiar with the way that ASAP Printing works, but we purchased the paper and other materials for your brochures upfront, and now we need to pay our bills for those materials.

E-Mail

Dear Mr. Allen:

I received your e-mail response to my last message regarding your overdue payment, but I have not received a check.

This is your second notice that payment of $5,329.43 for the printing of 10,000 copies of Connecticut Construction's Winter 2008 Brochure is overdue.

Please send us a check for the full amount immediately. If you have any questions or problems regarding this payment, please contact me directly at 555.555.5555.

Sincerely,

<e-mail signature, including name, title, company and contact information>

Third-Notice Letter of Collection (60 Days Overdue)

Purpose

- To notify a customer for the third time that his or her payment is overdue

Alternative Purposes

- To notify a first-time customer that payment is overdue
- To notify a long-time customer in good standing that payment is overdue
- To notify a chronically late-paying customer that payment is overdue

If you are notifying a long-time customer in good standing that payment is overdue:

I am sorry to say that your unpaid account will soon be out of my hands. It is the policy of …

If you are notifying a first-time customer that payment is overdue:

I have done everything I can think of to work with your company on resolving your overdue invoice. I am afraid that soon it will be out of my hands; it is the policy of …

If you are notifying a chronically late-paying customer that payment is overdue:

Your account is now more than 60 days past due. This letter constitutes your third notice regarding the outstanding balance of $5,329.43 for printing of 10,000 copies of the Winter 2008 Brochure.

It is the policy of ASAP Printing to give a customer three notices of an overdue invoice before we begin legal proceedings to recover our money.

May 4, 2008

Vernon Allen
Accounting Department
Connecticut Construction Co.
4900 N. Federal Pl.
Stamford, CT 28499

Dear Mr. Allen:

It is the policy of ASAP Printing to give a customer three notices of an overdue invoice before we begin legal proceedings to recover our money.

This letter constitutes the third notice that Connecticut Construction's payment of $5,329.43 for the printing of 10,000 copies of the Winter 2008 Brochure is overdue.

If we do not receive a check from you for the full amount by May 15, we will be forced to begin legal actions against your company. I hope that this final step can be avoided; please mail a check to my attention as soon as possible.

Sincerely,

Karen J. Greene
Accounts Receivable Manager

E-Mail

Dear Mr. Allen:

Please read this message carefully and print it out for your files.

It is the policy of ASAP Printing to give a customer three notices of an overdue invoice before we begin legal proceedings to recover our money.

This message constitutes the third notice that Connecticut Construction's payment of $5,329.43 for the printing of 10,000 copies of the Winter 2008 Brochure is overdue.

If we do not receive a check from you for the full amount by May 15, we will be forced to begin legal actions against your company.

I hope that this final step can be avoided; please mail a check to my attention as soon as possible.

Sincerely,

<e-mail signature, including name, title, company and contact information>

Letter Thanking Customer for a Payment

Purpose

- To thank a customer for payment received and acknowledge his or her business

Alternative Purposes

- To thank a customer for a large order or payment
- To thank a customer for his or her long-term business
- To thank a customer for an overdue payment

February 6, 2008

Monica Bauman
871 Rush St., Apt. 7A
Baton Rouge, LA 89255

Dear Ms. Bauman:

Thank you for your prompt payment on your latest order from Folk Artists of the Southwest (FAS).

We appreciate customers like you who respect our payment terms, and I hope that you are completely satisfied with the original artwork you purchased.

If you need anything else from us, whether it is a copy of our latest catalog or information on new works of art similar to the one you have purchased, please do not hesitate to contact us. Our customer service department is available at 555.555.5555 every day from 8:30 a.m. to 7 p.m. Central time.

Thank you again for your continued business.

Sincerely,

Inez M. Santiago
Customer Service Manager

If you are thanking a customer for a large order:

Thank you for your $1,250 payment on your latest order from Folk Artists of the Southwest (FAS). We value your business and want to make sure that you are completely satisfied ...

If you are thanking a long-term customer for his or her payment:

Thank you for your prompt payment on your latest order from Folk Artists of the Southwest (FAS). In processing the payment, I noticed that you have been a customer with us for more than 5 years now, and I want to personally thank you for your business.

If you are thanking a customer for an overdue payment:

Thank you for your payment on your latest order from Folk Artists of the Southwest (FAS). I am happy that we were able to resolve the issue, and want to let you know that we appreciate your business.

E-Mail

Dear Ms. Bauman:

This message is simply to say thank you for your prompt payment on your latest order from Folk Artists of the Southwest (FAS).

We appreciate customers like you who respect our payment terms and I hope that you are completely satisfied with the original artwork you purchased.

If you need anything else from us, whether it is a copy of our latest catalog or information on new works of art similar to the one you have purchased, please do not hesitate to contact us.

Thank you again for your continued business.

Sincerely,

<e-mail signature, including name, title, company and contact information>

Letter to Vendor or Supplier Noting Payment Terms

Purpose

- To introduce a new vendor to your organization's payment terms

Alternative Purposes

- To remind a current vendor about your payment terms
- To notify a vendor of a change in your payment terms
- To notify a vendor of an exception to your payment terms

If you are reminding a current supplier about your payment terms:

This letter is in response to your second invoice reminder (#583920) to BIS, which requested payment within 15 days. I would like to remind you of our payment terms, which you received last year. These terms clearly state that we will pay our suppliers within 45 days.

If you are notifying a supplier of a change in your payment terms:

Please note that effective immediately, BIS is implementing a new payment policy that affects all of our suppliers. We will no longer accept cash on delivery (c.o.d.) shipments. However, there are several other options for our suppliers who require payment in advance.

Enclosed you will find a revised list of payment …

If you are notifying a supplier of an exception to your payment terms:

I understand that VGB Binders Inc. requires payment within 30 days. It is our preference to pay in 60 days, but we are willing to make an exception to this. Therefore, we agree to pay within 30 days of receiving your invoice.

This exception is an addition to the enclosed list of payment terms for BIS suppliers, which includes our timeline …

January 24, 2008

Paul Mansfield
Customer Service Specialist
VGB Binders Inc.
772 N. Clinton St.
Omaha, NE 72844

Dear Mr. Mansfield:

We are delighted to welcome you as a supplier of Brink Information Services (BIS). I will be the contact for all financial aspects of your company's account. Our purchasing agent, Marianne Drover, passed your information on to me so that I can outline our payment terms to you before we place our first order for your binder products. Please share this information with your accounting department.

Enclosed you will find a comprehensive list of payment terms for BIS suppliers, including our timeline for payments, terms of credit and fees for late or incomplete shipments.

If you or your accounting department have any questions, please feel free to contact me at 555.555.5555.

Sincerely,

Veronica Perez
Accounts Receivable

E-Mail

Dear Mr. Mansfield:

We are delighted to welcome you as a supplier of Brink Information Services (BIS).

I will be the contact for all financial aspects of your company's account. Our purchasing agent, Marianne Drover, passed your information on to me so that I can outline our payment terms to you before we place our first order for your binder products.

Attached you will find a PDF containing a comprehensive list of payment terms for BIS suppliers, including our timeline for payments, terms of credit and fees for late or incomplete shipments. Please share this information with your accounting department.

If you or your accounting department have any questions, please feel free to contact me.

Sincerely,

<e-mail signature, including name, title, company and contact information>

Letter to Vendor Negotiating Price or Terms

Purpose

- To formally negotiate payment terms with a vendor or supplier

Alternative Purposes

- To counter a vendor's terms with non-negotiable terms of your own
- To negotiate price with a vendor
- To make a second attempt at negotiations

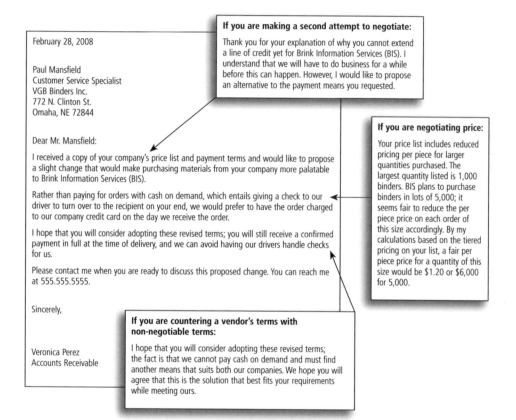

If you are making a second attempt to negotiate:

Thank you for your explanation of why you cannot extend a line of credit yet for Brink Information Services (BIS). I understand that we will have to do business for a while before this can happen. However, I would like to propose an alternative to the payment means you requested.

February 28, 2008

Paul Mansfield
Customer Service Specialist
VGB Binders Inc.
772 N. Clinton St.
Omaha, NE 72844

Dear Mr. Mansfield:

I received a copy of your company's price list and payment terms and would like to propose a slight change that would make purchasing materials from your company more palatable to Brink Information Services (BIS).

Rather than paying for orders with cash on demand, which entails giving a check to our driver to turn over to the recipient on your end, we would prefer to have the order charged to our company credit card on the day we receive the order.

I hope that you will consider adopting these revised terms; you will still receive a confirmed payment in full at the time of delivery, and we can avoid having our drivers handle checks for us.

Please contact me when you are ready to discuss this proposed change. You can reach me at 555.555.5555.

Sincerely,

Veronica Perez
Accounts Receivable

If you are negotiating price:

Your price list includes reduced pricing per piece for larger quantities purchased. The largest quantity listed is 1,000 binders. BIS plans to purchase binders in lots of 5,000; it seems fair to reduce the per piece price on each order of this size accordingly. By my calculations based on the tiered pricing on your list, a fair per piece price for a quantity of this size would be $1.20 or $6,000 for 5,000.

If you are countering a vendor's terms with non-negotiable terms:

I hope that you will consider adopting these revised terms; the fact is that we cannot pay cash on demand and must find another means that suits both our companies. We hope you will agree that this is the solution that best fits your requirements while meeting ours.

E-Mail

Dear Mr. Mansfield:

Thank you for forwarding your company's price list and payment terms. After reviewing it, I would like to propose a slight change that would make purchasing materials from your company more palatable to Brink Information Services (BIS).

Rather than paying for orders with cash on demand, which entails giving a check to our driver to turn over to the recipient on your end, we would prefer to have the order charged to our company credit card on the day we receive the order.

I hope that you will consider adopting these revised terms; you will still receive a confirmed payment in full at the time of delivery and we can avoid having our drivers handle checks for us.

Please contact me when you are ready to discuss this proposed change. You can reach me at 555.555.5555.

Sincerely,

<e-mail signature, including name, title, company and contact information>

Letter Requesting Business References for Vendor

Purpose

- To request financial or business references for a new or prospective vendor

Alternative Purposes

- To request correct or updated contact information for references
- To follow up on an initial request for references
- To report that business references were not acceptable

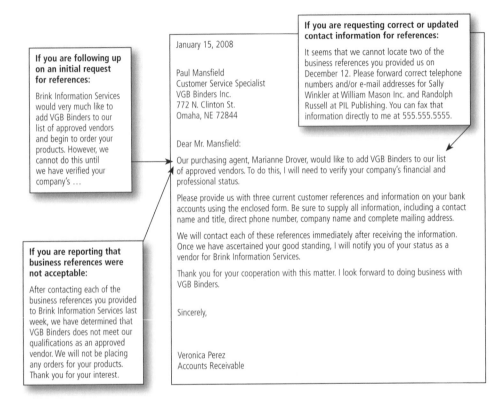

If you are following up on an initial request for references:

Brink Information Services would very much like to add VGB Binders to our list of approved vendors and begin to order your products. However, we cannot do this until we have verified your company's …

If you are reporting that business references were not acceptable:

After contacting each of the business references you provided to Brink Information Services last week, we have determined that VGB Binders does not meet our qualifications as an approved vendor. We will not be placing any orders for your products. Thank you for your interest.

January 15, 2008

Paul Mansfield
Customer Service Specialist
VGB Binders Inc.
772 N. Clinton St.
Omaha, NE 72844

Dear Mr. Mansfield:

Our purchasing agent, Marianne Drover, would like to add VGB Binders to our list of approved vendors. To do this, I will need to verify your company's financial and professional status.

Please provide us with three current customer references and information on your bank accounts using the enclosed form. Be sure to supply all information, including a contact name and title, direct phone number, company name and complete mailing address.

We will contact each of these references immediately after receiving the information. Once we have ascertained your good standing, I will notify you of your status as a vendor for Brink Information Services.

Thank you for your cooperation with this matter. I look forward to doing business with VGB Binders.

Sincerely,

Veronica Perez
Accounts Receivable

If you are requesting correct or updated contact information for references:

It seems that we cannot locate two of the business references you provided us on December 12. Please forward correct telephone numbers and/or e-mail addresses for Sally Winkler at William Mason Inc. and Randolph Russell at PIL Publishing. You can fax that information directly to me at 555.555.5555.

E-Mail

Dear Mr. Mansfield:

Brink Information Services (BIS) would like to begin ordering your company's products.

Before we do so, however, I need to verify your company's financial and professional status.

Please provide us with three current customer references and information on your bank accounts using the attached PDF. Be sure to supply all information, including a contact name and title, direct phone number, company name and complete mailing address.

We will contact each of these references immediately after receiving the information. Once we have ascertained your good standing, I will notify you of your status as a vendor for BIS.

Thank you for your cooperation in this matter. I look forward to doing business with VGB Binders.

Sincerely,

<e-mail signature, including name, title, company and contact information>

Letter Requesting That Vendor Adjust an Invoice

Purpose

- To respond to a received invoice with a request for correction or change

Alternative Purposes

- To request a goodwill discount
- To request correction of facts for record-keeping purposes
- To request a change in payment terms on invoice received

March 7, 2008

Paul Mansfield
Customer Service Specialist
VGB Binders Inc.
772 N. Clinton St.
Omaha, NE 72844

Dear Mr. Mansfield:

Today we received a VGB Binders invoice for our order #7492943. I wanted to contact you before this paperwork was sent to discuss a change to our agreement and I trust it is not too late.

As you know, this order for 5,000 binders did not go smoothly. We received the wrong materials initially and then had to wait more than a week to receive the correct binders. This delay caused a backup in our own customer orders.

Therefore, I think it would be fair for VGB Binders to reduce the costs on this order. I propose that a fair discount for our inconvenience and that of our customers would be 20 percent, making the cost of this invoice $4,985.

I realize that this invoice has already been processed on your end and that making this change will entail some backtracking. However, I would like to stress that Brink Information Services (BIS) would like to continue to rely on your company for our materials for a long time to come. Making the extra effort of revising this invoice will go a long way toward showing that your company also plans to pursue a long-standing and lucrative relationship with BIS.

If you would like to discuss this matter, please contact me directly at 555.555.5555.

Sincerely,

Veronica Perez
Accounts Receivable

If you are requesting a goodwill discount:

As you know, this is the second large order that Brink Information Services (BIS) has placed with VGB Binders. We are very happy with the quality of your materials and are now ready to rely solely on VGB Binders for all our binder needs.

With the promise of regular orders of the size of this last one, would you consider offering BIS a goodwill discount on this invoice? Giving us 20 percent off this bill would still net you $4,985.

If you are requesting a correction to facts on the invoice:

For our own records and accounting audit, we require that each invoice list the complete contents of each order, including any identifying item number used for each individual product. Can you resubmit this invoice with this detail and be sure to include it on all future invoices to Brink Information Services (BIS)?

If you are requesting a change in the payment terms on the invoice:

The invoice includes a notation that payment is due on receipt. The accounting procedures we have in place here at Brink Information Services (BIS) do not allow us to render payment that fast; we need time to verify that the order is satisfactory and complete, then submit the invoice for payment. All of this takes us several weeks and we typically pay invoices within 30 days.

I understand that you would prefer to be paid quickly; however, I would like to stress …

E-Mail

Dear Mr. Mansfield:

This message is in reference to a VGB Binders invoice for our order #7492943.

I had planned to contact you before this paperwork was sent to discuss a change to our agreement and I trust it is not too late.

As you know, this order for 5,000 binders did not go smoothly. We received the wrong materials initially and then had to wait more than a week to receive the correct binders. This delay caused a backup in our own customer orders.

Therefore, I think it would be fair for VGB Binders to reduce the costs on this order. I propose that a fair discount for our inconvenience and that of our customers would be 20 percent, making the cost of this invoice $4,985.

I realize that this invoice has already been processed on your end and that making this change will entail some backtracking. However, I would like to stress that Brink Information Services (BIS) would like to continue to rely on your company for our materials for a long time to come. Making the extra effort of revising this invoice will go a long way toward showing that your company also plans to pursue a long-standing and lucrative relationship with BIS.

If you would like to discuss this matter, please contact me at 555.555.5555.

Sincerely,

<e-mail signature, including name, title, company and contact information>

Letter to Vendor or Supplier Stating or Reiterating Your Policies

Purpose

- To introduce a new vendor to your organization's policies regarding payment, delivery and service

Alternative Purposes

- To remind a current vendor about your policies
- To notify a vendor of a change in your policies
- To notify a vendor of an exception to your policies

If you are reminding a current supplier about your policies:

This letter is in reference to our recent order of 5,000 binders, delivery of which was attempted on January 21. Our Vendor Policies clearly state that we will not accept cash on delivery (c.o.d.) shipments.

Please review the enclosed copy of …

If you are notifying a supplier of a change in your policies:

Please note that effective immediately, Brink Information Services is implementing a new payment policy that affects all of our suppliers. We will no longer accept c.o.d. shipments. However, there are several other options for our suppliers who require payment in advance.

Enclosed you will find a revised copy of Vendor Policies …

January 24, 2008
Paul Mansfield
Customer Service Specialist
VGB Binders Inc.
772 N. Clinton St.
Omaha, NE 72844

Dear Mr. Mansfield:

We are delighted to welcome you as a supplier for Brink Information Services (BIS). To ensure that our orders from your company are expedited smoothly and efficiently, I would like to explain how BIS operates.

Enclosed you will find a copy of Vendor Policies for BIS suppliers, including quality control standards, delivery specifications and payment terms. Please review this document and ensure that you are able to adhere to each policy.

If you have questions or concerns regarding anything in this document, please contact me directly at 555.555.5555.

Sincerely,

Veronica Perez
Accounts Receivable

If you are notifying a supplier of an exception to your policies:

I understand that VGB Binders Inc. requires payment within 30 days. It is our preference to pay in 60 days, but we are willing to make an exception to this. Therefore, we agree to pay within 30 days of receiving your invoice.

This exception is an addition to the enclosed copy of Vendor Policies …

E-Mail

Dear Mr. Mansfield:

We are delighted to welcome you as a supplier for Brink Information Services (BIS). To ensure that our orders from your company are expedited smoothly and efficiently, I would like to explain how BIS operates.

Attached is a PDF of Vendor Policies for BIS suppliers, including quality control standards, delivery specifications and payment terms. Please review this document and ensure that you are able to adhere to each policy.

If you have questions or concerns regarding anything in this document, please contact me.

Sincerely,

<e-mail signature, including name, title, company and contact information>

Letter to Vendor Refusing Payment

Purpose

- To notify a vendor that you will not pay on an invoice received

Alternative Purposes

- To announce that you will not pay due to damaged or missing goods
- To announce that you will not pay due to goods never received
- To announce that you will not pay due to double invoicing

March 7, 2008

Paul Mansfield
Customer Service Specialist
VGB Binders Inc.
772 N. Clinton St.
Omaha, NE 72844

Dear Mr. Mansfield:

Today we received a VGB Binders invoice for order #7492943 for 5,000 binders. I wanted to notify you immediately that we will not pay this invoice because what you delivered was not what we ordered.

After comparing the information on the invoice to that in our records, we found that the order attached to this invoice was incorrect and has yet to be replaced. We did order 5,000 of your standard padded binders, but the materials we received on February 8 did not match our order. Those materials, which included 4,000 5.5 x 8.5 binders and 2,000 vinyl portfolios, are still in our warehouse waiting for collection. Although our warehouse manager has repeatedly contacted your company for replacement of these materials with the 5,000 standard binders, no action has been taken.

Please check your own files to make sure that they accurately reflect this order. If there is a problem with the accounting system or general record-keeping at VGB Binders, I trust that you will personally make sure it is eliminated so that this does not happen again.

Sincerely,

Veronica Perez
Accounts Receivable

If the invoice is for a shipment that included missing or damaged goods:

After comparing the information on the invoice with that in our records, we discovered a problem. We did receive the order on February 8, but more than 50 percent of the binders shipped were in an unacceptable state due to water damage. Your department was alerted to this problem immediately, and the damaged binders were collected for return. We were left with approximately 2,250 usable binders.

If the invoice is for a shipment that was never received:

After comparing the information on the invoice with that in our records, we discovered a problem. We did indeed place this order with VGB Binders, but we never received the materials. The order is now more than a month overdue, and the only evidence we have seen of our binders is this invoice.

If you have already paid the invoice:

After comparing the information on the invoice with that in our records, we discovered a problem. Our payment records show that we sent you a check for full payment of this invoice last month. Specifically, check #4755 was mailed to the attention of your accounts payable department on February 17 and it has been cashed.

E-Mail

Dear Mr. Mansfield:

Yes, we did receive an invoice for order #7492943 for 5,000 VGB binders.

I wanted to notify you immediately that we will not pay this invoice. After comparing the information on the invoice with that in our records, we discovered a problem.

The order attached to this invoice was incorrect and has yet to be replaced. We did order 5,000 of your standard padded binders, but the materials we received on February 8 did not match our order. Those materials, which included 4,000 5.5 x 8.5 binders and 2,000 vinyl portfolios, are still in our warehouse waiting for collection.

Although our warehouse manager has repeatedly contacted your company for replacement of these materials with the 5,000 standard binders, no action has been taken.

Please check your own files to make sure that they accurately reflect this order.

If there is a problem with the accounting system or general record-keeping at VGB Binders, I trust that you will personally make sure it is eliminated so that this does not happen again.

Sincerely,

<e-mail signature, including name, title, company and contact information>

Letter Accompanying Vendor Payment

Purpose

- To highlight a payment made to a new vendor

Alternative Purposes

- To notify a vendor that you have enclosed a partial payment
- To notify a vendor that you have enclosed a late payment
- To notify a vendor that you have enclosed an advance payment

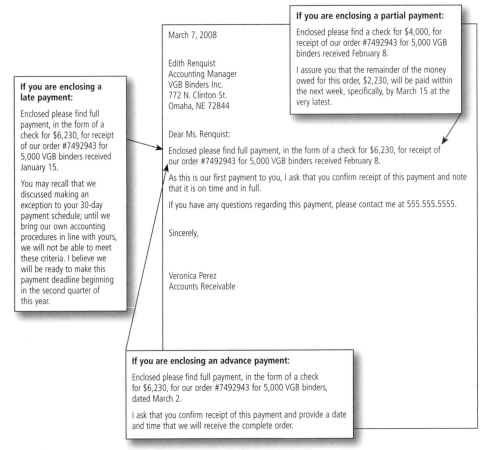

If you are enclosing a partial payment:

Enclosed please find a check for $4,000, for receipt of our order #7492943 for 5,000 VGB binders received February 8.

I assure you that the remainder of the money owed for this order, $2,230, will be paid within the next week, specifically, by March 15 at the very latest.

If you are enclosing a late payment:

Enclosed please find full payment, in the form of a check for $6,230, for receipt of our order #7492943 for 5,000 VGB binders received January 15.

You may recall that we discussed making an exception to your 30-day payment schedule; until we bring our own accounting procedures in line with yours, we will not be able to meet these criteria. I believe we will be ready to make this payment deadline beginning in the second quarter of this year.

If you are enclosing an advance payment:

Enclosed please find full payment, in the form of a check for $6,230, for our order #7492943 for 5,000 VGB binders, dated March 2.

I ask that you confirm receipt of this payment and provide a date and time that we will receive the complete order.

March 7, 2008

Edith Renquist
Accounting Manager
VGB Binders Inc.
772 N. Clinton St.
Omaha, NE 72844

Dear Ms. Renquist:

Enclosed please find full payment, in the form of a check for $6,230, for receipt of our order #7492943 for 5,000 VGB binders received February 8.

As this is our first payment to you, I ask that you confirm receipt of this payment and note that it is on time and in full.

If you have any questions regarding this payment, please contact me at 555.555.5555.

Sincerely,

Veronica Perez
Accounts Receivable

E-Mail

Dear Ms. Renquist:

This message is to let you know that we just mailed full payment, in the form of a check for $6,230, for receipt of our order #7492943 for 5,000 VGB binders received February 8.

As this is our first payment to you, I ask that you confirm receipt of this payment and note that it is on time and in full.

If you have any questions regarding this payment, please contact me.

Sincerely,

<e-mail signature, including name, title, company and contact information>

Letter Providing a Reference for a Vendor

Purpose

- To provide a professional or customer reference for an established vendor

Alternative Purposes

- To provide a noncommittal reference for a vendor
- To provide a reference for a past vendor
- To refuse to provide a reference for a vendor

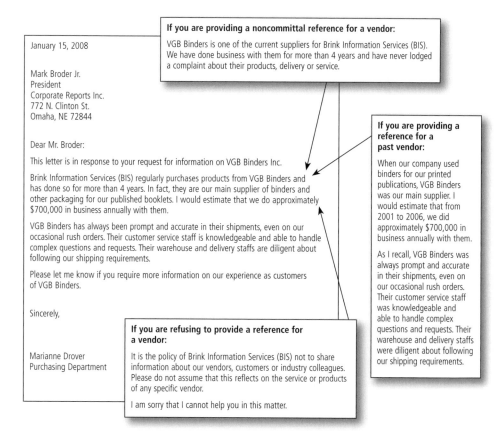

If you are providing a noncommittal reference for a vendor:

VGB Binders is one of the current suppliers for Brink Information Services (BIS). We have done business with them for more than 4 years and have never lodged a complaint about their products, delivery or service.

January 15, 2008

Mark Broder Jr.
President
Corporate Reports Inc.
772 N. Clinton St.
Omaha, NE 72844

Dear Mr. Broder:

This letter is in response to your request for information on VGB Binders Inc.

Brink Information Services (BIS) regularly purchases products from VGB Binders and has done so for more than 4 years. In fact, they are our main supplier of binders and other packaging for our published booklets. I would estimate that we do approximately $700,000 in business annually with them.

VGB Binders has always been prompt and accurate in their shipments, even on our occasional rush orders. Their customer service staff is knowledgeable and able to handle complex questions and requests. Their warehouse and delivery staffs are diligent about following our shipping requirements.

Please let me know if you require more information on our experience as customers of VGB Binders.

Sincerely,

Marianne Drover
Purchasing Department

If you are providing a reference for a past vendor:

When our company used binders for our printed publications, VGB Binders was our main supplier. I would estimate that from 2001 to 2006, we did approximately $700,000 in business annually with them.

As I recall, VGB Binders was always prompt and accurate in their shipments, even on our occasional rush orders. Their customer service staff was knowledgeable and able to handle complex questions and requests. Their warehouse and delivery staffs were diligent about following our shipping requirements.

If you are refusing to provide a reference for a vendor:

It is the policy of Brink Information Services (BIS) not to share information about our vendors, customers or industry colleagues. Please do not assume that this reflects on the service or products of any specific vendor.

I am sorry that I cannot help you in this matter.

E-Mail

Dear Mr. Broder:

I would be happy to provide a reference for VGB Binders Inc.

Brink Information Services (BIS) regularly purchases products from VGB Binders and has done so for more than 4 years. In fact, they are our main supplier of binders and other packaging for our published booklets. I would estimate that we do approximately $700,000 in business annually with them.

VGB Binders has always been prompt and accurate in their shipments, even on our occasional rush orders. Their customer service staff is knowledgeable and able to handle complex questions and requests. Their warehouse and delivery staffs are diligent about following our shipping requirements.

Sincerely,

<e-mail signature, including name, title, company and contact information>

Section Three

.....

Essential General
Administration Letters

Letter of Inquiry/Request for Information

Purpose

- To request specific information

Alternative Purposes

- To follow up on an initial meeting
- To request a brochure, catalog or other printed material
- To request a free sample or consultation

If you are following up on a meeting:

Although I did not get your name at the time, I spoke with you briefly at your booth at the Travel and Hospitality trade show last month.

February 12, 2008

Western Regional Representative
Executive Housing International
302 S. Wells St.
Sacramento, CA 98765

Dear Western Regional Representative:

I saw your company's short-term rental service advertised on a billboard in the Los Angeles airport and would like more information on your services.

Our Los Angeles headquarters frequently holds weeklong training sessions, which are attended by sales representatives and customers from across the country. We typically get hotel rooms for these travelers, but it may be more comfortable for them and more cost-efficient for my company if we were to rent several apartments for them for the duration of the training sessions.

If you are requesting a specific collateral piece:

Please send me the free brochure mentioned on the billboard.

Please send me information on your available Los Angeles area properties, pricing and contract terms. Feel free to call me at 555.555.5555 if you have any questions or need more information.

Sincerely,

If you are requesting a free sample or consultation:

The billboard ad mentioned an offer of one free night's stay in one of your rental apartments. I would like to schedule a night when our sales manager can try out one of your properties.

Sarah J. Taylor
Executive Sales Assistant

E-Mail

Dear Western Regional Representative:

Please send me information on your available Los Angeles area properties, pricing and contract terms. Feel free to call me at 555.555.5555 if you have any questions or need more information.

<e-mail signature, including name, title, company and contact information>

Letter Replying to Inquiry/Request for Information

Purpose

- To reply to a written request for specific information

Alternative Purposes

- To reply to a face-to-face or phone request for information
- To send a note to accompany a catalog or brochure
- To redirect request to a phone call or in-person meeting

If you are following up on a face-to-face request:

I enjoyed speaking with you at the Travel and Hospitality trade show in January. As I recall, your company hosts out-of-town guests for weeklong meetings.

February 16, 2008

Sarah J. Taylor
Executive Sales Assistant
Focal Financial Services Inc.
5943 Broadway, Suite 2300
Los Angeles, CA 90000

Dear Ms. Taylor:

Thank you for contacting me regarding your company's needs for short-term rental properties in the Los Angeles area. I am confident that Executive Housing International can provide accommodations that will make your out-of-town visitors more comfortable while saving you money on hotel rooms.

Please find enclosed a brochure that outlines our services, a map showing available apartment locations, a price list and a sample contract. I will call you within the week to follow up and see if I can provide further information to help you make a decision. If you or your sales manager would like a walk-through of one or more of our rental properties, I would be happy to schedule one.

Thank you again for your interest, and I will talk to you soon.

Sincerely,

Carmen Gutierrez
Western Regional Representative

If you are responding to a request for a specific collateral piece:

Please find enclosed the brochure you requested, along with a map …

If you prefer to speak with the person:

Rather than send you our standard sales brochure, I would like to set up an appointment to determine your company's unique needs so that we can discuss custom pricing and scheduling. I will call you within the week to see if we can find a time convenient to both of us.

E-Mail

Dear Ms. Taylor:

Thank you for contacting me regarding your company's needs for short-term rental properties in the Los Angeles area. I am confident that Executive Housing International can provide accommodations that will make your out-of-town visitors more comfortable while saving you money on hotel rooms.

Please find attached a brochure that outlines our services, along with some other information. I will call you within the week to see if I can provide further information.

If you or your sales manager would like a walk-through of one or more of our rental properties, I would be happy to schedule one.

Thank you again for your interest, and I will talk to you soon.

<e-mail signature, including name, title, company and contact information>

Follow-Up Letter to Reply to Inquiry/Request for Information

Purpose

- To encourage action after first reply to inquiry for specific information

Alternative Purposes

- To follow up on a reply to a face-to-face or phone request for information
- To follow up on a note to accompany a catalog or brochure
- To follow up on a redirect of request for a phone call or in-person meeting

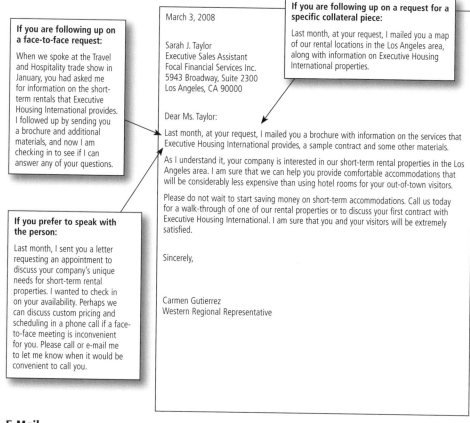

If you are following up on a request for a specific collateral piece:

Last month, at your request, I mailed you a map of our rental locations in the Los Angeles area, along with information on Executive Housing International properties.

If you are following up on a face-to-face request:

When we spoke at the Travel and Hospitality trade show in January, you had asked me for information on the short-term rentals that Executive Housing International provides. I followed up by sending you a brochure and additional materials, and now I am checking in to see if I can answer any of your questions.

If you prefer to speak with the person:

Last month, I sent you a letter requesting an appointment to discuss your company's unique needs for short-term rental properties. I wanted to check in on your availability. Perhaps we can discuss custom pricing and scheduling in a phone call if a face-to-face meeting is inconvenient for you. Please call or e-mail me to let me know when it would be convenient to call you.

March 3, 2008

Sarah J. Taylor
Executive Sales Assistant
Focal Financial Services Inc.
5943 Broadway, Suite 2300
Los Angeles, CA 90000

Dear Ms. Taylor:

Last month, at your request, I mailed you a brochure with information on the services that Executive Housing International provides, a sample contract and some other materials.

As I understand it, your company is interested in our short-term rental properties in the Los Angeles area. I am sure that we can help you provide comfortable accommodations that will be considerably less expensive than using hotel rooms for your out-of-town visitors.

Please do not wait to start saving money on short-term accommodations. Call us today for a walk-through of one of our rental properties or to discuss your first contract with Executive Housing International. I am sure that you and your visitors will be extremely satisfied.

Sincerely,

Carmen Gutierrez
Western Regional Representative

E-Mail

Dear Ms. Taylor:

Last month, at your request, I sent you a brochure with information on the services that Executive Housing International provides, along with some other materials.

As I understand it, your company is interested in our short-term rental properties in the Los Angeles area. I am sure that we can help you provide comfortable accommodations that will be considerably less expensive than using hotel rooms for your out-of-town visitors.

Please do not wait to start saving money on short-term accommodations. Respond today for a walk-through of one of our rental properties or to discuss your first contract with Executive Housing International.

I am sure that you and your visitors will be extremely satisfied.

<e-mail signature, including name, title, company and contact information>

Letter Requesting Appointment

Purpose

- To formally request a face-to-face appointment with an individual

Alternative Purposes

- To request a telephone appointment with an individual
- To request an appointment through an individual's assistant
- To request a meeting with a group or department

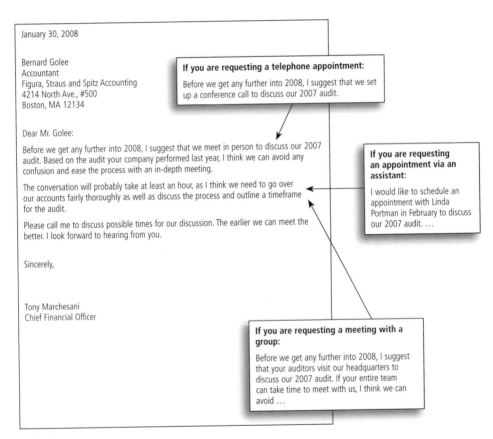

January 30, 2008

Bernard Golee
Accountant
Figura, Straus and Spitz Accounting
4214 North Ave., #500
Boston, MA 12134

Dear Mr. Golee:

Before we get any further into 2008, I suggest that we meet in person to discuss our 2007 audit. Based on the audit your company performed last year, I think we can avoid any confusion and ease the process with an in-depth meeting.

The conversation will probably take at least an hour, as I think we need to go over our accounts fairly thoroughly as well as discuss the process and outline a timeframe for the audit.

Please call me to discuss possible times for our discussion. The earlier we can meet the better. I look forward to hearing from you.

Sincerely,

Tony Marchesani
Chief Financial Officer

If you are requesting a telephone appointment:

Before we get any further into 2008, I suggest that we set up a conference call to discuss our 2007 audit.

If you are requesting an appointment via an assistant:

I would like to schedule an appointment with Linda Portman in February to discuss our 2007 audit. . . .

If you are requesting a meeting with a group:

Before we get any further into 2008, I suggest that your auditors visit our headquarters to discuss our 2007 audit. If your entire team can take time to meet with us, I think we can avoid . . .

E-Mail

Dear Mr. Golee:

Before we get any further into 2008, I suggest that we meet in person to discuss our 2007 audit. Based on the audit your company performed last year, I think we can avoid any confusion and ease the process with an in-depth meeting.

The conversation will probably take at least an hour, as I think we need to go over our accounts fairly thoroughly as well as discuss the process and outline a timeframe for the audit.

Please respond with some possible times for our discussion. The earlier we can meet the better.

I look forward to hearing from you.

Sincerely,

<e-mail signature, including name, title, company and contact information>

Letter Responding to Request for Appointment

Purpose

- To formally reply to a request for a face-to-face appointment

Alternative Purposes

- To reply to a request for a telephone appointment
- To reply to a request for an appointment on behalf of one's superior
- To reply to a request for a meeting with a group or department

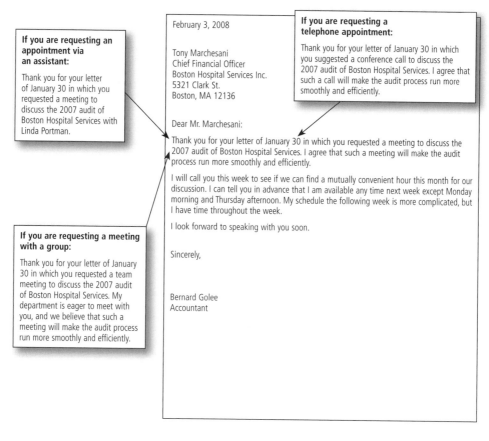

If you are requesting an appointment via an assistant:

Thank you for your letter of January 30 in which you requested a meeting to discuss the 2007 audit of Boston Hospital Services with Linda Portman.

If you are requesting a telephone appointment:

Thank you for your letter of January 30 in which you suggested a conference call to discuss the 2007 audit of Boston Hospital Services. I agree that such a call will make the audit process run more smoothly and efficiently.

If you are requesting a meeting with a group:

Thank you for your letter of January 30 in which you requested a team meeting to discuss the 2007 audit of Boston Hospital Services. My department is eager to meet with you, and we believe that such a meeting will make the audit process run more smoothly and efficiently.

February 3, 2008

Tony Marchesani
Chief Financial Officer
Boston Hospital Services Inc.
5321 Clark St.
Boston, MA 12136

Dear Mr. Marchesani:

Thank you for your letter of January 30 in which you requested a meeting to discuss the 2007 audit of Boston Hospital Services. I agree that such a meeting will make the audit process run more smoothly and efficiently.

I will call you this week to see if we can find a mutually convenient hour this month for our discussion. I can tell you in advance that I am available any time next week except Monday morning and Thursday afternoon. My schedule the following week is more complicated, but I have time throughout the week.

I look forward to speaking with you soon.

Sincerely,

Bernard Golee
Accountant

E-Mail

Dear Mr. Marchesani:

Thank you for your letter of January 30 in which you requested a meeting to discuss the 2007 audit of Boston Hospital Services. I agree that such a meeting will make the audit process run more smoothly and efficiently.

I hope that we can find a mutually convenient hour for our discussion within the next week or two. I am available any time next week except Monday morning and Thursday afternoon. Do you have time next week to meet with me? Please suggest a time convenient for you. I will get back to you promptly after checking my schedule.

Thank you,

<e-mail signature, including name, title, company and contact information>

Letter of Congratulations

Purpose

- To personally congratulate a colleague on a business achievement

Alternative Purposes

- To congratulate a colleague on a personal achievement
- To congratulate a customer or prospect on a business achievement
- To congratulate a customer or prospect on a personal achievement

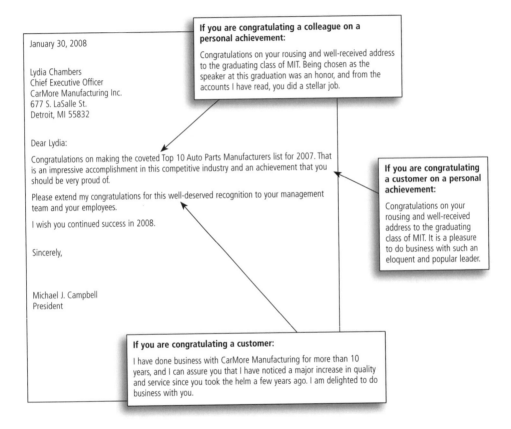

January 30, 2008

Lydia Chambers
Chief Executive Officer
CarMore Manufacturing Inc.
677 S. LaSalle St.
Detroit, MI 55832

Dear Lydia:

Congratulations on making the coveted Top 10 Auto Parts Manufacturers list for 2007. That is an impressive accomplishment in this competitive industry and an achievement that you should be very proud of.

Please extend my congratulations for this well-deserved recognition to your management team and your employees.

I wish you continued success in 2008.

Sincerely,

Michael J. Campbell
President

If you are congratulating a colleague on a personal achievement:

Congratulations on your rousing and well-received address to the graduating class of MIT. Being chosen as the speaker at this graduation was an honor, and from the accounts I have read, you did a stellar job.

If you are congratulating a customer on a personal achievement:

Congratulations on your rousing and well-received address to the graduating class of MIT. It is a pleasure to do business with such an eloquent and popular leader.

If you are congratulating a customer:

I have done business with CarMore Manufacturing for more than 10 years, and I can assure you that I have noticed a major increase in quality and service since you took the helm a few years ago. I am delighted to do business with you.

E-Mail

Dear Lydia:

Congratulations on making the coveted Top 10 Auto Parts Manufacturers list for 2007. That is an impressive accomplishment in this competitive industry and an achievement that you should be very proud of.

Please extend my congratulations for this well-deserved recognition to your management team and your employees. I wish you continued success in 2008.

<e-mail signature, including name, title, company and contact information>

Thank You Letter

Purpose

- To formally thank a colleague for a business favor

Alternative Purposes

- To thank a colleague for a personal favor
- To thank a customer for a business favor
- To thank a customer for a personal favor

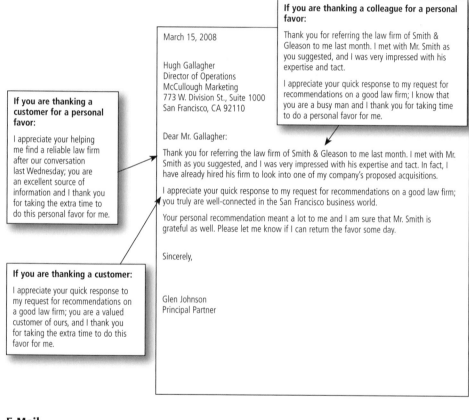

If you are thanking a colleague for a personal favor:

Thank you for referring the law firm of Smith & Gleason to me last month. I met with Mr. Smith as you suggested, and I was very impressed with his expertise and tact.

I appreciate your quick response to my request for recommendations on a good law firm; I know that you are a busy man and I thank you for taking time to do a personal favor for me.

If you are thanking a customer for a personal favor:

I appreciate your helping me find a reliable law firm after our conversation last Wednesday; you are an excellent source of information and I thank you for taking the extra time to do this personal favor for me.

If you are thanking a customer:

I appreciate your quick response to my request for recommendations on a good law firm; you are a valued customer of ours, and I thank you for taking the extra time to do this favor for me.

March 15, 2008

Hugh Gallagher
Director of Operations
McCullough Marketing
773 W. Division St., Suite 1000
San Francisco, CA 92110

Dear Mr. Gallagher:

Thank you for referring the law firm of Smith & Gleason to me last month. I met with Mr. Smith as you suggested, and I was very impressed with his expertise and tact. In fact, I have already hired his firm to look into one of my company's proposed acquisitions.

I appreciate your quick response to my request for recommendations on a good law firm; you truly are well-connected in the San Francisco business world.

Your personal recommendation meant a lot to me and I am sure that Mr. Smith is grateful as well. Please let me know if I can return the favor some day.

Sincerely,

Glen Johnson
Principal Partner

E-Mail

Dear Mr. Gallagher:

Thank you for referring the law firm of Smith & Gleason to me last month.

I met with Mr. Smith and was very impressed with his expertise and tact. In fact, I have already hired his firm to look into one of my company's proposed acquisitions.

I appreciate your quick response to my request for recommendations on a good law firm; you truly are well-connected in the San Francisco business world.

Your personal recommendation meant a lot to me and I am sure that Mr. Smith is grateful as well.

Please let me know if I can return the favor some day.

Sincerely,

<e-mail signature, including name, title, company and contact information>

Letter of Recognition

Purpose

- To formally recognize an employee's accomplishment

Alternative Purposes

- To formally recognize a business colleague's accomplishment
- To formally recognize an employee's efforts
- To formally recognize a business colleague's efforts

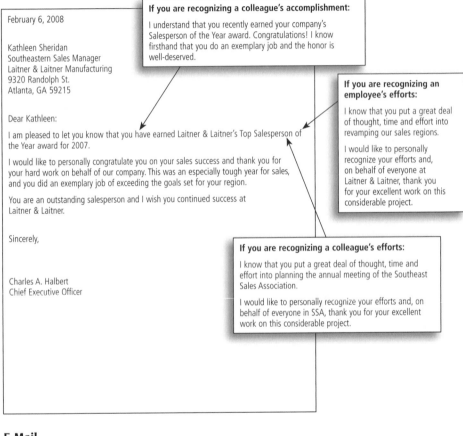

February 6, 2008

Kathleen Sheridan
Southeastern Sales Manager
Laitner & Laitner Manufacturing
9320 Randolph St.
Atlanta, GA 59215

Dear Kathleen:

I am pleased to let you know that you have earned Laitner & Laitner's Top Salesperson of the Year award for 2007.

I would like to personally congratulate you on your sales success and thank you for your hard work on behalf of our company. This was an especially tough year for sales, and you did an exemplary job of exceeding the goals set for your region.

You are an outstanding salesperson and I wish you continued success at Laitner & Laitner.

Sincerely,

Charles A. Halbert
Chief Executive Officer

If you are recognizing a colleague's accomplishment:

I understand that you recently earned your company's Salesperson of the Year award. Congratulations! I know firsthand that you do an exemplary job and the honor is well-deserved.

If you are recognizing an employee's efforts:

I know that you put a great deal of thought, time and effort into revamping our sales regions.

I would like to personally recognize your efforts and, on behalf of everyone at Laitner & Laitner, thank you for your excellent work on this considerable project.

If you are recognizing a colleague's efforts:

I know that you put a great deal of thought, time and effort into planning the annual meeting of the Southeast Sales Association.

I would like to personally recognize your efforts and, on behalf of everyone in SSA, thank you for your excellent work on this considerable project.

E-Mail

Dear Kathleen:

I am sending this e-mail because I wanted to give you some good news as soon as possible: You have earned Laitner & Laitner's Top Salesperson of the Year award for 2007.

Congratulations on your sales success and thank you for your hard work on behalf of our company. This was an especially tough year for sales, yet you still did an exemplary job of exceeding the goals set for your region.

You are an outstanding salesperson, and I wish you continued success at Laitner & Laitner.

Sincerely,

<e-mail signature, including name, title, company and contact information>

Letter of Complaint

Purpose

- To formally lodge a complaint with a business

Alternative Purposes

- To lodge a complaint about an ongoing problem
- To lodge a complaint about unacceptable service or customer contact
- To formally announce the end of business relations

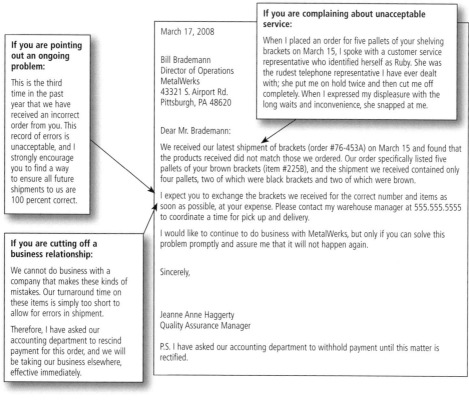

If you are pointing out an ongoing problem:

This is the third time in the past year that we have received an incorrect order from you. This record of errors is unacceptable, and I strongly encourage you to find a way to ensure all future shipments to us are 100 percent correct.

If you are cutting off a business relationship:

We cannot do business with a company that makes these kinds of mistakes. Our turnaround time on these items is simply too short to allow for errors in shipment.

Therefore, I have asked our accounting department to rescind payment for this order, and we will be taking our business elsewhere, effective immediately.

If you are complaining about unacceptable service:

When I placed an order for five pallets of your shelving brackets on March 15, I spoke with a customer service representative who identified herself as Ruby. She was the rudest telephone representative I have ever dealt with; she put me on hold twice and then cut me off completely. When I expressed my displeasure with the long waits and inconvenience, she snapped at me.

March 17, 2008

Bill Brademann
Director of Operations
MetalWerks
43321 S. Airport Rd.
Pittsburgh, PA 48620

Dear Mr. Brademann:

We received our latest shipment of brackets (order #76-453A) on March 15 and found that the products received did not match those we ordered. Our order specifically listed five pallets of your brown brackets (item #225B), and the shipment we received contained only four pallets, two of which were black brackets and two of which were brown.

I expect you to exchange the brackets we received for the correct number and items as soon as possible, at your expense. Please contact my warehouse manager at 555.555.5555 to coordinate a time for pick up and delivery.

I would like to continue to do business with MetalWerks, but only if you can solve this problem promptly and assure me that it will not happen again.

Sincerely,

Jeanne Anne Haggerty
Quality Assurance Manager

P.S. I have asked our accounting department to withhold payment until this matter is rectified.

E-Mail

Dear Mr. Brademann:

We received our latest shipment of brackets (order #76-453A) and found that the products received did not match those we ordered.

Our order specifically listed five pallets of your brown brackets (item #225B), and the shipment we received contained only four pallets, two of which were black brackets and two of which were brown.

I expect you to exchange the brackets we received for the correct number and items as soon as possible, at your expense.

Please contact my warehouse manager at 555.555.5555 to coordinate a time for pick up and delivery.

I would like to continue to do business with MetalWerks, but only if you can solve this problem promptly and assure me that it will not happen again.

Sincerely,

<e-mail signature, including name, title, company and contact information>

Reply to Letter of Complaint

Purpose

- To answer a customer complaint in writing

Alternative Purposes

- To answer a complaint about an ongoing problem
- To answer a complaint about unacceptable service or customer contact
- To answer an announcement of the end of business relations

March 22, 2008

Jeanne Anne Haggerty
Quality Assurance Manager
Closet Friends Inc.
3386 Clinton St.
Philadelphia, PA 40542

Dear Ms. Haggerty:

Thank you for your letter of March 17 in which you pointed out an error in the shipment of your order.

I would like to personally apologize for the mix-up and give you my word that this is the last time you will ever need to write such a letter.

I can tell you that we have found the source of the problem–an error on the loading dock–and have taken steps to ensure that this will not happen again. I personally oversaw the correct shipment of brown brackets, which left our dock an hour ago.

We thank you for your continued business with us, as we know that you have other vendors to choose from for your bracket needs.

Sincerely,

Bill Brademann
Director of Operations

If you are answering a letter cutting off a business relationship:

Please accept my sincere apology for the continued errors in your orders. I can assure you that as of yesterday, we have corrected the problems in our computerized stocking system and that these errors are now a thing of the past.

I hope that you will give MetalWerks another chance to fulfill your bracket needs; I would like to offer you a 20 percent discount on your next order as a way to compensate you for this error on our part.

If you are answering a letter on unacceptable service:

The customer service representative who treated you so rudely has been reassigned to a position where she does not deal with customers. Also, the manager of our order entry department has scheduled a series of training meetings to ensure all telephone representatives have the proper attitude and skills to deal with our valued customers.

If you are answering a letter on an ongoing problem:

I can tell you that we have found the source of the problem–an error on the loading dock–and have taken steps to ensure that this will not happen again. From now until I am completely confident that all trucks will be loaded accurately, I will be personally overseeing every order that goes out to you—starting with the correct shipment of brown brackets, which has just left our dock.

E-Mail

Dear Ms. Haggerty:

Thank you for your e-mail. I would like to personally apologize for the mix-up and give you my word that this is the last time you will ever need to write such a message.

I can tell you that we have found the source of the problem–an error on the loading dock–and have taken steps to ensure that this will not happen again. I personally oversaw the correct shipment of brown brackets, which left our dock an hour ago.

We thank you for your continued business with us, as we know that you have other vendors to choose from for your bracket needs.

Sincerely,

<e-mail signature, including name, title, company and contact information>

Letter of Apology

Purpose

- To formally apologize to a customer

Alternative Purposes

- To apologize to an employee
- To apologize to a superior
- To apologize to a business colleague

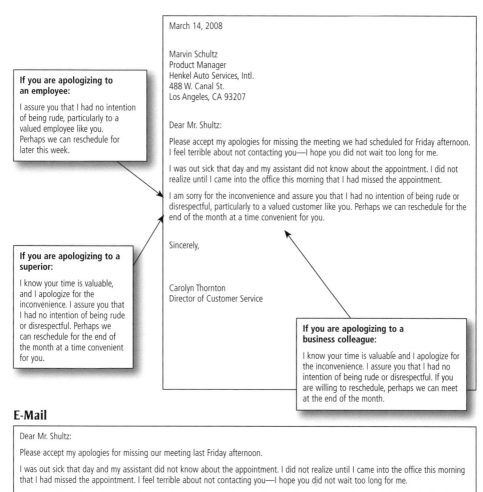

If you are apologizing to an employee:

I assure you that I had no intention of being rude, particularly to a valued employee like you. Perhaps we can reschedule for later this week.

If you are apologizing to a superior:

I know your time is valuable, and I apologize for the inconvenience. I assure you that I had no intention of being rude or disrespectful. Perhaps we can reschedule for the end of the month at a time convenient for you.

If you are apologizing to a business colleague:

I know your time is valuable and I apologize for the inconvenience. I assure you that I had no intention of being rude or disrespectful. If you are willing to reschedule, perhaps we can meet at the end of the month.

March 14, 2008

Marvin Schultz
Product Manager
Henkel Auto Services, Intl.
488 W. Canal St.
Los Angeles, CA 93207

Dear Mr. Shultz:

Please accept my apologies for missing the meeting we had scheduled for Friday afternoon. I feel terrible about not contacting you—I hope you did not wait too long for me.

I was out sick that day and my assistant did not know about the appointment. I did not realize until I came into the office this morning that I had missed the appointment.

I am sorry for the inconvenience and assure you that I had no intention of being rude or disrespectful, particularly to a valued customer like you. Perhaps we can reschedule for the end of the month at a time convenient for you.

Sincerely,

Carolyn Thornton
Director of Customer Service

E-Mail

Dear Mr. Shultz:

Please accept my apologies for missing our meeting last Friday afternoon.

I was out sick that day and my assistant did not know about the appointment. I did not realize until I came into the office this morning that I had missed the appointment. I feel terrible about not contacting you—I hope you did not wait too long for me.

I am sorry for the inconvenience and assure you that I had no intention of being rude or disrespectful, particularly to a valued customer like you.

Perhaps we can reschedule for the end of the month at a time convenient for you.

Sincerely,

<e-mail signature, including name, title, company and contact information>

Reply to Letter of Apology

Purpose

- To accept an apology in writing

Alternative Purposes

- To acknowledge an apology
- To refuse an apology
- To respond with your own apology

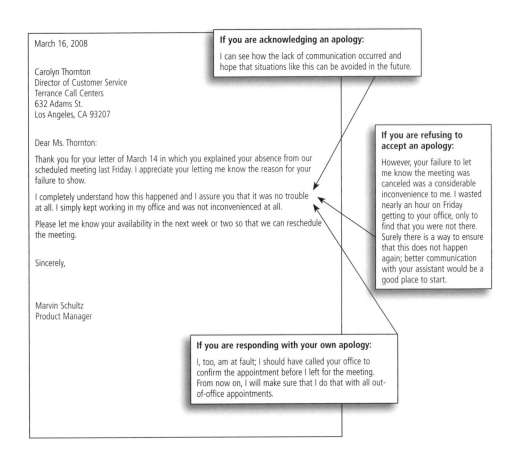

March 16, 2008

Carolyn Thornton
Director of Customer Service
Terrance Call Centers
632 Adams St.
Los Angeles, CA 93207

Dear Ms. Thornton:

Thank you for your letter of March 14 in which you explained your absence from our scheduled meeting last Friday. I appreciate your letting me know the reason for your failure to show.

I completely understand how this happened and I assure you that it was no trouble at all. I simply kept working in my office and was not inconvenienced at all.

Please let me know your availability in the next week or two so that we can reschedule the meeting.

Sincerely,

Marvin Schultz
Product Manager

If you are acknowledging an apology:

I can see how the lack of communication occurred and hope that situations like this can be avoided in the future.

If you are refusing to accept an apology:

However, your failure to let me know the meeting was canceled was a considerable inconvenience to me. I wasted nearly an hour on Friday getting to your office, only to find that you were not there. Surely there is a way to ensure that this does not happen again; better communication with your assistant would be a good place to start.

If you are responding with your own apology:

I, too, am at fault; I should have called your office to confirm the appointment before I left for the meeting. From now on, I will make sure that I do that with all out-of-office appointments.

E-Mail

Dear Ms. Thornton:

Thank you for your e-mail. I appreciate your letting me know the reason for your failure to show.

I completely understand how this happened and I assure you that it was no trouble at all. I simply kept working in my office and was not inconvenienced at all.

Please let me know your availability in the next week or two so that we can reschedule the meeting.

Sincerely,

<e-mail signature, including name, title, company and contact information>

Letter Requesting Donation

Purpose

- To request a monetary donation from a business on behalf of your business

Alternative Purposes

- To request a nonmonetary donation from a business on behalf of your business
- To personally request a monetary donation from a colleague
- To personally request a nonmonetary donation from a colleague

---

If you are personally requesting a monetary donation:

In addition to personally pledging $5,000 to the coalition, I have set a personal goal to raise $100,000 through my business associates and other professional contacts. I am sure that you have your own charitable causes that are near and dear to your heart, but a contribution of just $100 will provide food and shelter for five homeless people for a week; a contribution of $500 will help one person get off the street permanently.

Please help us help the coalition to alleviate homelessness in our community. Simply send a tax-deductible contribution…

If you are requesting a nonmonetary donation:

I am one of a committee that is setting up an auction to help raise funds for the coalition. Would Midwest Industries be able to donate a valuable item or service that can be auctioned off? Other companies have pledged tickets for sporting events, appliances and even travel packages.

Please help us help the coalition to alleviate homelessness in our community. Fill out the enclosed form to let me know what you can contribute to this important cause.

March 27, 2008

Thomas T. Brinks
Chief Executive Officer
Midwest Industries
822 N. Damen Ave., Suite 350
Indianapolis, IN 63903

Dear Mr. Brinks:

I believe it is important for businesses to give back to their communities. That is why Del Valle Enterprises is supporting the Indy Coalition to End Homelessness. We are raising funds for the coalition, encouraging our employees to volunteer and generally spreading the word about this important Indianapolis cause.

In addition to personally pledging $5,000 to the coalition, I have set a personal goal to raise $100,000 through my professional contacts. A corporate contribution of just $100 will provide food and shelter for five homeless people for a week; a contribution of $500 will help one person get off the street permanently.

Please help us help the coalition to alleviate homelessness in our community. Your organization can send a tax-deductible contribution using the enclosed form and envelope.

Sincerely,

Carlos Del Valle
President

If you are personally requesting a nonmonetary donation:

I am one of a committee that is setting up an auction to help raise funds for the coalition. Would you be able to donate a valuable item or service that can be auctioned off? Other executives have pledged tickets for sporting events, appliances and even travel packages.

Please help us help the coalition to alleviate homelessness in our community. Fill out the enclosed form to let me know what you can contribute to this important cause.

E-Mail

Dear Mr. Brinks:

I believe it is important for businesses to give back to their communities. That is why Del Valle Enterprises is supporting the Indy Coalition to End Homelessness. We are raising funds for the coalition, encouraging our employees to volunteer and generally spreading the word about this important Indianapolis cause.

In addition to personally pledging $5,000 to the coalition, I have set a personal goal to raise $100,000 through my professional contacts.

- A corporate contribution of just $100 will provide food and shelter for five homeless people for a week.
- A corporate contribution of $500 will help one person get off the street permanently.
- A corporate contribution of $1,000 will ensure a family is moved to low-income housing.

Please help us help the coalition to alleviate homelessness in our community. Your organization can send a tax-deductible contribution using the attached form.

Sincerely,

<e-mail signature, including name, title, company and contact information>

Letter Refusing Request for Donation

Purpose

- To respond negatively to a donation request

Alternative Purposes

- To respond negatively to a nonmonetary donation request
- To respond negatively with the possibility of a future contribution
- To respond with a firm no to a donation request

April 2, 2008

Carlos Del Valle
President
Del Valle Enterprises
934 S. Hubbard St.
Indianapolis, IN 63903

Dear Mr. Del Valle:

This letter is in response to your request for help for the Indy Coalition to End Homelessness.

Though I agree that this cause is an important one and believe that your efforts to support the coalition are commendable, we are unable to contribute at this time.

It is difficult to turn down your request, but Midwest Industries has limited funds available for charitable contributions and we have already allocated those funds to other causes.

Good luck with your fund raising efforts; I am sure that you will do an outstanding job.

Sincerely,

Thomas T. Brinks
Chief Executive Officer

If you are responding to a request for a nonmonetary donation:

It is difficult to turn down your request. Unfortunately, Midwest Industries does not have anything suitable to contribute to your auction and we do not have funds available to purchase anything.

If you would consider a future contribution:

It is difficult to turn down your request, but Midwest Industries has limited funds available for charitable contributions and we have already allocated those funds to other causes. If you are still seeking donations in 2009, please contact me before the end of the year and I will do my best to allocate some money for a contribution.

If you wish to prevent future requests for donations:

Our company has a policy against contributing to charitable organizations that are not on our approved list of national causes. Please do not direct requests for contributions to me or to Midwest Industries, as we will be unable to donate funds or goods.

E-Mail

Dear Mr. Del Valle:

Though I agree that the Indy Coalition to End Homelessness is an important cause and believe that your efforts to support the coalition are commendable, we are unable to contribute at this time.

It is difficult to turn down your request. Unfortunately, Midwest Industries has limited funds available for charitable contributions and we have already allocated those funds to other causes.

Good luck with your fund-raising efforts; I am sure that you will do an outstanding job.

Sincerely,

<e-mail signature, including name, title, company and contact information>

Letter Accompanying Donation

Purpose

- To acknowledge a donation request and detail the enclosed amount

Alternative Purposes

- To accept a nonmonetary donation request
- To promise a future donation
- To request more information regarding a donation

April 2, 2008

Carlos Del Valle
President
Del Valle Enterprises
934 S. Hubbard St.
Indianapolis, IN 63903

Dear Mr. Del Valle:

The Indy Coalition to End Homelessness is an excellent cause and we at Midwest Industries are happy to be able to join you in supporting it.

I too believe that companies should contribute to their communities, for both moral and business reasons. Therefore, I am enclosing a check from Midwest Industries for $500 to go toward the work of the Indy Coalition to End Homelessness.

Good luck with the remainder of your fund-raising efforts; I am sure that you will do an outstanding job on behalf of the coalition.

Sincerely,

Thomas T. Brinks
Chief Executive Officer

If you are promising a future donation:

The Indy Coalition to End Homelessness is an excellent cause and we at Midwest Industries would like to be able to join you in supporting it.

Although we do not have funds available right now for a contribution, I believe we will be able to allocate some money by June. Unless our plans change, I will send you a check for $500 at that time.

If you need more information regarding a donation:

The Indy Coalition to End Homelessness is an excellent cause, and we at Midwest Industries would like to be able to join you in supporting it.

However, before I can authorize payment for this cause, I need to know if contributions to the coalition are tax deductible and, if so, if we will be issued a receipt for our donation. As soon as you can personally confirm this, we will send a check for $500.

If you are accepting a nonmonetary donation request:

I too believe that companies should contribute to their communities, for both moral and business reasons. Therefore, Midwest Industries has agreed to donate four skybox tickets to the first Indianapolis Colts game of the season for your auction. Please contact me about where to send the tickets and to let me know how to get tickets to the auction.

E-Mail

Dear Mr. Del Valle:

The Indy Coalition to End Homelessness is an excellent cause and we at Midwest Industries are happy to be able to join you in supporting it.

We mailed a check today for $500 to the Indy Coalition to End Homelessness.

Good luck with the remainder of your fund-raising efforts; I am sure that you will do an outstanding job on behalf of the coalition.

Sincerely,

<e-mail signature, including name, title, company and contact information>

Thank You Letter for Donation

Purpose

- To personally thank a business colleague for a monetary donation

Alternative Purposes

- To personally thank a colleague for a nonmonetary donation
- To personally thank a colleague for work done for charity
- To acknowledge the promise of a future donation

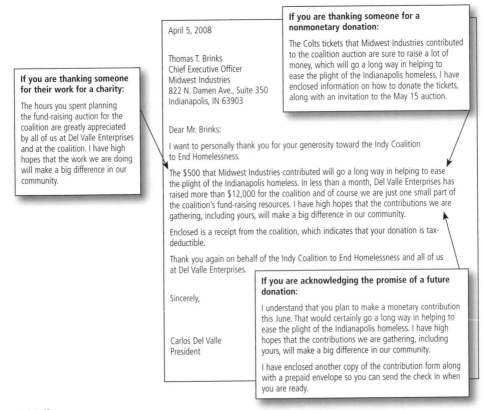

April 5, 2008

Thomas T. Brinks
Chief Executive Officer
Midwest Industries
822 N. Damen Ave., Suite 350
Indianapolis, IN 63903

Dear Mr. Brinks:

I want to personally thank you for your generosity toward the Indy Coalition to End Homelessness.

The $500 that Midwest Industries contributed will go a long way in helping to ease the plight of the Indianapolis homeless. In less than a month, Del Valle Enterprises has raised more than $12,000 for the coalition and of course we are just one small part of the coalition's fund-raising resources. I have high hopes that the contributions we are gathering, including yours, will make a big difference in our community.

Enclosed is a receipt from the coalition, which indicates that your donation is tax-deductible.

Thank you again on behalf of the Indy Coalition to End Homelessness and all of us at Del Valle Enterprises.

Sincerely,

Carlos Del Valle
President

If you are thanking someone for their work for a charity:

The hours you spent planning the fund-raising auction for the coalition are greatly appreciated by all of us at Del Valle Enterprises and at the coalition. I have high hopes that the work we are doing will make a big difference in our community.

If you are thanking someone for a nonmonetary donation:

The Colts tickets that Midwest Industries contributed to the coalition auction are sure to raise a lot of money, which will go a long way in helping to ease the plight of the Indianapolis homeless. I have enclosed information on how to donate the tickets, along with an invitation to the May 15 auction.

If you are acknowledging the promise of a future donation:

I understand that you plan to make a monetary contribution this June. That would certainly go a long way in helping to ease the plight of the Indianapolis homeless. I have high hopes that the contributions we are gathering, including yours, will make a big difference in our community.

I have enclosed another copy of the contribution form along with a prepaid envelope so you can send the check in when you are ready.

E-Mail

Dear Mr. Brinks:

I want to personally thank you for your generosity toward the Indy Coalition to End Homelessness.

The $500 that Midwest Industries contributed will go a long way in helping to ease the plight of the Indianapolis homeless. In less than a month, Del Valle Enterprises has raised more than $12,000 for the coalition and of course we are just one small part of the coalition's fund-raising resources. I have high hopes that the contributions we are gathering, including yours, will make a big difference in our community.

Attached is a receipt from the coalition, which indicates that your donation is tax-deductible.

Thank you again on behalf of the Indy Coalition to End Homelessness and all of us at Del Valle Enterprises.

Sincerely,

<e-mail signature, including name, title, company and contact information>

Letter to Shareholders Providing a General Update

Purpose

- To update your company's shareholders on the general state of the organization

Alternative Purposes

- To accompany a copy of your annual report
- To accompany a copy of a quarterly earnings report
- To alert your company's shareholders to an annual meeting

If you are sending the annual report:

Overall, consolidated revenues for 2007 were $3.2 million, a decrease of just six percent from the previous year. The enclosed annual report includes details and financial statements, including specific information on our operating income, earnings and retained earnings and much more.

If you are sending a quarterly earnings report:

The enclosed quarterly report outlines our profits and losses for the last quarter of 2007 and outlines the latest value of your shares in Stein Software.

January 23, 2008

Dear Shareholder:

Last year, despite a shaky economy, Stein Software managed to hold steady. We did lose a few clients—companies that went out of business, underwent acquisitions or simply lowered their IT budget—but we were able to make up for these losses with some cost controls and a reorganization.

Overall, consolidated revenues for 2007 were $3.2 million, a decrease of just six percent from the previous year.

Stein Software could not have succeeded so well in 2007 without the hard work and sacrifices of its staff and leadership. I would especially like to thank CEO Jillian Thomas for her leadership through these challenging times. And I would like to thank you, the shareholders, for your support of Stein Software.

We are looking forward to better things in 2008 and are confident that we can keep expenses low and thus increase our profits as we explore new markets and opportunities.

Sincerely,

Jason A. Tolbert
Chairman of the Board

If you are notifying shareholders of an annual meeting:

Enclosed is an invitation to our annual meeting of shareholders, to be held in the Stein Software auditorium on March 20, 2008, at 10 a.m. If you cannot attend the meeting, please sign and return the enclosed proxy form.

E-Mail

Dear Shareholder:

Last year, despite a shaky economy, Stein Software managed to hold steady. We did lose a few clients—companies that went out of business, underwent acquisitions or simply lowered their IT budget—but we were able to make up for these losses with some cost controls and a reorganization. Here are some financial highlights:

- Overall, consolidated revenues for 2007 were $3.2 million, a decrease of just six percent from the previous year.
- We managed to cut operating expenses from $1.6 million to $1.2 million by the end of the year.
- Net income for 2007 was $500,000 per share, a slight decrease from 2006.

Stein Software could not have succeeded so well in 2007 without the hard work and sacrifices of its staff and leadership. I would especially like to thank CEO Jillian Thomas for her leadership through these challenging times. And I would like to thank you, the shareholders, for your support of Stein Software.

We are looking forward to better things in 2008 and are confident that we can keep expenses low and thus increase our profits as we explore new markets and opportunities.

Sincerely,

<e-mail signature, including name, title, company and contact information>

Letter to Shareholders Providing Specific News

Purpose

- To alert your company's shareholders to a specific change in the organization

Alternative Purposes

- To alert your company's shareholders to a possible scandal
- To alert your company's shareholders to a change in management
- To alert your company's shareholders to a merger or acquisition

January 23, 2008

Dear Shareholder:

As a shareholder in Stein Software, you should hear major news about the corporation directly rather than reading it in the newspapers. That is why I am sending you this letter.

As you saw in our last annual report, we had plans to put some major cost controls into place in 2008. The first stage of that plan was implemented today, as we laid off 100 employees, or 14 percent of our workforce. Most of these layoffs occurred in our customer service department. As part of our new reorganization, our salespeople will take on customer service relations for their own clients. Also, Web-based and other automated programs will replace in-person communications.

You may see something about this subject in the press in the next few weeks. I want to assure you that everything is under control at Stein Software and ask for your continued support and goodwill as we handle this situation.

Sincerely,

Jason A. Tolbert
Chairman of the Board

If you are announcing a change in management:

Today, I gave my resignation to the Stein Software board of directors, effective March 31. The board will meet later this month to discuss my replacement. I will do my utmost to ensure that Stein Software has a smooth transition to a new chairman of the board.

If you are announcing a merger or acquisition:

Today, Stein Software officially closed a deal to acquire a small software development company called Diehard Developers. We are very excited to bring on board this innovative company, which is responsible for creating several Web-based programs for human resources departments. Their product line, employee expertise and market share makes them a terrific match for Stein Software.

You will be receiving a new prospectus with financial information and an update on the state of your shares by the end of this quarter.

If you are alerting shareholders to a scandal:

This week, Stein Software was served with a lawsuit citing copyright infringement. Our competitor, Digitull Systems, has accused us of using some sections of the programming code used in their payroll systems software in our new Benefits Plus software package.

Our lawyers assure us that the suit has no merit, and we are confident that we can avoid being embroiled in a long, drawn-out legal battle.

E-Mail

Dear Shareholder:

As a shareholder in Stein Software, you should hear major news about the corporation directly rather than reading it in the newspapers. That is why I am sending you this e-mail message.

As you saw in our last annual report, we had plans to put some major cost controls into place in 2008. The first stage of that plan was implemented today, as we laid off 100 employees, or 14 percent of our workforce.

Most of these layoffs occurred in our customer service department. As part of our new reorganization, our salespeople will take on customer service relations for their own clients. Also, Web-based and other automated programs will replace in-person communications.

You may see something about this subject in the press in the next few weeks. I want to assure you that everything is under control at Stein Software and ask for your continued support and goodwill as we handle this situation.

Sincerely,

<e-mail signature, including name, title, company and contact information>

Positive Response to Unsolicited Sales Letter

Purpose

- To respond formally to a direct mail or personal solicitation letter

Alternative Purposes

- To request additional information
- To request a meeting
- To place an order or accept an offer

If you need additional information to make a decision:

Your letter did not mention anything about pricing. Can you forward me an outline of how your fees work? Do you require an annual contract? If so, what is the fee structure? I would appreciate any information, even a price range, which would help me compare your company with our current support team.

If you are placing an order or accepting an offer:

I would like to contract with your company to provide technical support for our office. I have enclosed the application form you sent; please let me know if there is anything else you need from me to start the process.

February 18, 2008

Albert Lee
Director of Sales and Marketing
Help Desk Enterprises
8371 S. Columbus Drive
Lincoln, NE 49210

Dear Mr. Lee:

You sent me a letter dated February 2 that outlined your company's tech support services for small and midsized offices. Although I was not familiar with Help Desk Enterprises, it sounds like you would be a good fit for our support needs.

Heil & Heil has 20 employees working in our office, along with several offsite consultants who access our computer network via their laptops. Our network is on an XP Windows server running Linux.

I would be interested in hearing what types of services Help Desk Enterprises can offer us and at what price. Please contact me at 555.555.5555 to discuss the next steps.

I look forward to hearing from you.

Sincerely,

Carolyn Frey
Office Manager

If you want to set up a meeting:

I would like to set up a meeting in our office with one of your sales representatives, our network administrator and myself. Please call me at the number above to see if we can find a convenient time to meet.

E-Mail

Dear Mr. Lee:

Based on the information in your previous e-mail, it sounds like you would be a good fit for the support needs of Heil & Heil.

We have 20 employees working in our office, along with several offsite consultants who access our computer network via their laptops. Our network is on a 2-year-old Linux-Windows server.

I would be interested in hearing what types of services Help Desk Enterprises can offer us and at what price. Please contact me to discuss next steps.

Sincerely,

<e-mail signature, including name, title, company and contact information>

Negative Response to Unsolicited Sales Letter

Purpose

- To formally respond to a direct mail or personal solicitation letter

Alternative Purposes

- To alert the sender to erroneous information
- To recommend another contact for future mailings
- To request to be taken off a mailing list

February 18, 2008

Albert Lee
Director of Sales and Marketing
Help Desk Enterprises
8371 S. Columbus Drive
Lincoln, NE 49210

Dear Mr. Lee:

You sent me a letter dated February 2 that outlined your company's tech support services.

I want to let you know that although Heil & Heil is a relatively small firm, we do have our own in-house technical support. We have no need to hire outside help now or in the foreseeable future.

I will keep your letter on file in the unlikely event that this situation changes. In the meantime, please make a note that we do not require your services.

Sincerely,

Carolyn Frey
Office Manager

If you are alerting the sender to erroneous information:

I want to let you know that although Heil & Heil is a two-person company, we are not in the market for tech support services. I suggest that you double-check the source of your mailing list, as we are much too small a company to be a legitimate prospect for your mailings.

If you want to recommend another contact:

Please direct all future correspondence to Ned Drummond, our network administrator. He would be the person most likely to make decisions about using your company's services. I did forward your letter on to him.

If you no longer wish to receive mailings:

Please remove my name and the names of any other contacts you have at Heil & Heil from your company's mailing list. We do not wish to receive any more mailings from your company.

E-Mail

Dear Mr. Lee:

In response to your message, I want to let you know that Heil & Heil has no need of hiring outside tech support now or in the foreseeable future. Although we are a relatively small firm, we have our own in-house technical support.

I will keep your message on file in the unlikely event that this situation changes. In the meantime, please make a note that we do not require your services.

Sincerely,

<e-mail signature, including name, title, company and contact information>

Letter Accompanying Application for Business License

Purpose

- To notify the appropriate person that you are submitting an application for a business license

Alternative Purposes

- To notify the appropriate person that you are submitting a renewal for a business license
- To notify the appropriate person that you are submitting an incomplete application for a business license
- To notify the appropriate person that you are submitting a permit for your business

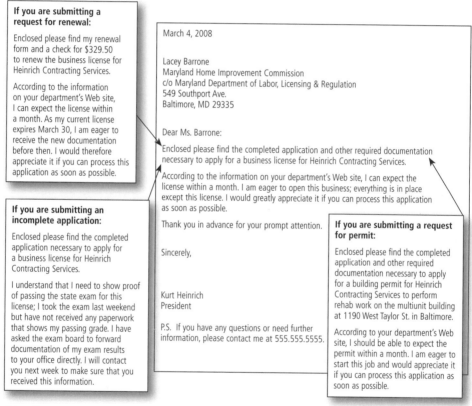

If you are submitting a request for renewal:

Enclosed please find my renewal form and a check for $329.50 to renew the business license for Heinrich Contracting Services.

According to the information on your department's Web site, I can expect the license within a month. As my current license expires March 30, I am eager to receive the new documentation before then. I would therefore appreciate it if you can process this application as soon as possible.

If you are submitting an incomplete application:

Enclosed please find the completed application necessary to apply for a business license for Heinrich Contracting Services.

I understand that I need to show proof of passing the state exam for this license; I took the exam last weekend but have not received any paperwork that shows my passing grade. I have asked the exam board to forward documentation of my exam results to your office directly. I will contact you next week to make sure that you received this information.

March 4, 2008

Lacey Barrone
Maryland Home Improvement Commission
c/o Maryland Department of Labor, Licensing & Regulation
549 Southport Ave.
Baltimore, MD 29335

Dear Ms. Barrone:

Enclosed please find the completed application and other required documentation necessary to apply for a business license for Heinrich Contracting Services.

According to the information on your department's Web site, I can expect the license within a month. I am eager to open this business; everything is in place except this license. I would greatly appreciate it if you can process this application as soon as possible.

Thank you in advance for your prompt attention.

Sincerely,

Kurt Heinrich
President

P.S. If you have any questions or need further information, please contact me at 555.555.5555.

If you are submitting a request for permit:

Enclosed please find the completed application and other required documentation necessary to apply for a building permit for Heinrich Contracting Services to perform rehab work on the multiunit building at 1190 West Taylor St. in Baltimore.

According to your department's Web site, I should be able to expect the permit within a month. I am eager to start this job and would appreciate it if you can process this application as soon as possible.

E-Mail

Dear Ms. Barrone:

Attached please find the completed application necessary to apply for a business license for Heinrich Contracting Services.

According to the information on your department's Web site, I can expect the license within a month. I am eager to open this business; everything is in place except this license. I would greatly appreciate it if you can process this application as soon as possible. If you have any questions or need further information, please respond to this message.

Thank you in advance for your prompt attention.

Sincerely,

<e-mail signature, including name, title, company and contact information>

Letter to Landlord Negotiating Terms of Lease

Purpose

- To formally open negotiations on a new or continued lease

Alternative Purposes

- To propose a longer lease contract
- To propose adding more space to your current location
- To propose new payment terms

March 16, 2008

Ellen Constantino
Property Manager
Culver & Culver Real Estate
624 N. Polk St.
San Diego, CA 93402

Dear Ms. Constantino:

As I am sure you are aware, the lease for Pacific Construction's office space and warehouse at 4338 N. Ashland Ave. will expire at the end of June. I would like to assure you that we are interested in renewing that lease but would like a change in the terms of our lease.

The current rental market in San Diego favors tenants, and we have many options for moving and saving money on rent. However, there are a number of reasons why we would prefer to stay at this location and continue to rent from Culver & Culver.

Therefore, I propose that we renew our lease for the standard time frame of 3 years with a five percent decrease in our rent. This decrease would bring our payments more in line with the current market, and we would be willing to accept this minor reduction in order to avoid the costs of moving. You would benefit by ensuring you have a paying tenant for the next 3 years with no effort on your part.

Please let me know if this proposition suits you. I will need an answer by the end of the month so we can make any necessary plans to move.

Thank you for your consideration in this matter.

Sincerely,

Yolanda Cruz
Chief Financial Officer

If you are proposing the addition of space:

Our business has grown, and while our office space is sufficient, we will need more warehouse space in the near future. We would like to rent an additional 10,000-square-foot space with a loading dock from you, located anywhere in our building.

If you have space available, I propose that we add that to our lease for the same amount we are paying for our current space.

If you are proposing new payment terms:

This year, we have implemented a new accounting system that is reconciled quarterly rather than monthly. I would like to propose that we pay our rent to you each quarter, in a lump sum rather than monthly. This would dovetail with our system, and you would receive the same amount of money—in advance, of course.

If you are proposing a longer lease:

Therefore, I am proposing that we will renew our lease for 5 years rather than the standard time frame of 3 years. This extension would lock us in at our current rent and benefit us by ensuring our expenditure until 2003. You would benefit by ensuring you have a paying tenant for the next 5 years, no matter how loose the rental market may become.

E-Mail

Dear Ms. Constantino:

As I am sure you are aware, the lease for Pacific Construction's office space and warehouse at 4338 N. Ashland Ave. will expire at the end of June. I would like to assure you that we are interested in renewing that lease but would like a change in terms.

The current rental market in San Diego favors tenants, and we have many options for moving and saving money on rent. However, there are a number of reasons why we would prefer to stay at this location and continue to rent from Culver & Culver.

Therefore, I am proposing that we will renew our lease for the standard time frame of 3 years with a five percent decrease in the monthly rent. This decrease would bring our payments more in line with the current market, and we would be willing to accept this minor reduction in order to avoid the costs of moving. You would benefit by ensuring you have a paying tenant for the next 3 years with no effort on your part.

Please let me know if this proposition suits you. I will need an answer by the end of the month so we can make any necessary plans to move.

Thank you for your consideration in this matter.

Sincerely,

<e-mail signature, including name, title, company and contact information>

Letter to Congressman Supporting Specific Legislation

Purpose

- To encourage your state or U.S. representative in Congress to support specific legislation that is beneficial to your business

Alternative Purposes

- To encourage your representative to vote against legislation that is not beneficial to your business
- To ask your representative to introduce specific legislation
- To ask your representative to do a specific favor for your business

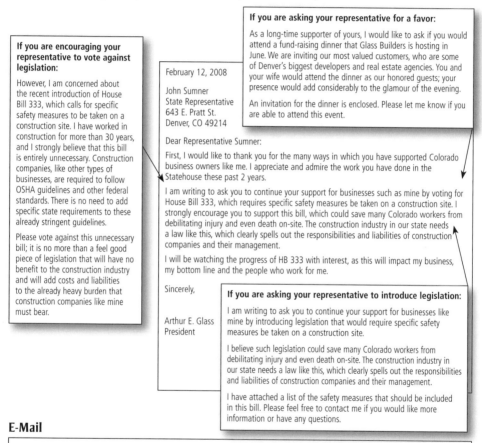

If you are asking your representative for a favor:

As a long-time supporter of yours, I would like to ask if you would attend a fund-raising dinner that Glass Builders is hosting in June. We are inviting our most valued customers, who are some of Denver's biggest developers and real estate agencies. You and your wife would attend the dinner as our honored guests; your presence would add considerably to the glamour of the evening.

An invitation for the dinner is enclosed. Please let me know if you are able to attend this event.

If you are encouraging your representative to vote against legislation:

However, I am concerned about the recent introduction of House Bill 333, which calls for specific safety measures to be taken on a construction site. I have worked in construction for more than 30 years, and I strongly believe that this bill is entirely unnecessary. Construction companies, like other types of businesses, are required to follow OSHA guidelines and other federal standards. There is no need to add specific state requirements to these already stringent guidelines.

Please vote against this unnecessary bill; it is no more than a feel good piece of legislation that will have no benefit to the construction industry and will add costs and liabilities to the already heavy burden that construction companies like mine must bear.

February 12, 2008

John Sumner
State Representative
643 E. Pratt St.
Denver, CO 49214

Dear Representative Sumner:

First, I would like to thank you for the many ways in which you have supported Colorado business owners like me. I appreciate and admire the work you have done in the Statehouse these past 2 years.

I am writing to ask you to continue your support for businesses such as mine by voting for House Bill 333, which requires specific safety measures be taken on a construction site. I strongly encourage you to support this bill, which could save many Colorado workers from debilitating injury and even death on-site. The construction industry in our state needs a law like this, which clearly spells out the responsibilities and liabilities of construction companies and their management.

I will be watching the progress of HB 333 with interest, as this will impact my business, my bottom line and the people who work for me.

Sincerely,

Arthur E. Glass
President

If you are asking your representative to introduce legislation:

I am writing to ask you to continue your support for businesses like mine by introducing legislation that would require specific safety measures be taken on a construction site.

I believe such legislation could save many Colorado workers from debilitating injury and even death on-site. The construction industry in our state needs a law like this, which clearly spells out the responsibilities and liabilities of construction companies and their management.

I have attached a list of the safety measures that should be included in this bill. Please feel free to contact me if you would like more information or have any questions.

E-Mail

Dear Representative Sumner:

First, I would like to thank you for the many ways in which you have supported Colorado business owners like me. I appreciate and admire the work you have done in the Statehouse these past 2 years.

I am asking you to continue your support for businesses such as mine by voting for House Bill 333, which requires specific safety measures be taken on a construction site. I strongly encourage you to support this bill, which could save many Colorado workers from debilitating injury and even death on-site. The construction industry in our state needs a law like this, which clearly spells out the responsibilities and liabilities of construction companies and their management.

I will be watching the progress of HB 333 with interest, as this will impact my business, my bottom line and the people who work for me.

Sincerely,

<e-mail signature, including name, title, company and contact information>

Letter to Media Suggesting Coverage of Your Company

Purpose

- To alert a member of the media to a newsworthy aspect of your business

Alternative Purposes

- To alert a member of the media to a newsworthy product of your business
- To alert a member of the media to a newsworthy event at your business
- To alert a member of the media to a newsworthy change of personnel at your business

February 24, 2008

Rebecca Fleishmann
Senior Editor
Grocers World Journal
9321 W. Rush St.
Iowa City, IA 59981

Dear Ms. Fleishmann:

Never before have Americans consumed so much exotic tea. In fact, this past year marked the first year that tea sales exceeded sales of bulk coffees. Special Teas Inc.–a wholesaler of exotic, high-end teas from Asia that sells to major retail chains and smaller specialty stores around the U.S.–has statistics on geographic sales in supermarkets to show buying patterns.

This is exciting news for all of us here at Special Teas Inc. and I believe readers of Grocers World Journal would be interested in learning about this news. I have read your journal regularly and it seems this article would be a natural fit for your editorial content.

If you are interested in writing an article on this subject or would like to learn more, please contact me. I would be happy to answer any questions you may have and to set up interviews with the appropriate people within Special Teas Inc.

I look forward to hearing from you.

Sincerely,

Jay Bulicek
Marketing Manager

If you are alerting the media regarding a new product:

For the first time, a U.S. tea plantation will have exotic teas available in American supermarkets and other retail outlets. This week, Special Teas Inc–a wholesaler of exotic, high-end teas from Asia that sells to major retail chains as well as smaller specialty stores around the U.S.–signed a contract with a tea plantation in Hawaii called Aloha Tea. We will begin selling Aloha Teas to our retail customers this summer with special "Made in America" packaging.

If you are alerting the media regarding a company event:

This spring, Special Teas Inc. will host an international forum on the tea industry. We are inviting leading tea growers from around the world to join us in Dallas, Texas, May 12-14, for this first-ever forum.

If you are alerting the media regarding a change of personnel:

Our founder, Alan Su, not only started up Special Teas Inc. on a shoestring budget in 1983, he has led the company to greater and greater success over the past 25 years. Alan has announced his plans to retire at the end of May, and he will be succeeded as Special Teas' CEO by his daughter, Linda Su Lemoyne.

E-Mail

Dear Ms. Fleishmann:

Never before have Americans consumed so much exotic tea. In fact, this past year marked the first year that tea sales exceeded sales of bulk coffees. Special Teas Inc.–a wholesaler of exotic, high-end teas from Asia that sells to major retail chains and smaller specialty stores around the U.S.–has statistics on geographic sales in supermarkets to show buying patterns.

This trend is exciting news for all of us here at Special Teas Inc. and I believe readers of Grocers World Journal would be interested in learning about this news.

If you are interested in writing an article on this subject, or would like to learn more, please contact me. I would be happy to answer any questions you may have and to set up interviews with the appropriate people within Special Teas Inc.

Sincerely,

<e-mail signature, including name, title, company and contact information>

Letter Welcoming New Leader

Purpose

- To personally welcome a new addition to your company's board of directors

Alternative Purposes

- To welcome a new addition to your advisory board or panel
- To welcome an outside consultant as a new addition to a committee
- To welcome an employee as a new addition to a committee

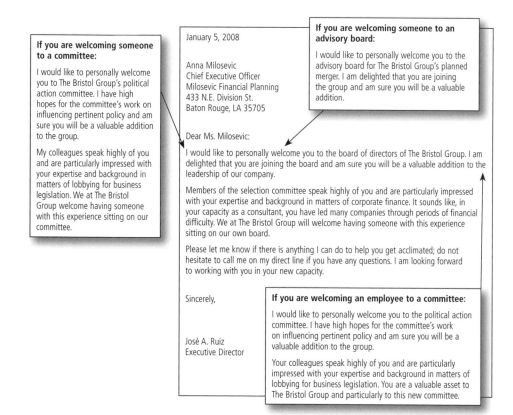

If you are welcoming someone to a committee:

I would like to personally welcome you to The Bristol Group's political action committee. I have high hopes for the committee's work on influencing pertinent policy and am sure you will be a valuable addition to the group.

My colleagues speak highly of you and are particularly impressed with your expertise and background in matters of lobbying for business legislation. We at The Bristol Group welcome having someone with this experience sitting on our committee.

If you are welcoming someone to an advisory board:

I would like to personally welcome you to the advisory board for The Bristol Group's planned merger. I am delighted that you are joining the group and am sure you will be a valuable addition.

January 5, 2008

Anna Milosevic
Chief Executive Officer
Milosevic Financial Planning
433 N.E. Division St.
Baton Rouge, LA 35705

Dear Ms. Milosevic:

I would like to personally welcome you to the board of directors of The Bristol Group. I am delighted that you are joining the board and am sure you will be a valuable addition to the leadership of our company.

Members of the selection committee speak highly of you and are particularly impressed with your expertise and background in matters of corporate finance. It sounds like, in your capacity as a consultant, you have led many companies through periods of financial difficulty. We at The Bristol Group will welcome having someone with this experience sitting on our own board.

Please let me know if there is anything I can do to help you get acclimated; do not hesitate to call me on my direct line if you have any questions. I am looking forward to working with you in your new capacity.

Sincerely,

José A. Ruiz
Executive Director

If you are welcoming an employee to a committee:

I would like to personally welcome you to the political action committee. I have high hopes for the committee's work on influencing pertinent policy and am sure you will be a valuable addition to the group.

Your colleagues speak highly of you and are particularly impressed with your expertise and background in matters of lobbying for business legislation. You are a valuable asset to The Bristol Group and particularly to this new committee.

E-Mail

Dear Ms. Milosevic:

I would like to personally welcome you to the board of directors of The Bristol Group. I am delighted that you are joining the board and am sure you will be a valuable addition to the leadership of our company.

Members of the selection committee speak highly of you and are particularly impressed with your expertise and background in matters of corporate finance. It sounds like, in your capacity as a consultant, you have led many companies through periods of financial difficulty. We at The Bristol Group will welcome having someone with this experience sitting on our own board.

Please let me know if there is anything I can do to help you get acclimated and do not hesitate to contact me if you have any questions.

I am looking forward to working with you in your new capacity.

Sincerely,

<e-mail signature, including name, title, company and contact information>

Invitation to Speak at a Company Event

Purpose

- To formally invite an individual to speak at your company event

Alternative Purposes

- To invite an employee to speak at your company event
- To invite your superior to speak at your company event
- To invite a professional speaker to speak at your company event

---

March 30, 2008

Elena Panazzo
President
Panazzo Consulting Group
4794 W. Wabash Ave.
Cincinnati, OH 47099

Dear Ms. Panazzo:

On May 12, our company will hold its annual sales meeting, when approximately 125 salespeople from around the country will come to Columbus to hear about the company's status, learn what is in store for the coming year and receive training on our new and upcoming products.

This year, we thought it would add value to the event if we started the meeting with a keynote speaker. Your role in helping to create our newest product makes you an excellent choice. Would you be willing to give a short presentation on the planning and development process behind the debut of the LF-12 horizontal milling machine?

Please let me know if you are willing and able to speak on May 12. Your presentation would be approximately 15 minutes and would take place between 9 a.m. and 9:30 a.m. I would be happy to discuss this with you and answer any questions you may have. You can reach me at 555.555.5555. I look forward to hearing from you soon.

Sincerely,

Pamela J. Nash
Meeting Planner

If you are asking an employee to speak:

This year, we thought it would add value to the event if we started the meeting with a keynote speaker. As the top salesperson for 2007, you would be an excellent presenter. Would you be willing to share insights into your success with your peers?

If you are asking your superior to speak:

This year, we thought it would add value to the event if we started the meeting with a keynote speaker. Would you consider opening the sales meeting with a brief presentation on how the company is doing?

If you are asking a professional speaker to speak:

This year, we thought it would add value to the event if we started the meeting with a keynote speaker, and we would be delighted to get a leading expert in our industry and a popular speaker such as yourself.

E-Mail

Dear Ms. Panazzo:

On May 12, our company will hold its annual sales meeting, when approximately 125 salespeople from around the country will come to Columbus to hear about the company's status, learn what is in store for the coming year and receive training on our new and upcoming products.

This year, we thought it would add value to the event if we started the meeting with a keynote speaker. Your role in helping to create our newest product makes you an excellent choice.

Would you be willing to give a short presentation on the planning and development process behind the debut of the LF-12 horizontal milling machine?

Please let me know if you are willing and able to speak on May 12. Your presentation would be approximately 15 minutes and would take place between 9 a.m. and 9:30 a.m.

I would be happy to discuss this with you and answer any questions you may have. I look forward to hearing from you soon.

<e-mail signature, including name, title, company and contact information>

Reply to Invitation to Speak at a Company Event

Purpose

- To accept an invitation to speak at a business event

Alternative Purposes

- To decline an invitation to speak at a business event
- To request more information on speaking at a business event
- To recommend a colleague to speak at a business event

April 4, 2008

Pamela J. Nash
Meeting Planner
Bristol Group
6321 W. Clark St.
Columbus, OH 47324

Dear Ms. Nash:

Thank you for the invitation to speak at the Bristol Group's national sales meeting on May 12 in Columbus. I am flattered that you asked me to be your keynote speaker.

I would be delighted to give a 15-minute presentation to the sales force on the development of the LF-12. I have some anecdotes and some statistics that should surprise them as well as detailed information that should help them sell this new machine.

Please forward all available information about the meeting as it becomes available. Meanwhile, I will begin drafting my presentation.

Thank you again for this opportunity.

Sincerely,

Elena Panazzo
President

If you are declining the invitation:

I am sorry, but I cannot accept your invitation. My company has a policy that prohibits employees from speaking publicly about our projects, even to the customer who owns the project.

If you are requesting more information:

I am interested in this speaking opportunity, but would like more information before I accept. Specifically, I would like to know if Bristol Group plans to pay a speaking fee and if they will pay for travel expenses.

Please call me to discuss the financial support you can offer.

If you are recommending a colleague:

I would like to suggest that my partner, Alan Howard, would be a better choice as a speaker. Alan is more knowledgeable than me on the development of the LF-12 and he is an established speaker.

I have forwarded your original letter to Alan. If you would like to discuss the keynote address with him, you can reach him at 555.555.5555.

E-Mail

Dear Ms. Nash:

Thank you for the invitation to speak at the Bristol Group's national sales meeting. I am flattered that you asked me to be your keynote speaker.

I would be delighted to give a 15-minute presentation on the development of the LF-12. I have some anecdotes and some statistics that should surprise the sales force as well as detailed information that should help them sell this new machine.

Please forward all available information about the meeting as it becomes available. Meanwhile, I will begin drafting my presentation.

Thank you again for this opportunity.

<e-mail signature, including name, title, company and contact information>

Letter Acknowledging Speaker at Company Event

Purpose

- To formally thank an individual for speaking at your company event

Alternative Purposes

- To offer extensive praise for the speaker
- To offer feedback to the speaker
- To offer a referral to the speaker

If you are offering extensive praise:

With your informative and motivational presentation, you set the bar high for future keynote speakers. Your speech certainly set the tone for an excellent and productive day, and we credit you with the energy and excitement felt throughout the day.

May 18, 2008

Elena Panazzo
President
Panazzo Consulting Group
4794 W. Wabash Ave.
Cincinnati, OH 47099

Dear Ms. Panazzo:

On behalf of the CEO, the salespeople and everyone here at the Bristol Group, I would like to thank you for presenting the keynote address at our May 12 sales meeting. We appreciate your time and effort both in preparing your speech and in attending our opening session.

Your speech helped set the tone for an exciting and productive meeting.

I have enclosed a videotape of the opening session, including your presentation. Please feel free to use the segment with your speech for any promotional purposes.

Sincerely,

Pamela J. Nash
Meeting Planner

If you are offering feedback:

Your speech was highly informative and I am sure that the salespeople learned a lot. I did hear some comments that your voice could not be heard very well in the back of the room; if you plan to continue speaking to large groups you might want to consider practicing projection techniques.

If you are suggesting a referral:

Your speech helped set the tone for an exciting and productive meeting. One of our attendees, Peter Barnes, is on the planning committee for the industry's upcoming conference. He was so impressed with your poise and confidence at the podium that he suggested you should consider speaking at the conference. If you are interested, you can contact Peter at 555.555.5555.

E-Mail

Dear Ms. Panazzo:

Thank you so much for presenting the keynote address at our May 12 sales meeting. We appreciate your time and effort both in preparing your speech and in attending our opening session.

Your speech helped set the tone for an exciting and productive meeting.

I have attached a file that is a videotape of your presentation. Please feel free to use this for any promotional purposes.

<e-mail signature, including name, title, company and contact information>

Response to Communication Addressed to Departed Employee

Purpose

- To alert the recipient that his or her contact is no longer employed at your business

Alternative Purposes

- To direct the recipient to employee's replacement
- To let the recipient know you have forwarded his or her letter
- To request that all future communications stop

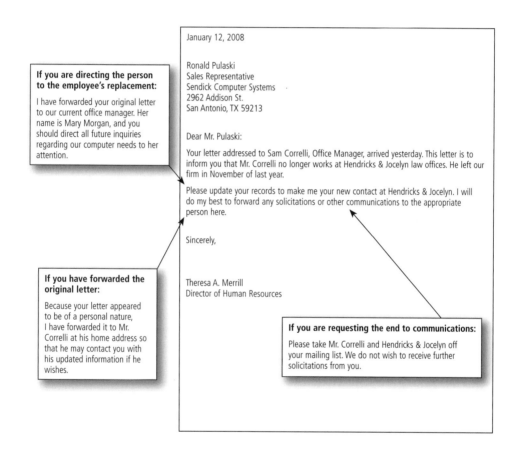

If you are directing the person to the employee's replacement:

I have forwarded your original letter to our current office manager. Her name is Mary Morgan, and you should direct all future inquiries regarding our computer needs to her attention.

If you have forwarded the original letter:

Because your letter appeared to be of a personal nature, I have forwarded it to Mr. Correlli at his home address so that he may contact you with his updated information if he wishes.

If you are requesting the end to communications:

Please take Mr. Correlli and Hendricks & Jocelyn off your mailing list. We do not wish to receive further solicitations from you.

January 12, 2008

Ronald Pulaski
Sales Representative
Sendick Computer Systems
2962 Addison St.
San Antonio, TX 59213

Dear Mr. Pulaski:

Your letter addressed to Sam Correlli, Office Manager, arrived yesterday. This letter is to inform you that Mr. Correlli no longer works at Hendricks & Jocelyn law offices. He left our firm in November of last year.

Please update your records to make me your new contact at Hendricks & Jocelyn. I will do my best to forward any solicitations or other communications to the appropriate person here.

Sincerely,

Theresa A. Merrill
Director of Human Resources

E-Mail

Dear Mr. Pulaski:

Your e-mail to Sam Correlli (**scorrelli@hendricks.jocelyn.com**) arrived yesterday. This message is to inform you that Mr. Correlli no longer works at Hendricks & Jocelyn law offices. He left our firm in November of last year.

Please update your records to make me your new contact at Hendricks & Jocelyn. I will do my best to forward any solicitations or other communications to the appropriate person here.

Sincerely,

<e-mail signature, including name, title, company and contact information>

Section Four

·····

Essential Human
Resources Letters

Follow-Up Letter to Job Candidate after Interview

Purpose

- To acknowledge receipt of a job application or resume

Alternative Purposes

- To invite the person to come to an interview
- To reject the applicant
- To inform the person that the position has been filled

If you are rejecting the applicant:

Your cover letter and resume indicate that you have the necessary technical knowledge and skills for this position; however, we are looking for someone with 2 or more years of supervisory experience. If you are interested in working in another capacity in our IT department, please keep an eye on our online job listings at **www.greggmatherinc.com/jobs.**

If the position has been filled:

Your cover letter and resume indicate that you are well-qualified for this position, but we officially hired someone for the job 2 days before I received your information.

March 18, 2008

Sarah J. Thornton
5921 S. Clybourn Ave.
Baton Rouge, LA 49302

Dear Ms. Thornton:

Thank you for submitting your resume for the position of IT manager here at Gregg Mather.

Your cover letter and resume indicate that you are well-qualified for this position, but as I am sure you can imagine, we received many applications. Once we review our top choices, we will contact you regarding the next steps; at this point, we will either set up a phone interview with you or let you know that we have selected other candidates ahead of you. I would estimate that we will contact you within the next week.

Again, thank you for your interest in working at Gregg Mather.

Sincerely,

Jason Leavitt
Human Resources Director

If you are inviting the person to come to an interview:

Your cover letter and resume indicate that you are well-qualified for this position. I would like to set up an initial interview between you and one of my HR associates next week. Please contact my assistant, Jerilynn Adams at 555.555.5555 to set up this appointment.

E-Mail

Dear Ms. Thornton:

Thank you for submitting your resume for the position of IT manager here at Gregg Mather.

Your e-mail and resume both indicate that you are well-qualified for this position, but as I am sure you can imagine, we received many such applications.

Once we review our top choices, we will contact you regarding the next steps; at this point, we will either set up a phone interview with you or let you know that we have selected other candidates ahead of you.

I would estimate that we will contact you within the next week.

Again, thank you for your interest in working at Gregg Mather.

Sincerely,

< e-mail signature, including name, title, company and contact information>

Letter Responding to Unsolicited Resume

Purpose

- To respond to an unsolicited job application or resume

Alternative Purposes

- To inform the sender that you will file his or her resume for future reference
- To set up a job interview with the sender
- To reject the resume

March 19, 2008

Sarah J. Thornton
5921 S. Clybourn Ave.
Baton Rouge, LA 49302

Dear Ms. Thornton:

Earlier this week, I received the resume and cover letter you sent to Gregg Mather in hopes of interviewing for a position in our IT department.

We do not have any current openings in this department and do not anticipate any. You can check our company Web site for a listing of job openings in our Baton Rouge office and across the country. That listing can be found by visiting our home page at **www.greggmatherinc.com** and clicking on "About Us," then selecting "Employment Opportunities."

Thank you for your interest in working at Gregg Mather. I wish you luck in your job search.

Sincerely,

Jason Leavitt
Human Resources Director

If you are filing the resume for future reference:

We do not have any current openings in this department and do not anticipate any. However, your level of experience and skill set is a good fit for this department, so I will file your resume in case something opens up unexpectedly.

If you are inviting the person to come to an interview:

We may have a job opening for an IT associate. Your cover letter and resume indicate that you are well-qualified for this position. I would like to have you come in for a preliminary interview with our human resources department. Please call Jerilynn Adams, my assistant, at 555.555.5555 to set up this appointment.

If you are rejecting the unsolicited resume:

Please note that we do not accept unsolicited resumes or job applications; the volume of mail is simply too much. You can check our company Web site …

E-Mail

Dear Ms. Thornton:

We do not have any current openings in our IT department and do not anticipate any.

You can check our company Web site for a listing of job openings in our Baton Rouge office and across the country. That listing can be found by visiting our home page at **www.greggmatherinc.com** and clicking on "About Us," then selecting "Employment Opportunities."

Thank you for your interest in working at Gregg Mather. I wish you luck in your job search.

Sincerely,

< e-mail signature, including name, title, company and contact information>

Letter to Employees Requesting Job Candidate Referrals

Purpose

- To personally ask your employees to refer candidates for an open position

Alternative Purposes

- To ask for a referral for a specific position
- To offer a finder's fee for recommending a new employee
- To acknowledge employees who have referred job candidates

If you are offering a finder's fee:

… and then submit a completed Employee Referral Form (attached) to the human resources department. If we hire a candidate originally recommended by you, you will receive a $300 finder's fee. This money will be given to you after the candidate is hired and completes their 3-month probationary period.

If you are acknowledging employees who have referred job candidates:

This memo is a reminder that any employee can personally refer individuals for our specific job openings. This is a terrific opportunity for you to help your friends and professional colleagues while you help your company.

I would like to personally thank the following employees, who are responsible for finding great matches for four of our recent job openings:

Ricardo Gomez
Jackie Martinson
Terrance Smith
Ed Withers

If you know someone who is a good fit for an open position …

March 8, 2008

To: All Employees of Gregg Mather Inc.
From: Jason Leavitt, Human Resources Director
Re: Referral of New Job Candidates

Dear Employee:

This month, your human resources department will implement a program that will allow you to help your friends and professional colleagues while you help your company.

Gregg Mather is offering all employees the opportunity to personally refer individuals for our specific job openings. If you know someone who is a good fit for an open position, I ask that you first ensure that person is interested in the job and then submit a completed Employee Referral Form (attached) to the human resources department.

We will give priority to those candidates who were referred by our employees, assuming that the candidate is qualified for the specific job and his or her information is current and correct.

If you have any questions regarding the referral process, please contact me or anyone else in the human resources department.

Thank you in advance for your help in building a stronger team here at Gregg Mather.

Sincerely,

Jason Leavitt

If you are asking for a referral for a specific position:

We are currently seeking a sales manager to fill the position left by Sally Cortez last month. If you know someone with previous experience managing a regional sales force, and is familiar with our market, please contact him or her and direct him or her to the position description on our Web site at **www.greggmatherinc.com/about/jobs**. We will give priority …

E-Mail

Dear Employee:

This month, your human resources department will implement a program that will allow you to help your friends and professional colleagues while you help your company.

Gregg Mather is offering all employees the opportunity to personally refer individuals for our specific job openings. If you know someone who is a good fit for an open position, please:

- ensure that person is interested in the job, then
- submit a completed Employee Referral Form (attached) to the human resources department.

We will give priority to those candidates who were referred by our employees, assuming that the candidate is qualified for the specific job and his or her information is current and correct.

If you have any questions regarding the referral process, please contact me or anyone else in the human resources department.

Thank you in advance for your help in building a stronger team here at Gregg Mather.

Sincerely,

< e-mail signature, including name, title, company and contact information>

Letter Requesting Information from References

Purpose

- To officially request information on a job candidate from a current or previous employer

Alternative Purposes

- To request information on a job candidate from his or her personal reference
- To ask for verification of employment
- To ask for a financial background check

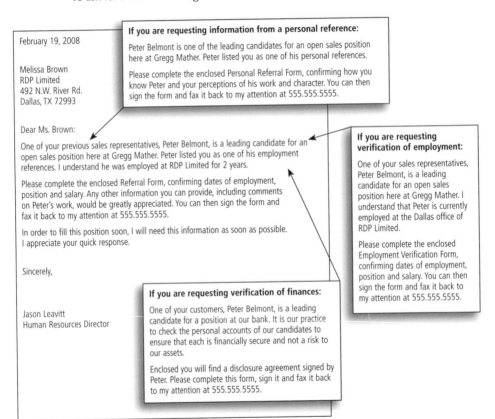

February 19, 2008

Melissa Brown
RDP Limited
492 N.W. River Rd.
Dallas, TX 72993

Dear Ms. Brown:

One of your previous sales representatives, Peter Belmont, is a leading candidate for an open sales position here at Gregg Mather. Peter listed you as one of his employment references. I understand he was employed at RDP Limited for 2 years.

Please complete the enclosed Referral Form, confirming dates of employment, position and salary. Any other information you can provide, including comments on Peter's work, would be greatly appreciated. You can then sign the form and fax it back to my attention at 555.555.5555.

In order to fill this position soon, I will need this information as soon as possible. I appreciate your quick response.

Sincerely,

Jason Leavitt
Human Resources Director

If you are requesting information from a personal reference:

Peter Belmont is one of the leading candidates for an open sales position here at Gregg Mather. Peter listed you as one of his personal references.

Please complete the enclosed Personal Referral Form, confirming how you know Peter and your perceptions of his work and character. You can then sign the form and fax it back to my attention at 555.555.5555.

If you are requesting verification of employment:

One of your sales representatives, Peter Belmont, is a leading candidate for an open sales position here at Gregg Mather. I understand that Peter is currently employed at the Dallas office of RDP Limited.

Please complete the enclosed Employment Verification Form, confirming dates of employment, position and salary. You can then sign the form and fax it back to my attention at 555.555.5555.

If you are requesting verification of finances:

One of your customers, Peter Belmont, is a leading candidate for a position at our bank. It is our practice to check the personal accounts of our candidates to ensure that each is financially secure and not a risk to our assets.

Enclosed you will find a disclosure agreement signed by Peter. Please complete this form, sign it and fax it back to my attention at 555.555.5555.

E-Mail

Dear Ms. Brown:

One of your previous sales representatives, Peter Belmont, is a leading candidate for an open sales position here at Gregg Mather. Peter listed you as one of his employment references. I understand he was employed at RDP Limited for 2 years.

Please print out and complete the attached PDF of our Referral Form, confirming dates of employment, position and salary.

Any other information you can provide, including comments on Peter's work, would be greatly appreciated.

You can then sign the form and fax it back to my attention at 555.555.5555.

In order to fill this position soon, I will need this information as soon as possible. I appreciate your quick response.

Sincerely,

< e-mail signature, including name, title, company and contact information>

Follow-Up Letter to Job Candidate after Interview

Purpose

- To thank a management candidate for an in-person interview and inform him or her of the next steps

Alternative Purposes

- To request a second or third interview
- To request more information from the candidate
- To reject the candidate

If you are requesting another interview:

Your qualifications, work experience and personality seem like a good fit for this position. I would like to set up an interview for you with the CEO of Gregg Mather and, more briefly, with some of our other executives. This meeting will take 1 to 2 hours.

Please check your calendar and let me know if you can come in sometime next Tuesday afternoon or Wednesday morning. You can contact me directly to set up this appointment.

If you are rejecting the candidate:

After reviewing your excellent qualifications and work experience, we have decided that another candidate for the position will be a better fit.

Thank you again for your interest in working at Gregg Mather, and I wish you luck with your job search.

March 27, 2008

Sarah J. Thornton
5921 S. Clybourn Ave.
Baton Rouge, LA 49302

Dear Ms. Thornton:

Thank you for taking the time to come in and meet with me regarding the position of chief information officer here at Gregg Mather.

I want to keep you informed on how the interview process is going. We have narrowed the field to four leading candidates, including you. I will be contacting each to schedule an interview with the CEO of Gregg Mather and, more briefly, with some of our other executives.

I will be in touch with you soon with several possible interview times. In the meantime, if you have any questions about Gregg Mather or about the position, please do not hesitate to call me directly.

Sincerely,

Jason Leavitt
Human Resources Director

If you are requesting more information:

Your qualifications, work experience and personality seem like a good fit for this position. The next step in our interview process calls for reference checks. Please forward me the names, titles and contact information for three references. You can e-mail the information to me at **jleavitt@greggmather.com**.

Thank you in advance for this information. If you have any questions …

E-Mail

Dear Ms. Thornton:

Thank you for taking the time to come in and meet with me regarding the position of chief information officer here at Gregg Mather.

I want to keep you informed on how the interview process is going.

We have narrowed the field to four leading candidates, including you. I will be contacting each to schedule an interview with the CEO of Gregg Mather and, more briefly, with some of our other executives.

I will be in touch with you soon with several possible interview times. In the meantime, if you have any questions about Gregg Mather or about the position, please do not hesitate to call me directly.

Sincerely,

<e-mail signature, including name, title, company and contact information>

Letter Outlining Job Offer, Benefits and Salary

Purpose

- To formally confirm a job offer and provide all necessary details of employment

Alternative Purposes

- To initiate a job offer in writing
- To outline final steps before official employment
- To enclose a contract for the candidate to sign

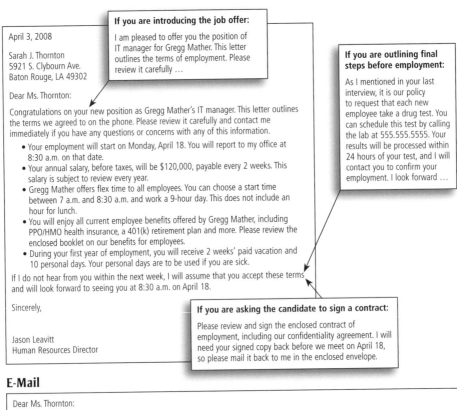

If you are introducing the job offer:

I am pleased to offer you the position of IT manager for Gregg Mather. This letter outlines the terms of employment. Please review it carefully ...

If you are outlining final steps before employment:

As I mentioned in your last interview, it is our policy to request that each new employee take a drug test. You can schedule this test by calling the lab at 555.555.5555. Your results will be processed within 24 hours of your test, and I will contact you to confirm your employment. I look forward ...

April 3, 2008

Sarah J. Thornton
5921 S. Clybourn Ave.
Baton Rouge, LA 49302

Dear Ms. Thornton:

Congratulations on your new position as Gregg Mather's IT manager. This letter outlines the terms we agreed to on the phone. Please review it carefully and contact me immediately if you have any questions or concerns with any of this information.

- Your employment will start on Monday, April 18. You will report to my office at 8:30 a.m. on that date.
- Your annual salary, before taxes, will be $120,000, payable every 2 weeks. This salary is subject to review every year.
- Gregg Mather offers flex time to all employees. You can choose a start time between 7 a.m. and 8:30 a.m. and work a 9-hour day. This does not include an hour for lunch.
- You will enjoy all current employee benefits offered by Gregg Mather, including PPO/HMO health insurance, a 401(k) retirement plan and more. Please review the enclosed booklet on our benefits for employees.
- During your first year of employment, you will receive 2 weeks' paid vacation and 10 personal days. Your personal days are to be used if you are sick.

If I do not hear from you within the next week, I will assume that you accept these terms and will look forward to seeing you at 8:30 a.m. on April 18.

Sincerely,

Jason Leavitt
Human Resources Director

If you are asking the candidate to sign a contract:

Please review and sign the enclosed contract of employment, including our confidentiality agreement. I will need your signed copy back before we meet on April 18, so please mail it back to me in the enclosed envelope.

E-Mail

Dear Ms. Thornton:

Congratulations on your new position as Gregg Mather's IT manager.

This message outlines the terms we agreed to on the phone. Please review it carefully and reply immediately if you have any questions or concerns with any of this information.

- Your employment will start on Monday, April 18. You will report to my office at 8:30 a.m. on that date.
- Your annual salary, before taxes, will be $120,000, payable every 2 weeks. This salary is subject to review every year.
- Gregg Mather offers flex time to all employees. You can choose a start time between 7 a.m. and 8:30 a.m. and work a 9-hour day. This does not include an hour for lunch.
- You will enjoy all current employee benefits offered by Gregg Mather, including PPO/HMO health insurance, a 401(k) retirement plan and more. Please review the enclosed booklet on our benefits for employees.
- During your first year of employment, you will receive 2 weeks' paid vacation and 10 personal days. Your personal days are to be used if you are sick.

If I do not hear from you within the next week, I will assume that you accept these terms and will look forward to seeing you at 8:30 a.m. on April 18.

Sincerely,

<e-mail signature, including name, title, company and contact information>

Letter of Acceptance to a Job Candidate

Purpose

- To formally offer a job to a candidate

Alternative Purposes

- To request a meeting in order to offer the job
- To outline final steps before official employment
- To enclose a contract for the candidate to sign

If you are outlining final steps before employment:

… standard employee benefit package. It is also contingent upon your passing a drug test. Our company policy requires that each new employee take a drug test; you can schedule your test by calling the lab at 555.555.5555. Your results will be processed within 24 hours of your test, and I will contact you to confirm your employment.

April 3, 2008

Sarah J. Thornton
5921 S. Clybourn Ave.
Baton Rouge, LA 49302

Dear Ms. Thornton:

I am pleased to offer you the position of IT manager for Gregg Mather.

This offer is contingent upon your agreement to the terms of employment. These terms include the salary I quoted in our last interview of $120,000 gross annual salary and our standard employee benefit package.

Please respond to this offer by calling me directly at 555.555.5555. I would be happy to answer any questions or address any concerns. However, I need to hear from you by the end of this week so that we can make other plans if you cannot accept this offer.

I hope that I am not premature in offering you congratulations on your new position and welcoming you to Gregg Mather.

Sincerely,

Jason Leavitt
Human Resources Director

If you are requesting an in-person meeting to offer the job:

I would like to schedule one more pre-employment meeting with you to discuss the terms of your employment and confirm your agreement. I can meet with you midday on Tuesday or on Thursday morning. Please call my assistant, Jerilynn Adams, at 555.555.5555 to set up this appointment.

If you are asking the candidate to sign a contract:

Please review and sign the enclosed contract of employment, including our confidentiality agreement. Feel free to call me if you have any questions or concerns. Otherwise, I will expect a copy of your signed contract by April 15 at the latest.

E-Mail

Dear Ms. Thornton:

I am pleased to offer you the position of IT manager for Gregg Mather.

This offer is contingent upon your agreement to the terms of employment. These terms include the salary I quoted in our last interview of $120,000 gross annual salary and our standard employee benefit package.

Please respond to this offer by replying to this message. I would be happy to answer any questions or address any concerns.

I hope that I am not premature in offering you congratulations on your new position and welcoming you to Gregg Mather.

Sincerely,

<e-mail signature, including name, title, company and contact information>

Letter of Rejection to a Job Candidate

Purpose

- To inform a finalist job candidate that you have selected someone else

Alternative Purposes

- To inform a job candidate that the position is no longer being offered
- To inform a job candidate that his or her references or background check were negative
- To inform a job candidate that you cannot meet his or her negotiated terms

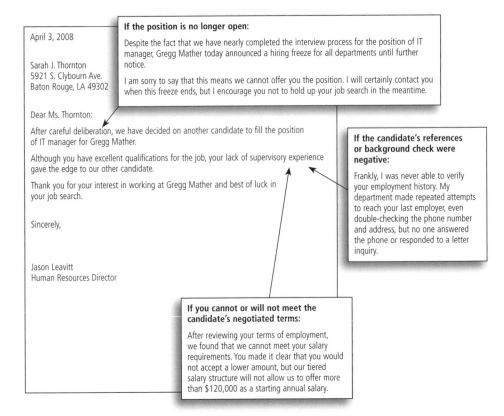

April 3, 2008

Sarah J. Thornton
5921 S. Clybourn Ave.
Baton Rouge, LA 49302

Dear Ms. Thornton:

After careful deliberation, we have decided on another candidate to fill the position of IT manager for Gregg Mather.

Although you have excellent qualifications for the job, your lack of supervisory experience gave the edge to our other candidate.

Thank you for your interest in working at Gregg Mather and best of luck in your job search.

Sincerely,

Jason Leavitt
Human Resources Director

If the position is no longer open:

Despite the fact that we have nearly completed the interview process for the position of IT manager, Gregg Mather today announced a hiring freeze for all departments until further notice.

I am sorry to say that this means we cannot offer you the position. I will certainly contact you when this freeze ends, but I encourage you not to hold up your job search in the meantime.

If the candidate's references or background check were negative:

Frankly, I was never able to verify your employment history. My department made repeated attempts to reach your last employer, even double-checking the phone number and address, but no one answered the phone or responded to a letter inquiry.

If you cannot or will not meet the candidate's negotiated terms:

After reviewing your terms of employment, we found that we cannot meet your salary requirements. You made it clear that you would not accept a lower amount, but our tiered salary structure will not allow us to offer more than $120,000 as a starting annual salary.

E-Mail

Dear Ms. Thornton:

I am sending this e-mail because I wanted to let you know as soon as possible: After careful deliberation, we have decided on another candidate to fill the position of IT manager for Gregg Mather.

Although you have excellent qualifications for the job, your lack of supervisory experience gave the edge to our other candidate.

Thank you for your interest in working at Gregg Mather and best of luck in your job search.

Sincerely,

<e-mail signature, including name, title, company and contact information>

Letter Introducing New Employee to Staff

Purpose

- To formally introduce a new hire to your staff

Alternative Purposes

- To introduce a new manager to the staff he or she will oversee
- To announce the departure of an employee and name his or her replacement
- To introduce a consultant who will be working with the staff

---

April 18, 2008

To: All Employees of Gregg Mather Inc.
From: Jason Leavitt, Human Resources Director
Re: Meet Your New IT Manager

Dear Employee:

Our new IT manager will begin work at Gregg Mather this Thursday. Please take a moment to welcome Sarah J. Thornton to our team.

Sarah has nearly 20 years' experience in the information technology field. She comes to us from her position as IT manager at Ohio Glass Co., where she managed a staff of nine, running the midrange computer system at the company's Dayton office and providing desktop support. In 2007, Sarah oversaw her department's upgrade to an i5.

Sarah holds an MIS degree from Ohio State and has the expertise to run the computer systems in our office.

I encourage each of you to introduce yourself to Sarah during her first few days here and make her feel welcome.

Sincerely,

Jason Leavitt

If you are introducing a new manager to the staff:

Let me introduce the new manager of your department: Sarah J. Thornton will step into the position of Gregg Mather's IT manager starting this Thursday. She will manage the entire IT staff and will report to Bob Roll, our chief information officer.

If you are introducing a consultant who will be working with the staff:

Starting this Thursday, you will see a new face in the IT department. Sarah J. Thornton is a technology consultant with Repinger-Allen, and she will be working in our offices 3 days a week, helping us convert to Linux-based architecture.

If you are announcing the departure of an employee and naming his or her replacement:

As of last Friday, Bob Roll no longer works at Gregg Mather. We wish Bob well as he pursues other interests.

Our IT associate, Sarah J. Thornton, will assume the position of IT manager, effective immediately. Sarah's 7 years of experience working in our IT department ensures that this transition will be a seamless one.

E-Mail

Dear Employee:

Our new IT manager will begin work at Gregg Mather this Thursday.

Please take a moment to welcome Sarah J. Thornton to our team.

Sarah has nearly 20 years' experience in the information technology field. She comes to us from her position as IT manager at Ohio Glass Co., where she managed a staff of nine, running the midrange computer system at the company's Dayton office and providing desktop support.

Sarah holds an MIS degree from Ohio State and has the expertise to run the computer systems in our office.

I encourage each of you to introduce yourself to Sarah during her first few days here and make her feel welcome.

Sincerely,

<e-mail signature, including name, title, company and contact information>

Letter Requesting Salary Increase or Promotion

Purpose

- To formally request an increase in salary for your current job

Alternative Purposes

- To request a promotion
- To request additional responsibilities
- To request special benefits, such as flex time or additional time off

---

January 18, 2008

To: Lawrence Gallagher, Director of Marketing
From: Beth Cahill
Re: My Annual Review

Dear Lawrence:

My annual review is coming up in February. Therefore, I want to make a case in advance for special consideration for my work.

Over the past year, I have taken on more and more responsibility as TRX's marketing has ramped up to include public relations and internal communications. Specifically, I have added full responsibility for press relations and press releases to my regular workload.

I have reviewed the TRX employee handbook and know that a standard salary increase for an employee with a good or excellent review is six percent. I believe that due to the circumstances of my increased responsibilities and the excellent quality of all my work, I should be eligible for an exception to this policy. I am asking that you consider increasing my current salary by 10 percent.

Thank you for considering this proposal. I look forward to discussing it in more detail during my review.

Sincerely,

Beth Cahill
Marketing Communications Associate

If you are requesting additional responsibilities:

I have been sending out press releases at your request for 7 months now and feel that I have a good sense of what is newsworthy and important to TRX. I am asking that you consider turning over responsibility to me for deciding what our releases should cover.

If you are requesting special benefits:

These added hours have made my evening commute a lot slower. If I could leave the office earlier, it would save a great deal of wasted time in my car. Therefore, I am asking that you consider letting me start each day at 7 a.m. and leave at 4:30 p.m. If I have work left over at the end of the day, I can take it home with me, if applicable, or stay past 4:30 p.m. to finish it.

If you are requesting a promotion:

I believe that my new everyday responsibilities exceed those of an associate. I am asking that you consider promoting me to a marketing communications director level; this title is more appropriate for the main press contact for TRX, and I feel that my increased level of expertise warrants a promotion.

E-Mail

Dear Lawrence:

My annual review is coming up in February. Therefore, I want to make a case in advance for special consideration for my work.

Over the past year, I have taken on more and more responsibility as TRX's marketing has ramped up to include public relations and internal communications. Specifically, I have added full responsibility for press relations and press releases to my regular workload.

I have reviewed the TRX employee handbook and know that a standard salary increase for an employee with a good or excellent review is six percent.

I believe that due to the circumstances of my increased responsibilities and the excellent quality of all my work, I should be eligible for an exception to this policy. I am asking that you consider increasing my current salary by 10 percent.

Thank you for considering this proposal. I look forward to discussing it in more detail during my review.

Sincerely,

<e-mail signature, including name, title, company and contact information>

Letter Outlining Salary Increase or Promotion

Purpose

- To officially outline the terms of a new salary increase

Alternative Purposes

- To outline the terms of a promotion
- To outline the terms of additional responsibilities
- To outline the terms of special benefits, such as flex time or additional time off

If you are outlining the terms of a promotion:

Effective March 1, your new title will be Marketing Communications Director. Your salary will increase to a new director's level of $75,000.

You will continue to report to me, and you will have no staff reporting to you. It is possible that one or more associates might start to report to you later this year, but we can discuss this after you have settled into your new position.

If you are outlining the terms of special benefits:

Effective March 1, your daily hours will be those you requested: 7 a.m. to 4:30 p.m. It is your responsibility to maintain these hours and to let your fellow employees and your media contacts know when you will be available.

February 19, 2008

To: Beth Cahill
From: Lawrence Gallagher
Re: Salary Considerations

Dear Beth:

This memo confirms the changes agreed to in our discussion during your annual review on February 15.

With your three percent increase, your new annual salary will be $73,500. Your March 14 paycheck will include this increase, retroactive to February 15. Please note that your deductions for state and federal taxes and your 401(k) contribution will be slightly higher because of this increase.

If you have any questions or concerns regarding your paychecks or benefits beginning in mid-April, please contact our human resources department.

Once again, congratulations on your excellent review.

Sincerely,

Lawrence Gallagher
Director of Marketing

If you are outlining the terms of additional responsibilities:

Your job description has been amended to include your public relations duties. Please find a copy of the new job description attached.

E-Mail

Dear Beth:

This e-mail confirms the changes agreed to in our discussion during your annual review on February 15.

With your three percent increase, your new annual salary will be $73,500. Your March 14 paycheck will include this increase, retroactive to February 15. Please note that your deductions for state and federal taxes and your 401(k) contribution will be slightly higher because of this increase.

If you have any questions or concerns regarding your paychecks or benefits beginning in mid-April, please contact our human resources department.

Once again, congratulations on your excellent review.

Sincerely,

<e-mail signature, including name, title, company and contact information>

Letter Refusing Request for Salary Increase or Promotion

Purpose

- To outline the reasons why an employee's request for a salary increase cannot be met

Alternative Purposes

- To outline the reasons why a request for promotion cannot be met
- To outline the reasons why a request for additional responsibilities cannot be met
- To outline the reasons why a request for special benefits cannot be met

January 24, 2008

To: Beth Cahill
From: Lawrence Gallagher
Re: Salary Considerations

Dear Beth:

I received your note of January 18 regarding your upcoming annual review. Rather than wait for our in-person meeting in February, I wanted to respond immediately.

First, let me reinforce that TRX has a set salary range for each position, and no exceptions can be made to those ranges. The salary range for your position is $60,000 to $70,000. As long as you stay in your current job, and until those salary ranges are adjusted by TRX's human resources department, your salary cannot exceed $70,000.

Second, though I understand that you have been doing additional work in the past few months, I must point out that everyone here (and, indeed, in most companies in the United States) is working harder than ever. This is the state of our economy; we must all work harder than we used to. While I agree that your work is of excellent quality, I cannot reward you for handling additional responsibilities, as this is true of every employee here at TRX.

When we sit down for your annual review, I would be happy to discuss how I perceive your work. However, I want to stress that your initial request is unrealistic.

Sincerely,

Lawrence Gallagher
Director of Marketing

If you are outlining the reasons that a request for additional responsibilities cannot be met:

I will not be able to fulfill your request for additional decision-making responsibilities. The topics of our press releases, which you suggested you can determine, mesh with a larger marketing mix that you do not have access to. A master plan of all future press releases through the end of this year has already been established.

If you are outlining the reasons that a request for promotion cannot be met:

A promotion to marketing manager is more than just a change of title and a larger salary. The job description for a TRX marketing manager includes the duties of supervising one or more other marketing staff. The hierarchy of our department is already set, and I have no plans to reassign management duties at this time.

Perhaps we can discuss the skills and expertise you need to develop in order to become a marketing manager in the future.

If you are outlining the reasons that a request for special benefits cannot be met:

I will not be able to fulfill your request for earlier work hours. Unfortunately, TRX does not currently offer flex time; our stated office hours apply to everyone. If you find you are working late hours, perhaps you could come in early to ensure that you leave on time, but that time must be 5:30 p.m.

E-Mail

Dear Beth:

Rather than wait for our in-person meeting in February, I wanted to respond to your e-mail immediately.

First, let me reinforce that TRX has a set salary range for each position, and no exceptions can be made to those ranges.

The salary range for your position is $60,000 to $70,000. As long as you stay in your current job, and until those salary ranges are adjusted by TRX's human resources department, your salary cannot exceed $70,000.

Second, though I understand that you have been doing additional work in the past few months, I must point out that everyone here (and, indeed, in most companies in the United States) is working harder than ever. This is the state of our economy; we must all work harder than we used to.

Though I agree that your work is of excellent quality, I cannot reward you for handling additional responsibilities, as this is true of every employee here at TRX.

When we sit down for your annual review, I would be happy to discuss how I perceive your work. However, I want to stress that your initial request is unrealistic.

Sincerely,

<e-mail signature, including name, title, company and contact information>

Letter Outlining an Employee Problem

Purpose

- To formally note that an employee is causing problems in the workplace

Alternative Purposes

- To address a personal issue
- To address a general bad attitude
- To address insubordination

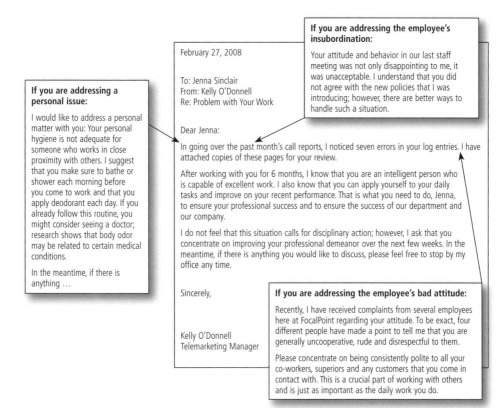

If you are addressing the employee's insubordination:

Your attitude and behavior in our last staff meeting was not only disappointing to me, it was unacceptable. I understand that you did not agree with the new policies that I was introducing; however, there are better ways to handle such a situation.

If you are addressing a personal issue:

I would like to address a personal matter with you: Your personal hygiene is not adequate for someone who works in close proximity with others. I suggest that you make sure to bathe or shower each morning before you come to work and that you apply deodorant each day. If you already follow this routine, you might consider seeing a doctor; research shows that body odor may be related to certain medical conditions.

In the meantime, if there is anything …

February 27, 2008

To: Jenna Sinclair
From: Kelly O'Donnell
Re: Problem with Your Work

Dear Jenna:

In going over the past month's call reports, I noticed seven errors in your log entries. I have attached copies of these pages for your review.

After working with you for 6 months, I know that you are an intelligent person who is capable of excellent work. I also know that you can apply yourself to your daily tasks and improve on your recent performance. That is what you need to do, Jenna, to ensure your professional success and to ensure the success of our department and our company.

I do not feel that this situation calls for disciplinary action; however, I ask that you concentrate on improving your professional demeanor over the next few weeks. In the meantime, if there is anything you would like to discuss, please feel free to stop by my office any time.

Sincerely,

Kelly O'Donnell
Telemarketing Manager

If you are addressing the employee's bad attitude:

Recently, I have received complaints from several employees here at FocalPoint regarding your attitude. To be exact, four different people have made a point to tell me that you are generally uncooperative, rude and disrespectful to them.

Please concentrate on being consistently polite to all your co-workers, superiors and any customers that you come in contact with. This is a crucial part of working with others and is just as important as the daily work you do.

E-Mail

Dear Jenna:

In going over the past month's call reports, I noticed seven errors in your log entries. I have attached PDFs of these pages for your review.

After working with you for 6 months, I know that you are an intelligent person who is capable of excellent work.

I also know that you can apply yourself to your daily tasks and improve on your recent performance. That is what you need to do, Jenna, to ensure your professional success and to ensure the success of our department and our company.

I do not feel that this situation calls for disciplinary action; however, I ask that you concentrate on improving your professional demeanor over the next few weeks.

In the meantime, if there is anything you would like to discuss, please feel free to stop by my office any time.

Sincerely,

<e-mail signature, including name, title, company and contact information>

Letter Outlining Employee Problem and Disciplinary Course of Action

Purpose

- To formally note that an employee has broken a rule or policy and inform him or her of the disciplinary action

Alternative Purposes

- To ask the employee to provide his or her side of the argument in writing
- To ask the employee to meet with you
- To ask the employee to meet with a mediator

If you are asking the employee to meet with you:

It is time we had a formal meeting about this problem. Please come to the south conference room at 3 p.m. on Tuesday, March 4 to see if we can resolve this issue before it goes any further.

If you are asking the employee to provide his or her side:

I would like to give you an opportunity to add your side of the story to your file. If you are interested, you can type up the reasons why you have been late so frequently and submit that document to me. I will place it in your file along with this letter, and it will become part of your permanent file.

February 27, 2008

To: Jenna Sinclair
From: Kelly O'Donnell
Re: Your Late Arrival

Dear Jenna:

Yesterday, February 26, and today, I noticed that you were 20 minutes late and 45 minutes late, respectively. Jenna, we have discussed your chronic late arrivals several times in person, but the message does not seem to be getting through: It is very important that you be at your desk and ready to answer your phone by 8:45 a.m. every workday morning.

A copy of this letter will be placed in your permanent personnel file, and if further problems occur, this record will be taken into account. Our company policy states that if you are late one more time after receiving this letter, the next step will be to place you on probation, and the step after that will be immediate termination. I certainly hope that it does not come to that, but I would like to stress that this has become a serious issue and we need to ensure that you change this bad habit before it costs you your job.

If you have any questions regarding this course of disciplinary action, please come and talk to me.

Sincerely,

Kelly O'Donnell
Telemarketing Manager

If you are asking the employee to meet with a mediator:

It is time to bring in some outside help to address this problem. Please come to the south conference room at 3 p.m. on Tuesday, March 4 to meet with me and Frank Saunders, the personnel manager. Frank can help us both come to a resolution on this issue.

E-Mail

Dear Jenna:

Yesterday and today, I noticed that you were 20 minutes late and 45 minutes late, respectively.

Jenna, we have discussed your chronic late arrivals several times in person, but the message does not seem to be getting through: It is very important that you be at your desk and ready to answer your phone by 8:45 a.m. every workday morning.

A printed copy of this e-mail will be placed in your permanent personnel file and if further problems occur, this record will be taken into account. Our company policy states that if you are late one more time after receiving this letter, the next step will be to place you on probation, and the step after that will be immediate termination. I certainly hope that it does not come to that, but I would like to stress that this has become a serious issue and we need to ensure that you change this bad habit before it costs you your job.

If you have any questions regarding this course of disciplinary action, please come and talk to me any time that I am free.

Sincerely,

<e-mail signature, including name, title, company and contact information>

Letter of Dismissal

Purpose

- To formally notify someone that you are terminating his or her employment

Alternative Purposes

- To notify an employee that his or her position has been eliminated
- To notify an employee that the company or office is closing
- To notify an employee on leave that his or her job will not be waiting for him or her

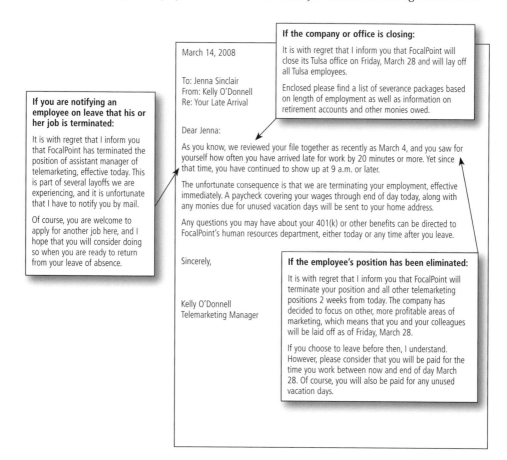

If the company or office is closing:

It is with regret that I inform you that FocalPoint will close its Tulsa office on Friday, March 28 and will lay off all Tulsa employees.

Enclosed please find a list of severance packages based on length of employment as well as information on retirement accounts and other monies owed.

March 14, 2008

To: Jenna Sinclair
From: Kelly O'Donnell
Re: Your Late Arrival

If you are notifying an employee on leave that his or her job is terminated:

It is with regret that I inform you that FocalPoint has terminated the position of assistant manager of telemarketing, effective today. This is part of several layoffs we are experiencing, and it is unfortunate that I have to notify you by mail.

Of course, you are welcome to apply for another job here, and I hope that you will consider doing so when you are ready to return from your leave of absence.

Dear Jenna:

As you know, we reviewed your file together as recently as March 4, and you saw for yourself how often you have arrived late for work by 20 minutes or more. Yet since that time, you have continued to show up at 9 a.m. or later.

The unfortunate consequence is that we are terminating your employment, effective immediately. A paycheck covering your wages through end of day today, along with any monies due for unused vacation days will be sent to your home address.

Any questions you may have about your 401(k) or other benefits can be directed to FocalPoint's human resources department, either today or any time after you leave.

Sincerely,

Kelly O'Donnell
Telemarketing Manager

If the employee's position has been eliminated:

It is with regret that I inform you that FocalPoint will terminate your position and all other telemarketing positions 2 weeks from today. The company has decided to focus on other, more profitable areas of marketing, which means that you and your colleagues will be laid off as of Friday, March 28.

If you choose to leave before then, I understand. However, please consider that you will be paid for the time you work between now and end of day March 28. Of course, you will also be paid for any unused vacation days.

E-Mail

Dear Jenna:

As you know, we reviewed your file together as recently as March 4, and you saw for yourself how often you have arrived late for work by 20 minutes or more. Yet since that time, you have continued to show up at 9 a.m. or later.

Please come to see me in my office today at 2:30 p.m. to discuss next steps for addressing this continuing problem.

Sincerely,

<e-mail signature, including name, title, company and contact information>

Letter of Recommendation for an Employee to an Outside Company

Purpose

- To provide a personal recommendation for an employee who is leaving your company

Alternative Purposes

- To provide a personal recommendation for a consultant or freelance employee
- To provide a personal recommendation for a past employee
- To provide confirmation of employment for an employee who is leaving your company

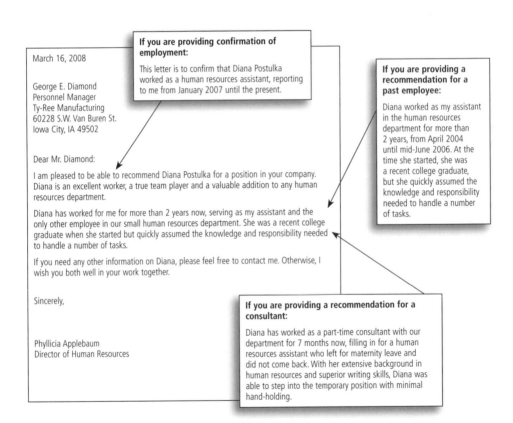

March 16, 2008

George E. Diamond
Personnel Manager
Ty-Ree Manufacturing
60228 S.W. Van Buren St.
Iowa City, IA 49502

Dear Mr. Diamond:

I am pleased to be able to recommend Diana Postulka for a position in your company. Diana is an excellent worker, a true team player and a valuable addition to any human resources department.

Diana has worked for me for more than 2 years now, serving as my assistant and the only other employee in our small human resources department. She was a recent college graduate when she started but quickly assumed the knowledge and responsibility needed to handle a number of tasks.

If you need any other information on Diana, please feel free to contact me. Otherwise, I wish you both well in your work together.

Sincerely,

Phyllicia Applebaum
Director of Human Resources

If you are providing confirmation of employment:

This letter is to confirm that Diana Postulka worked as a human resources assistant, reporting to me from January 2007 until the present.

If you are providing a recommendation for a past employee:

Diana worked as my assistant in the human resources department for more than 2 years, from April 2004 until mid-June 2006. At the time she started, she was a recent college graduate, but she quickly assumed the knowledge and responsibility needed to handle a number of tasks.

If you are providing a recommendation for a consultant:

Diana has worked as a part-time consultant with our department for 7 months now, filling in for a human resources assistant who left for maternity leave and did not come back. With her extensive background in human resources and superior writing skills, Diana was able to step into the temporary position with minimal hand-holding.

E-Mail

Dear Mr. Diamond:

This e-mail is in response to your request for a reference for Diana Postulka for a position in your company.

Diana is an excellent worker, a true team player and a valuable addition to any human resources department. She has worked for me for more than 2 years now, serving as my assistant and the only other employee in our small human resources department. Diana was a recent college graduate when she started but quickly assumed the knowledge and responsibility needed to handle a number of tasks.

I wish you both well in your work together.

Sincerely,

<e-mail signature, including name, title, company and contact information>

Letter of Recommendation for an Employee to Another Supervisor in Your Organization

Purpose

- To provide a personal recommendation for an employee to another supervisor in your organization

Alternative Purposes

- To provide a personal recommendation for a consultant or freelance employee
- To provide a personal recommendation for a past employee
- To provide a personal recommendation for an employee up for a promotion

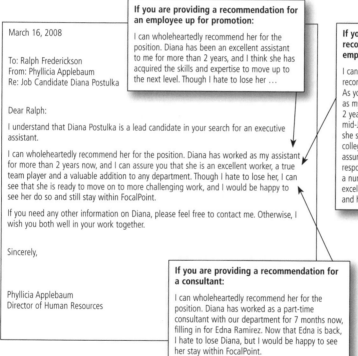

If you are providing a recommendation for an employee up for promotion:

I can wholeheartedly recommend her for the position. Diana has been an excellent assistant to me for more than 2 years, and I think she has acquired the skills and expertise to move up to the next level. Though I hate to lose her …

If you are providing a recommendation for a past employee:

I can wholeheartedly recommend her for the position. As you may recall, Diana worked as my assistant for more than 2 years, from April 2004 until mid-June 2006. At the time she started, she was a recent college graduate, but she quickly assumed the knowledge and responsibility needed to handle a number of tasks. She was an excellent worker, a self-starter and highly detail-oriented.

If you are providing a recommendation for a consultant:

I can wholeheartedly recommend her for the position. Diana has worked as a part-time consultant with our department for 7 months now, filling in for Edna Ramirez. Now that Edna is back, I hate to lose Diana, but I would be happy to see her stay within FocalPoint.

March 16, 2008

To: Ralph Frederickson
From: Phyllicia Applebaum
Re: Job Candidate Diana Postulka

Dear Ralph:

I understand that Diana Postulka is a lead candidate in your search for an executive assistant.

I can wholeheartedly recommend her for the position. Diana has worked as my assistant for more than 2 years now, and I can assure you that she is an excellent worker, a true team player and a valuable addition to any department. Though I hate to lose her, I can see that she is ready to move on to more challenging work, and I would be happy to see her do so and still stay within FocalPoint.

If you need any other information on Diana, please feel free to contact me. Otherwise, I wish you both well in your work together.

Sincerely,

Phyllicia Applebaum
Director of Human Resources

E-Mail

Dear Ralph:

I understand that Diana Postulka is a lead candidate in your search for an executive assistant.

I can wholeheartedly recommend her for the position.

Diana has worked as my assistant for more than 2 years now, and I can assure you that she is an excellent worker, a true team player and a valuable addition to any department. Though I hate to lose her, I can see that she is ready to move on to more challenging work, and I would be happy to see her do so and still stay within FocalPoint.

If you need any other information on Diana, please feel free to ask.

Otherwise, I wish you both well in your work together.

Sincerely,

<e-mail signature, including name, title, company and contact information>

Letter of Recommendation for an Outside Contractor

Purpose

- To provide a personal recommendation for a vendor, freelance worker or consultant

Alternative Purposes

- To provide a personal recommendation for a consultant to another manager in your organization
- To provide a personal recommendation for a past contractor
- To provide a personal recommendation for a vendor

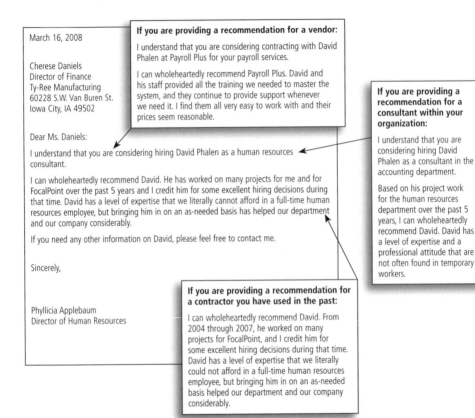

March 16, 2008

Cherese Daniels
Director of Finance
Ty-Ree Manufacturing
60228 S.W. Van Buren St.
Iowa City, IA 49502

Dear Ms. Daniels:

I understand that you are considering hiring David Phalen as a human resources consultant.

I can wholeheartedly recommend David. He has worked on many projects for me and for FocalPoint over the past 5 years and I credit him for some excellent hiring decisions during that time. David has a level of expertise that we literally cannot afford in a full-time human resources employee, but bringing him in on an as-needed basis has helped our department and our company considerably.

If you need any other information on David, please feel free to contact me.

Sincerely,

Phyllicia Applebaum
Director of Human Resources

If you are providing a recommendation for a vendor:

I understand that you are considering contracting with David Phalen at Payroll Plus for your payroll services.

I can wholeheartedly recommend Payroll Plus. David and his staff provided all the training we needed to master the system, and they continue to provide support whenever we need it. I find them all very easy to work with and their prices seem reasonable.

If you are providing a recommendation for a consultant within your organization:

I understand that you are considering hiring David Phalen as a consultant in the accounting department.

Based on his project work for the human resources department over the past 5 years, I can wholeheartedly recommend David. David has a level of expertise and a professional attitude that are not often found in temporary workers.

If you are providing a recommendation for a contractor you have used in the past:

I can wholeheartedly recommend David. From 2004 through 2007, he worked on many projects for FocalPoint, and I credit him for some excellent hiring decisions during that time. David has a level of expertise that we literally could not afford in a full-time human resources employee, but bringing him in on an as-needed basis helped our department and our company considerably.

E-Mail

Dear Ms. Daniels:

I am writing to you at the request of David Phalen. I understand that you are considering hiring him as a human resources consultant.

I can wholeheartedly recommend David. He has worked on many projects for me and for FocalPoint over the past 5 years and I credit him for some excellent hiring decisions during that time. David has a level of expertise that we literally cannot afford in a full-time human resources employee, but bringing him in on an as-needed basis has helped our department and our company considerably.

If you need any other information on David, please feel free to respond to this message.

Sincerely,

<e-mail signature, including name, title, company and contact information>

Letter to Departing Employee

Purpose

- To personally acknowledge an employee who is leaving the company

Alternative Purposes

- To thank a long-time employee
- To offer to act as a future reference
- To remind the employee of a noncompete or other contractual agreement

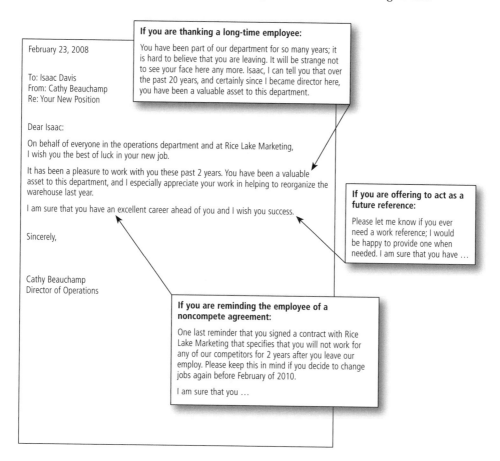

February 23, 2008

To: Isaac Davis
From: Cathy Beauchamp
Re: Your New Position

Dear Isaac:

On behalf of everyone in the operations department and at Rice Lake Marketing, I wish you the best of luck in your new job.

It has been a pleasure to work with you these past 2 years. You have been a valuable asset to this department, and I especially appreciate your work in helping to reorganize the warehouse last year.

I am sure that you have an excellent career ahead of you and I wish you success.

Sincerely,

Cathy Beauchamp
Director of Operations

If you are thanking a long-time employee:

You have been part of our department for so many years; it is hard to believe that you are leaving. It will be strange not to see your face here any more. Isaac, I can tell you that over the past 20 years, and certainly since I became director here, you have been a valuable asset to this department.

If you are offering to act as a future reference:

Please let me know if you ever need a work reference; I would be happy to provide one when needed. I am sure that you have …

If you are reminding the employee of a noncompete agreement:

One last reminder that you signed a contract with Rice Lake Marketing that specifies that you will not work for any of our competitors for 2 years after you leave our employ. Please keep this in mind if you decide to change jobs again before February of 2010.

I am sure that you …

E-Mail

Dear Isaac:

I want to wish you the best of luck in your new job.

It has been a pleasure to work with you these past 2 years. You have been a valuable asset to this department and I especially appreciate your work in helping to reorganize the warehouse last year.

I am sure that you have an excellent career ahead of you and I wish you success.

Sincerely,

<e-mail signature, including name, title, company and contact information>

Letter of Resignation—Leaving on Good Terms

Purpose

- To officially announce your resignation to your supervisor

Alternative Purposes

- To offer more than 2 weeks' notice
- To request a personal reference
- To outline the monies owed you by your employer

February 9, 2008

To: Cathy Beauchamp
From: Isaac Davis
Re: Letter of Resignation

Dear Cathy:

I hope that it will not come as too much of a surprise to you that I have accepted a position with another company. Because of the current conditions at Rice Lake Marketing, including the recent layoffs, I thought it best for my future if I found employment elsewhere.

With this letter, I am giving my 2 weeks' notice; February 23 will be my last day of work before I start my new job as operations manager at Gershon Press Inc.

It has been a pleasure to work for you, and I wish you and all my colleagues in the operations department good luck in the months ahead.

Sincerely,

Isaac Davis
Warehouse Manager

If you are outlining the monies owed you by the company:

… Gershon Press Inc. By my calculations, I have accumulated 13 unused vacation days to date and am entitled to pay for those days. Please check my personnel file and see if your records reflect this.

If you are offering more than two weeks' notice:

I know that the standard policy for our company is to provide 2 weeks' notice. I am in a position where I can stay on for longer if it would help the transition to a new warehouse manager. My departure date can be any time between now and the end of March. Please consider how long you would like me to stay and we can discuss this in person when you are ready.

If you are requesting your supervisor to act as a future reference:

I would be honored if you would agree to act as a reference for me when I seek new employment. If you are willing, can you provide me with a letter of recommendation before I leave Rice Lake Marketing?

It has been a pleasure …

E-Mail

Dear Cathy:

I hope that it will not come as too much of a surprise to you that I have accepted a position with another company.

Because of the current conditions at Rice Lake Marketing, including the recent layoffs, I thought it best for my future if I found employment elsewhere.

With this message, I am giving my 2 weeks' notice; February 23 will be my last day of work before I start my new job as operations manager at Gershon Press Inc.

It has been a pleasure to work for you, and I wish you and all my colleagues in the operations department good luck in the months ahead.

Sincerely,

<e-mail signature, including name, title, company and contact information>

Letter of Resignation—Leaving on Bad Terms

Purpose

- To officially announce your resignation to your supervisor

Alternative Purposes

- To offer no notice
- To go over your supervisor's head
- To outline the monies owed you by your employer

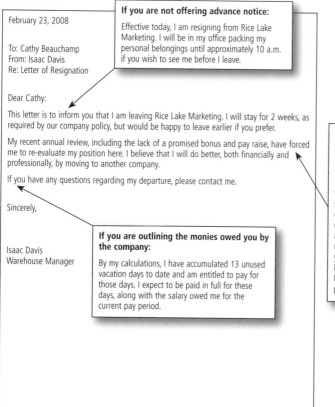

February 23, 2008

To: Cathy Beauchamp
From: Isaac Davis
Re: Letter of Resignation

Dear Cathy:

This letter is to inform you that I am leaving Rice Lake Marketing. I will stay for 2 weeks, as required by our company policy, but would be happy to leave earlier if you prefer.

My recent annual review, including the lack of a promised bonus and pay raise, have forced me to re-evaluate my position here. I believe that I will do better, both financially and professionally, by moving to another company.

If you have any questions regarding my departure, please contact me.

Sincerely,

Isaac Davis
Warehouse Manager

If you are not offering advance notice:

Effective today, I am resigning from Rice Lake Marketing. I will be in my office packing my personal belongings until approximately 10 a.m. if you wish to see me before I leave.

If you are resigning because of your direct supervisor:

My personal difficulties in dealing with Marcia Beals have escalated to the point where I can no longer work with her. Her dramatic mood swings, forgetfulness and lack of organization have made my job so difficult that I feel I am no longer able to be productive. I hope that my resignation will encourage you to take an objective look at Miss Beals' effect on the Rice Lake Marketing warehouse and staff productivity there.

If you are outlining the monies owed you by the company:

By my calculations, I have accumulated 13 unused vacation days to date and am entitled to pay for those days. I expect to be paid in full for these days, along with the salary owed me for the current pay period.

E-Mail

Dear Cathy:

This message is to inform you that I am leaving Rice Lake Marketing.

I will stay for 2 weeks, as required by our company policy, but would be happy to leave earlier if you prefer.

My recent annual review, including the lack of a promised bonus and pay raise, have forced me to re-evaluate my position here. I believe that I will do better, both financially and professionally, by moving to another company.

If you have any questions regarding my departure, please contact me.

Sincerely,

<e-mail signature, including name, title, company and contact information>

Letter Acknowledging Employee Suggestion

Purpose

- To acknowledge that an employee's suggestion has been received

Alternative Purposes

- To explain how the suggestion will be implemented
- To explain why the suggestion cannot be implemented
- To offer a reward for the suggestion

If you are explaining how the suggestion will be implemented:

This is an excellent idea; I have passed it along to the CEO and recommended that he discuss the viability of scheduling such meetings with each department head.

March 17, 2008

To: Marvin Edelmann
From: Tom Thompson
Re: Suggestion for Weekly Departmental Meetings

Dear Marvin:

Thank you for submitting your suggestion of holding weekly departmental meetings throughout El-tronics.

Holding weekly departmental meetings is an interesting idea. I have passed this along to the CEO to discuss with upper management.

Marvin, I want you to know that regardless of what action is taken regarding your suggestion, I appreciate your time and effort in considering ways to improve productivity here at El-tronics and I hope that you will continue to do so.

Sincerely,

Tom Thompson
Human Resources Manager

If you are explaining why the suggestion cannot be implemented:

Though I can see the merits of regular communications, weekly meetings do not seem like the most time-efficient way to stay informed. If you feel that staff working in your department need more regular communications, perhaps you can ask your supervisor to send out a weekly e-mail or other updates to her staff.

If you are offering a reward for the suggestion:

The attached gift certificate is our way of saying thank you for taking the time and effort to consider ways to improve productivity here at El-tronics. Regardless of what action is taken regarding your suggestion, we hope you will continue to submit your ideas.

E-Mail

Dear Marvin:

Thank you for your suggestion.

Holding weekly departmental meetings is an interesting idea. I have passed this along to the CEO to discuss with upper management.

Marvin, I want you to know that regardless of what action is taken regarding your suggestion, I appreciate your time and effort in considering ways to improve productivity here at El-tronics and I hope that you will continue to do so.

Sincerely,

<e-mail signature, including name, title, company and contact information>

Letter of Appreciation to Employee

Purpose

- To personally express appreciation to an individual employee

Alternative Purposes

- To express appreciation for participation on a committee or task force
- To express appreciation for a presentation
- To express appreciation for extra work

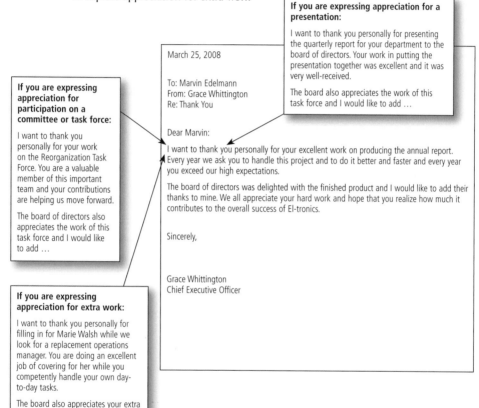

If you are expressing appreciation for a presentation:

I want to thank you personally for presenting the quarterly report for your department to the board of directors. Your work in putting the presentation together was excellent and it was very well-received.

The board also appreciates the work of this task force and I would like to add …

If you are expressing appreciation for participation on a committee or task force:

I want to thank you personally for your work on the Reorganization Task Force. You are a valuable member of this important team and your contributions are helping us move forward.

The board of directors also appreciates the work of this task force and I would like to add …

If you are expressing appreciation for extra work:

I want to thank you personally for filling in for Marie Walsh while we look for a replacement operations manager. You are doing an excellent job of covering for her while you competently handle your own day-to-day tasks.

The board also appreciates your extra efforts and I would like to add …

March 25, 2008

To: Marvin Edelmann
From: Grace Whittington
Re: Thank You

Dear Marvin:

I want to thank you personally for your excellent work on producing the annual report. Every year we ask you to handle this project and to do it better and faster and every year you exceed our high expectations.

The board of directors was delighted with the finished product and I would like to add their thanks to mine. We all appreciate your hard work and hope that you realize how much it contributes to the overall success of EI-tronics.

Sincerely,

Grace Whittington
Chief Executive Officer

E-Mail

Dear Marvin:

I want to thank you personally for your excellent work on producing the annual report.

Every year we ask you to handle this project and to do it better and faster and every year you exceed our high expectations.

The board of directors was delighted with the finished product and I would like to add their thanks to mine.

We all appreciate your hard work and hope that you realize how much it contributes to the overall success of EI-tronics.

Sincerely,

<e-mail signature, including name, title, company and contact information>

Letter Marking Employee Work Anniversary

Purpose

- To personally congratulate an employee on a work anniversary

Alternative Purposes

- To note the anniversary of an employee who reports to you
- To note the anniversary of a board member
- To offer a gift for the anniversary

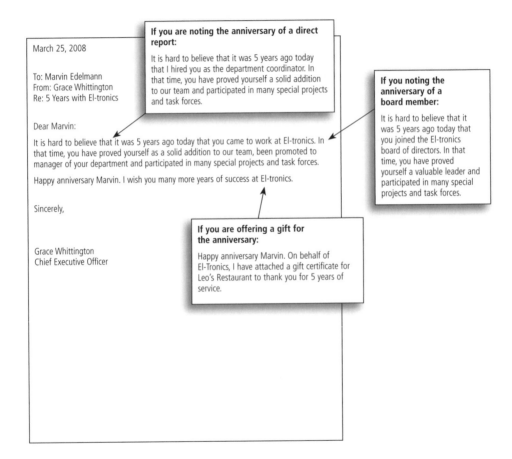

March 25, 2008

To: Marvin Edelmann
From: Grace Whittington
Re: 5 Years with El-tronics

Dear Marvin:

It is hard to believe that it was 5 years ago today that you came to work at El-tronics. In that time, you have proved yourself as a solid addition to our team, been promoted to manager of your department and participated in many special projects and task forces.

Happy anniversary Marvin. I wish you many more years of success at El-tronics.

Sincerely,

Grace Whittington
Chief Executive Officer

If you are noting the anniversary of a direct report:

It is hard to believe that it was 5 years ago today that I hired you as the department coordinator. In that time, you have proved yourself a solid addition to our team and participated in many special projects and task forces.

If you noting the anniversary of a board member:

It is hard to believe that it was 5 years ago today that you joined the El-tronics board of directors. In that time, you have proved yourself a valuable leader and participated in many special projects and task forces.

If you are offering a gift for the anniversary:

Happy anniversary Marvin. On behalf of El-Tronics, I have attached a gift certificate for Leo's Restaurant to thank you for 5 years of service.

E-Mail

Marvin:

It is hard to believe that it was 5 years ago today that you came to work at El-tronics.

In that time, you have proved yourself as a solid addition to our team, been promoted to manager of your department and participated in many special projects and task forces.

Happy anniversary Marvin. I wish you many more years of success at El-tronics.

Sincerely,

<e-mail signature, including name, title, company and contact information>

Letter Requesting a Meeting with Your Supervisor

Purpose

- To ask your immediate supervisor for a meeting to discuss a specific topic

Alternative Purposes

- To remind your supervisor of a promised meeting
- To ask your supervisor for a meeting to address a problem
- To ask several managers for a group meeting

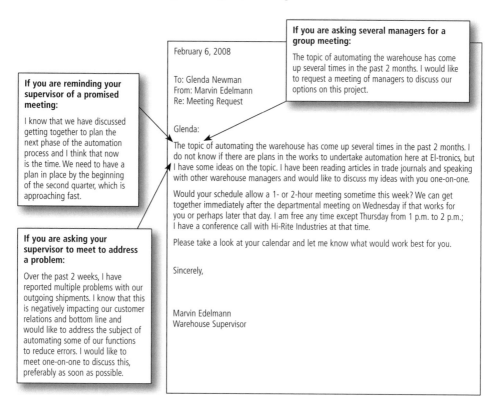

If you are asking several managers for a group meeting:

The topic of automating the warehouse has come up several times in the past 2 months. I would like to request a meeting of managers to discuss our options on this project.

If you are reminding your supervisor of a promised meeting:

I know that we have discussed getting together to plan the next phase of the automation process and I think that now is the time. We need to have a plan in place by the beginning of the second quarter, which is approaching fast.

If you are asking your supervisor to meet to address a problem:

Over the past 2 weeks, I have reported multiple problems with our outgoing shipments. I know that this is negatively impacting our customer relations and bottom line and would like to address the subject of automating some of our functions to reduce errors. I would like to meet one-on-one to discuss this, preferably as soon as possible.

February 6, 2008

To: Glenda Newman
From: Marvin Edelmann
Re: Meeting Request

Glenda:

The topic of automating the warehouse has come up several times in the past 2 months. I do not know if there are plans in the works to undertake automation here at El-tronics, but I have some ideas on the topic. I have been reading articles in trade journals and speaking with other warehouse managers and would like to discuss my ideas with you one-on-one.

Would your schedule allow a 1- or 2-hour meeting sometime this week? We can get together immediately after the departmental meeting on Wednesday if that works for you or perhaps later that day. I am free any time except Thursday from 1 p.m. to 2 p.m.; I have a conference call with Hi-Rite Industries at that time.

Please take a look at your calendar and let me know what would work best for you.

Sincerely,

Marvin Edelmann
Warehouse Supervisor

E-Mail

Glenda:

I know that the topic of automating the warehouse has come up several times in the past 2 months. I am unsure whether there are plans to undertake automation here at El-tronics, but I have some ideas on the topic. I have been reading articles in trade journals and speaking with other warehouse managers and would like to discuss my ideas with you one-on-one.

Would your schedule allow a 1- or 2-hour meeting sometime this week?

We can get together immediately after the departmental meeting on Wednesday or perhaps later that day. I am free any time except Thursday from 1 p.m. to 2 p.m.

Please take a look at your calendar and let me know what would work best for you.

<e-mail signature, including name, title, company and contact information>

Employee Letter of Concern

Purpose

- To alert your superior to a specific problem or concern

Alternative Purposes

- To alert a human resources contact to a specific problem or concern
- To alert upper management to a specific problem or concern
- To follow up on an initial letter of concern

February 21, 2008

To: Tom Thompson
From: Marvin Edelmann
Re: Warehouse Safety Concern

Dear Tom:

I am writing because I want to go on record with this: I am concerned about the safety of the forklifts in the warehouse.

These machines are more than 10 years old and should be replaced, both because they are unreliable and because I believe them to be unsafe for anyone driving them. Compared with newer forklifts, ours are easy to overbalance; those of us who have been driving them for a while are used to their load limitations, but I am finding that our newer employees, who are used to more modern equipment, are prone to overload the machines. Although each new warehouse employee's orientation includes training on the forklifts, I think it is time we invested in some new technology.

I would be happy to pull together some recommendations and pricing for replacing the existing equipment. Let me know if you would like that information. In the meantime, I would appreciate hearing your thoughts on this matter.

Sincerely,

Marvin Edelmann
Warehouse Supervisor

If you are addressing upper management:

I am writing because we in the warehouse have a problem that could concern the entire company: I am concerned about the safety of the forklifts in the warehouse and the threat of a lawsuit from an employee if an accident should occur.

If you are following up on an initial letter of concern:

In November, I wrote to you about the state of our forklifts and my concerns about employee safety. I thought that action would be taken, or at least initiated, by the beginning of this year. However, I have not heard of any plans to replace the machinery and the risks continue to build.

If you are addressing a human resources contact:

I am writing because we in the warehouse have a problem that is worthy of your attention: I believe that our forklifts are so old that they may not be in compliance with OSHA regulations.

E-Mail

Dear Tom:

I am writing because I want to go on record with this: I am concerned about the safety of the forklifts in the warehouse.

These machines are more than 10 years old and should be replaced, both because they are unreliable and because I believe them to be unsafe for anyone driving them.

Compared with newer forklifts, ours are easy to overbalance; those of us who have been driving them for a while are used to their load limitations, but I am finding that our newer employees, who are used to more modern equipment, are prone to overload the machines. Although each new warehouse employee's orientation includes training on the forklifts, I think it is time we invested in some new technology.

I would be happy to pull together some recommendations and pricing for replacing the existing equipment. Let me know if you would like that information.

In the meantime, I would appreciate hearing your thoughts on this matter.

Sincerely,

<e-mail signature, including name, title, company and contact information>

Thank You Letter to Employee for Charitable Donation

Purpose

- To personally thank an employee who has donated money to a company-sponsored charitable cause

Alternative Purposes

- To thank an employee for donating his or her time
- To thank an employee for donating goods
- To thank an employee for raising funds

If you are thanking an employee for donating goods:

I am so grateful to you and to all the El-tronics employees who donated canned goods and other food to the Help for the Homeless Fund this year. I understand that our combined efforts resulted in enough nonperishable goods to feed 10 families for the next month—that is very commendable!

If you are thanking an employee for raising funds:

I am so grateful to you and to everyone here at El-tronics who worked to raise money for the Help for the Homeless Fund this year. I understand that our combined efforts totaled more than $6,000 for the fund, which will go a long way toward getting homeless people in our community clothed, fed and off the streets into homes or shelters.

If you are thanking an employee for donating time:

I am so grateful to you and to all the El-tronics employees who spent their personal time last Saturday working for the Help for the Homeless Fund. Your efforts went a long way toward making some less fortunate people in our community more comfortable, both physically and socially.

March 5, 2008

To: Marvin Edelmann
From: Grace Whittington
Re: Thank You

Dear Marvin:

I am so grateful to you and to all the El-tronics employees who donated to the Help for the Homeless Fund this year. Together we managed to raise $4,235 for the fund, which will go a long way toward getting homeless people in our community clothed, fed and off the streets into homes or shelters.

I would like to personally thank you for your contribution. I appreciate your support of this worthy cause.

Sincerely,

Grace Whittington
Chief Executive Officer

E-Mail

Dear Marvin:

I am so grateful to you and to all the El-tronics employees who donated to the Help for the Homeless Fund.

Together, we managed to raise $4,235 for the fund, which will go a long way toward getting homeless people in our community clothed, fed and off the streets into homes or shelters.

I would like to personally thank you for your contribution. I appreciate your support of this worthy cause.

Sincerely,

<e-mail signature, including name, title, company and contact information>

Letter Inviting an Employee to a Company Function

Purpose

- To personally invite your employee to a company party

Alternative Purposes

- To invite an employee to an industry event
- To invite an employee to a charitable event
- To invite an employee to an event as a reward or thank you

March 5, 2008

To: Marvin Edelmann
From: Grace Whittington
Re: Thank You

Dear Marvin:

Next month marks the 50th anniversary of El-tronics. I plan to celebrate the occasion with a companywide cocktail party, to take place next door at Gingrich's Pub immediately after work on Friday, April 20. Light hors d'oeuvres will be served in addition to an open bar. Past employees are also invited, including my predecessor, Erin Newcomb.

You are an important member of our team, Marvin, and I hope that you can attend this special occasion. Please R.S.V.P. to my assistant, Ursula Ringold, by March 14.

Sincerely,

Grace Whittington
Chief Executive Officer

If you are inviting an employee to an industry event:

The American Association of Electronics Manufacturers is holding their 2008 convention in our city next month. I would like you to be my guest at the banquet there. The dinner is at 8 p.m. on Friday, April 20—I have reserved a table for 10 of our managers.

If you are inviting an employee to a charitable event:

I would be pleased if you and your wife can join me at the April 20 banquet for the Help for the Homeless Fund. I have purchased a table at the banquet, so you would attend as my guests. The dinner is at 8 p.m. on Friday, April 20.

If you are inviting an employee to an event as a reward or thank you:

In appreciation for your excellent work in helping to automate the warehouse, I would like to invite you and your wife to be my guest at the Wilmington Yacht Club for dinner and dancing. I am inviting several of the key players in the automation project to join me at 8 p.m. on Friday, April 20.

E-Mail

Dear Marvin:

Next month marks the 50th anniversary of El-tronics.

I plan to celebrate the occasion with a companywide cocktail party, to take place next door at Gingrich's Pub immediately after work on Friday, April 20. Light hors d'oeuvres will be served in addition to an open bar. Past employees are also invited, including my predecessor, Erin Newcomb.

You are an important member of our team, Marvin, and I hope that you can attend this special occasion.

Please R.S.V.P. to Ursula Ringold by March 14.

Sincerely,

<e-mail signature, including name, title, company and contact information>

Letter Announcing an Employee's Promotion

Purpose

- To announce to your company or department that an employee has been promoted

Alternative Purposes

- To announce a new management hire
- To announce the addition of a new employee
- To announce an employee's lateral move

If you are announcing a new management hire:

I am pleased to announce that we have hired a new manager for your department. Josie Bergman will join us as director of marketing beginning February 1.

Josie will oversee the entire marketing staff and will report directly to me.

If you are announcing an employee's lateral move:

I am pleased to announce that Josie Bergman will take over as Internet sales specialist beginning February 1.

Josie will be responsible for creating and maintaining an Internet sales site. We are looking for someone to fill her current position in marketing; any recommendations for a replacement are welcome.

If you are announcing the addition of a new employee:

I am pleased to announce that your department will gain an Internet sales specialist beginning February 1. We have hired Josie Bergman to fill this new position.

Josie will be responsible for creating and maintaining an Internet sales site and will work within the sales and marketing department. She will have extensive interaction with this department as well as with the warehouse and the sales floor.

January 13, 2008

To: Marketing Department
From: Caleb Keeler
Re: New Marketing Director

I am pleased to announce that Josie Bergman will take over as director of marketing beginning February 1.

Josie will oversee the entire marketing staff and will report directly to me. We are looking for someone to fill her current position in marketing; any recommendations for a replacement are welcome.

Josie began her career in 2001 as a marketing associate at PDK Sales in Los Angeles and joined Eureka Fittings as a marketing communications specialist in 2006. She recently earned an MBA from the Broad Graduate School of Management at Michigan State University.

I am sure that you will all make Josie feel welcome in her new position.

Sincerely,

Caleb Keeler
Director, Sales & Marketing

E-Mail

I am pleased to let you know that Josie Bergman will take over as director of marketing beginning Wednesday, February 1.

In her new position, Josie will oversee the entire marketing staff and will report directly to me.

We are looking for someone to fill her current position in marketing; any recommendations for a replacement are welcome.

Josie began her career in 2001 as a marketing associate at PDK Sales in Los Angeles and joined Eureka Fittings as a marketing communications specialist in 2006. She recently earned an MBA from the Broad Graduate School of Management at Michigan State University.

I am sure that you will all make Josie feel welcome in her new position.

Sincerely,

<e-mail signature, including name, title, company and contact information>

Letter Announcing the Departure of a Manager

Purpose

- To announce to your company or department that a manager is leaving

Alternative Purposes

- To announce that an employee is leaving
- To announce that you are leaving
- To announce that a position has been eliminated

January 13, 2008

To: Marketing Department
From: Caleb Keeler
Re: Josie Bergman

There is an ancient quote that says, "The only constant is change," and we at Eureka Fittings can certainly attest to that. We have seen a number of changes here, and I am sure that it will continue—change is healthy, both for businesses and for people.

Josie Bergman has decided to make a change. Yesterday she submitted her letter of resignation and has left our department to take a new position. I know that this is sudden, but we are working to make this transition as seamless as possible.

I will assume the duties of director of marketing until the position is filled. If anyone is interested in applying for the position, please contact the human resources director about the application process.

In the meantime, if you have any questions or concerns, please feel free to stop by my office.

Sincerely,

Caleb Keeler
Director, Sales & Marketing

If you are announcing that an employee is leaving:

Josie Bergman has decided to make a change. Yesterday she submitted her letter of resignation and has left our department to take a new position.

We will start searching for a new marketing communications specialist this week. If anyone is interested in applying for the position, please contact the human resources director about the application process.

If you are announcing that a position has been eliminated:

We are making some changes to the marketing department. Specifically, we are eliminating the position of Internet sales specialist. Josie Bergman will take a standard sales position with Eureka Fittings, and we will discontinue our efforts at Internet sales.

Let me assure you that this will not impact any other jobs. We simply tried a new sales venue and decided it was not right for us; we do not plan to eliminate any other marketing or sales positions.

If you are announcing that you are leaving:

I have decided to make a change. Yesterday I submitted my letter of resignation, and January 31 will be my last day with Eureka Fittings. I know that this is sudden, but we are working to make this transition as seamless as possible.

Josie Bergman will assume the duties of director of sales and marketing until the position is filled. I am confident that she will keep the department running on an even keel and I encourage all of you to help out however you can.

E-Mail

This message is to let everyone in the marketing department know that your manager, Josie Bergman, has left Eureka Fittings to take a new position at another company.

I know that this is sudden, but we are working to make this transition as seamless as possible.

I will assume the duties of director of marketing until the position is filled. If anyone is interested in applying for the position, please contact the human resources director about the application process.

In the meantime, if you have any questions or concerns, please feel free to stop by my office.

Sincerely,

<e-mail signature, including name, title, company and contact information>

Letter Announcing Change in Benefits

Purpose

- To announce a change in employee benefits to your staff

Alternative Purposes

- To announce an increase in health insurance costs
- To announce a decrease in health insurance costs
- To announce a change in available retirement accounts

If you are announcing a change in available retirement accounts:

The result of our latest review is that beginning next quarter, on April 1, you will have different mutual funds to choose from for your 401(k) retirement fund. We will continue to work with the same company, but the fund choices will change.

Please watch your personal mail in March for a list of the choices you will have and details on the new funds.

If you are announcing a decrease in health insurance costs:

The result of our latest review is that beginning next quarter, on April 1, we will be decreasing employee contributions for health insurance coverage. This is because we are bypassing our current broker and working directly with our insurance provider, Hellington Mutual Insurance Co.

Starting in April, you will see a decrease of approximately five percent in the amount deducted from your salary for health insurance coverage. The exact decrease depends on the coverage plan you have chosen and how many family members are included in your health insurance plan.

February 9, 2008

To: All Employees
From: Iris Krink
Re: Change in Benefits

Every 2 years, your human resources department reviews Englehart Whittaker's employee benefit offerings to see if we can find better benefits for you or save money on specific offerings.

The result of our latest review is that beginning next quarter, on April 1, we will replace our current health insurance provider with Hellington Mutual Insurance Co. Our new health insurance will offer the options of an HMO or PPO, similar to the choice you have now.

I have attached a breakdown of the employee costs per option, including your contribution per check, deductibles and copay information. Please review the options and, when you receive the changeover paperwork early next month, be prepared to select the HMO or PPO option for this new coverage. A list of providers for both programs will also be provided at that time.

Attached please find a revised employee handbook, which has been updated with complete details on these changes. Be sure to replace your old handbook with this one. As always, please contact me if you have any questions.

Sincerely,

Iris Krink
Director, Human Resources

If you are announcing an increase in health insurance costs:

The result of our latest review is that beginning next quarter, on April 1, we will be increasing employee contributions for health insurance coverage. I am sure that you are aware that health care costs have increased dramatically in recent years.

Starting in April, you will see an increase of approximately five percent in the amount deducted from your salary for health insurance coverage. The exact increase depends on the coverage plan you have chosen and how many family members are included in your health insurance plan.

E-Mail

Please note: Beginning next quarter, on April 1, we will replace our current health insurance provider with Hellington Mutual Insurance Co. Our new health insurance will offer the options of an HMO or PPO, similar to the choice you have now.

I have attached a PDF that includes a breakdown of employee costs per option, including your contribution per check, deductibles and copay information. Please review the options and, when you receive the changeover paperwork early next month, be prepared to select the HMO or PPO option for this new coverage. A list of providers for both programs will also be provided at that time.

This change is a result of a benefits review that the human resources department conducts every year, during which we examine Englehart Whittaker's employee benefit offerings to see if we can find better benefits for you or save money on specific offerings.

Please contact me if you have any questions on this change.

Sincerely,

<e-mail signature, including name, title, company and contact information>

**Brooks - Cork Library
Shelton State
Community College**

Letter Announcing Change in Work Hours

Purpose

- To announce a change in daily work schedule to your staff

Alternative Purposes

- To announce a temporary change in work schedule
- To announce a change to flex time
- To announce a change in overtime work schedules

March 17, 2008

To: All Employees
From: Iris Krink
Re: Change in Work Schedule

Englehart Whittaker is expanding our business hours so that we can have better communications with customers and vendors on the East Coast. The workday for all employees, both hourly and salaried, is changing to 8:30 a.m. to 5:30 p.m. With your current two 15-minute breaks and 1 hour for lunch, you will work 8 hours per day. This is in line with most U.S. companies today.

This change in hours is effective beginning Monday, February 2. If you have special circumstances, such as child care availability that may prevent you from changing your hours in 2 weeks, please discuss your options with the manager of your department within the next week. Anyone who cannot work the new schedule must let their manager know before the schedule change takes place.

Please contact me or any member of the human resources staff if you have questions regarding the new schedule.

Sincerely,

Iris Krink
Director, Human Resources

If you are announcing a change in overtime work schedules:

Beginning June 15, Englehart Whittaker will implement a policy limiting overtime. All hourly employees will be restricted to no more than 10 hours of overtime per pay period unless they receive written approval from a director ahead of time.

If you are announcing a temporary change in work schedule:

Beginning June 15, Englehart Whittaker will implement summer hours. This means that all employees will work 9-hour workdays and receive Friday afternoons off until the week after Labor Day.

Please discuss your hours with your supervisor and determine your temporary daily schedule, then make any necessary plans regarding childcare, transportation, etc., so you will be prepared to start earlier and leave later beginning June 15.

If you are announcing a change to flex time:

This spring, Englehart Whittaker will implement a flex time option for all employees. Beginning April 1, individuals can choose a start time between 7 a.m. and 8:30 a.m. and work a 9-hour day (including a lunch hour), then leave between 4 p.m. and 5:30 p.m.

All schedules must be approved by your immediate supervisor, and once you choose a schedule, you must adhere to it.

E-Mail

Please note that your hours of work will change beginning in February.

Englehart Whittaker is expanding our business hours so that we can have better communications with customers and vendors on the East Coast.

The workday for all employees, both hourly and salaried, is changing to 8:30 a.m. to 5:30 p.m. With your current two 15-minute breaks and 1 hour for lunch, you will work 8 hours per day. This is in line with most U.S. companies today.

This change in hours is effective beginning Monday, February 2.

If you have special circumstances, such as child care availability that may prevent you from changing your hours in 2 weeks, please discuss your options with the manager of your department within the next week. Anyone who cannot work the new schedule must let their manager know before the schedule change takes place.

Sincerely,

<e-mail signature, including name, title, company and contact information>

Letter to Employees Announcing Merger or Acquisition

Purpose

- To announce to all staff that your company is merging with another

Alternative Purposes

- To announce an acquisition
- To announce changes due to a merger
- To announce radical changes

If you are announcing an acquisition:

I want you to be the first to know before a public announcement is made that Englehart Whittaker has been acquired by Grebe Communications, our top competitor.

This friendly acquisition can mean good things for all of us. It gives our combined companies an extremely strong position in the marketplace and unites the strengths of Grebe Communications with our own.

If you are announcing radical changes:

Because the papers were signed today, it is too early to determine what impact this will have on individual departments. Though our company name and headquarters location will remain the same, our new combined management team will be looking for ways to integrate and improve each department, drawing from personnel, ideas and cultures from both companies.

I know that this may seem an unsettling prospect for some of you, but I encourage you to be patient and optimistic; good changes are going to come. Meanwhile, I promise to keep every member of our staff updated in the months ahead as we plan our course as a larger, stronger organization.

January 30, 2008

To: All Employees
From: Rodney J. Doyle
Re: Changes Ahead for Englehart Whittaker

I want you to be the first to know before a public announcement is made that Englehart Whittaker is merging with Grebe Communications, our top competitor.

This friendly merger means good things for all of us. It gives our company an extremely strong position in the marketplace and adds the strengths of Grebe Communications to our own.

Because the deal just took place today, it is too early to outline any specific changes that may take place. But I can assure you that our company name and headquarters location will remain the same. We will be making some changes to our employee benefits packages as we merge the two companies, but the plans are basically the same, so you should not see much difference in the quality and coverage of your current benefits.

Other than that it is too soon to outline what will happen in the future. However, I promise to keep every member of our staff updated in the months ahead as we plan our course as a larger, stronger organization.

Sincerely,

Rodney J. Doyle
President and CEO

If you are announcing changes due to a merger:

Because the deal just took place today, it is too early to outline all the changes that may take place. I can assure you that our company name and headquarters location will remain the same and that our employee benefits package will probably see some slight changes.

We will be changing and consolidating jobs in certain departments as we incorporate the staff, processes and structure of Grebe Communications here. I promise to keep every member of our staff updated in the months ahead as we plan our course as a larger, stronger organization.

E-Mail

IMPORTANT: Please read immediately

I want you to be the first to know before a public announcement is made that Englehart Whittaker is merging with Grebe Communications, our top competitor. The papers were signed just this morning.

This friendly merger means good things for all of us. It gives our company an extremely strong position in the marketplace and adds the strengths of Grebe Communications to our own.

Because the deal just took place today, it is too early to outline any specific changes that may take place. But I can assure you that our company name and headquarters location will remain the same. We will be making some changes to our employee benefits packages as we merge the two companies, but the plans are basically the same, so you should not see much difference in the quality and coverage of your current benefits.

Other than that it is too soon to outline what will happen in the future. However, I promise to keep every member of our staff updated in the months ahead as we plan our course as a larger, stronger organization.

Sincerely,

<e-mail signature, including name, title, company and contact information>

Letter Announcing a Change to an Employee's Job Description

Purpose

- To alert staff to a change in an employee's job description

Alternative Purposes

- To alert staff to a new reporting structure
- To alert staff to increased responsibilities for everyone
- To alert staff to a shift in departments

> **If you are announcing an employee's lateral move:**
>
> Effective immediately, Art Director Emily Tazlo is taking over the position of print production coordinator. In her new job, Emily will handle all aspects of print production for the department. She will act as liaison to printing companies, from getting estimates to going on press checks.
>
> Please join me in congratulating Emily on her new position and in wishing her well.

March 28, 2008

To: Marketing Department
From: Caleb Keeler
Re: Redistribution of Duties

After reviewing the work that the marketing department does and the division of duties within it, I have decided that it is time for a change. I hope that by shifting some responsibilities around, we will all be able to work more efficiently.

Effective immediately, Art Director Emily Tazlo will handle all aspects of print production for the department. For those of you planning and designing marketing pieces that require printing, you should work directly with Emily. She will act as liaison to printing companies, from getting estimates to going on press checks.

This change will enable our product managers and graphic designers to focus on their important tasks. It should also save on printing costs when Emily batches various jobs.

The reporting structure of the department will not change and Emily will still handle some graphic design responsibilities, as her schedule allows.

Please feel free to stop by my office if you have any questions about this new division of duties.

Sincerely,

Caleb Keeler
Director, Sales & Marketing

> **If you are alerting staff to a new reporting structure:**
>
> In her new capacity, Emily will report to me and will not oversee any staff. All other graphic designers will report directly to Josie Bergman, Director of Marketing.

> **If you are alerting staff to increased responsibilities for everyone:**
>
> Emily's new responsibilities will allow all other graphic designers to focus on their important tasks. However, we do not plan to add any more staff in this department, so all of you will have more design work to cover. I am sure that by focusing your efforts on layout and design, you will be able to handle this extra workload.

E-Mail

This message is important for the entire marketing department, but it especially applies to all those who oversee print production, including securing printing estimates.

Effective immediately, Art Director Emily Tazlo will handle all aspects of print production for the department. Those of you planning and designing marketing pieces that require printing should work directly with Emily. She will act as your liaison to printing companies, from getting estimates to going on press checks.

I hope that by shifting some responsibilities around, we will all be able to work more efficiently. This will enable our product managers and graphic designers to focus on their important tasks. It should also save on printing costs when Emily batches various jobs.

The reporting structure of the department will not change, and Emily will still handle some graphic design responsibilities, as her schedule allows.

Please feel free to stop by my office if you have any questions about this new division of duties.

Sincerely,

<e-mail signature, including name, title, company and contact information>

Request for Meeting with Group of Employees

Purpose

- To announce a meeting for a department, team or other group of employees

Alternative Purposes

- To announce a conference call
- To set up an initial meeting of a task force or committee
- To request that individuals prepare reports for a meeting

February 9, 2008

To: Members of Customer Care Task Force
From: Caleb Keeler
Re: February 15 Meeting

Our task force will meet next Tuesday, February 15, from 2:30 p.m. to 4 p.m. in conference room C.

We will be reviewing our progress to date and brainstorming ideas for the next phase of our project: reaching out to former customers. I will distribute an agenda sometime next Monday or Tuesday.

It is important that all of you be present, so please rearrange your schedule as needed to ensure that you can attend this meeting.

Sincerely,

Caleb Keeler
Director, Sales & Marketing

If you are announcing a conference call:

Please plan to participate in a conference call for our task force Tuesday, February 15, from 2:30 p.m. to 4 p.m. Central time. You can call in to 555.555.5555 and use the code 5555 to join the call.

If you are setting up an initial meeting of a committee:

Thank you all for agreeing to serve on the Eureka Fittings Customer Care Task Force. Our first meeting is scheduled for next Tuesday, February 15, from 2:30 p.m. to 4 p.m. in conference room C.

After a brief review of our purpose and goals, we will brainstorm ideas for how to reach out to our former customers. I will distribute ...

If you are requesting that individuals prepare reports for a meeting:

We will be reviewing our progress to date. Please come prepared to present a brief report on what your department has accomplished in the past month and a half. Also, I ask that you submit your report in writing to me by Monday the 14th so that I can distribute notes to all attendees.

E-Mail

Mark your calendar: Our task force will meet next Tuesday, February 15, from 2:30 p.m. to 4 p.m. in conference room C.

We will be reviewing our progress to date and brainstorming ideas for the next phase of our project: reaching out to former customers. I will distribute an agenda sometime next Monday or Tuesday.

It is important that all of you be present, so please rearrange your schedule as needed to ensure that you can attend this meeting.

Sincerely,

<e-mail signature, including name, title, company and contact information>

Letter Requesting Employee Donations to Charity

Purpose

- To ask your employees to donate to a company-sponsored charity

Alternative Purposes

- To ask employees to donate time
- To ask employees to donate goods
- To ask employees to raise funds

> **If you are asking employees to donate time:**
>
> I am asking each of you to consider signing up for an evening of charity work. You can choose to prepare and/or distribute food, organize the food pantry, set up cots in the shelter or help with counseling.
>
> Please use the enclosed form to select which activity you prefer and when you are available. If you would like to get a group together from your department or other colleagues here at El-tronics, feel free to organize this on your own.

February 2, 2008

To: All El-tronics Employees
From: Grace Whittington
Re: Help for the Homeless Fund

Every year, we select a good cause for El-tronics to adopt. In years past, we have helped to build houses with Habitat for Humanity, supported needy children in Sierra Leone and given our time and money to charities for the families of Sept. 11 victims.

This year, El-tronics has selected a local cause. The Help for the Homeless Fund is a charity based here in Cleveland that not only feeds and shelters the homeless in our metropolitan areas, but provides counseling and funding to help get some of these people off the streets and employed.

I am asking each of you to consider making a cash donation to this good cause. It need not be a large donation, but whatever you give, the company will match. For example, if you donate $50, we will give an additional $50.

Please use the enclosed envelope and form to make your donation directly to the fund. All donations must be in by March 15, and at that time, I will write a check matching the total amount of funds given by El-tronics employees.

I hope that you will participate in helping this cause; together, we can make a difference in getting homeless people in our community clothed, fed, off the streets and into homes or shelters.

Sincerely,

Grace Whittington
Chief Executive Officer

> **If you are asking employees to donate goods:**
>
> I am asking each of you to consider participating in a food drive for the fund. From now until March 15, we will put out baskets throughout the building where you can drop off canned goods and other nonperishable food items. I have attached a list from the fund that recommends which foods are most needed.

> **If you are asking employees to raise funds:**
>
> I am asking each of you to consider participating in a fund-raising effort for the fund. Kits are available with everything you need to collect monetary contributions from family, friends and acquaintances. The fund-raising drive will take place from this week until March 15 and all monies need to be collected and turned in by April 1.

E-Mail

As you are aware, every year we select a good cause for El-tronics to adopt.

In years past, we have helped to build houses with Habitat for Humanity, supported needy children in Sierra Leone and given our time and money to charities for the families of Sept.11 victims.

This year, El-tronics has selected a local cause. The Help for the Homeless Fund is a charity based here in Cleveland that not only feeds and shelters the homeless in our metropolitan area, but provides counseling and funding to help get some of these people off the streets and employed.

I am asking each of you to consider making a cash donation to this good cause. It need not be a large contribution, but whatever you give, the company will match. For example, if you donate $50, we will give an additional $50.

Please use the enclosed envelope and form to make your donation directly to the fund.

All donations must be in by March 15, and at that time, I will write a check matching the total amount of funds given by El-tronics employees.

I hope that you will participate in helping this cause; together, we can make a difference in getting homeless people in our community clothed, fed, off the streets and into homes or shelters.

Sincerely,

<e-mail signature, including name, title, company and contact information>

Section Five

. . . . .

Essential Customer
Service Letters

Letter Accompanying Refund

Purpose

- To return a customer's payment because you cannot fulfill his or her order

Alternative Purposes

- To stop an order and refund payment at the customer's request
- To issue a refund due to overpayment
- To issue a refund for poor service or defective product

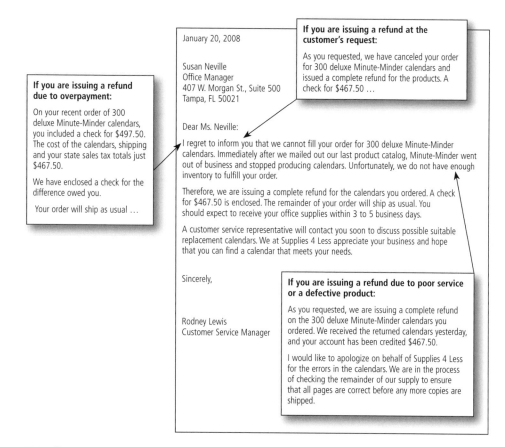

January 20, 2008

Susan Neville
Office Manager
407 W. Morgan St., Suite 500
Tampa, FL 50021

Dear Ms. Neville:

I regret to inform you that we cannot fill your order for 300 deluxe Minute-Minder calendars. Immediately after we mailed out our last product catalog, Minute-Minder went out of business and stopped producing calendars. Unfortunately, we do not have enough inventory to fulfill your order.

Therefore, we are issuing a complete refund for the calendars you ordered. A check for $467.50 is enclosed. The remainder of your order will ship as usual. You should expect to receive your office supplies within 3 to 5 business days.

A customer service representative will contact you soon to discuss possible suitable replacement calendars. We at Supplies 4 Less appreciate your business and hope that you can find a calendar that meets your needs.

Sincerely,

Rodney Lewis
Customer Service Manager

If you are issuing a refund due to overpayment:

On your recent order of 300 deluxe Minute-Minder calendars, you included a check for $497.50. The cost of the calendars, shipping and your state sales tax totals just $467.50.

We have enclosed a check for the difference owed you.

Your order will ship as usual ...

If you are issuing a refund at the customer's request:

As you requested, we have canceled your order for 300 deluxe Minute-Minder calendars and issued a complete refund for the products. A check for $467.50 ...

If you are issuing a refund due to poor service or a defective product:

As you requested, we are issuing a complete refund on the 300 deluxe Minute-Minder calendars you ordered. We received the returned calendars yesterday, and your account has been credited $467.50.

I would like to apologize on behalf of Supplies 4 Less for the errors in the calendars. We are in the process of checking the remainder of our supply to ensure that all pages are correct before any more copies are shipped.

E-Mail

I regret to inform you that we cannot fill your order for 300 deluxe Minute-Minder calendars. Immediately after we mailed out our last product catalog, Minute-Minder went out of business and stopped producing calendars. Unfortunately, we do not have enough inventory to fulfill your order.

Therefore, we are issuing a complete refund for the calendars you ordered, and $467.50 has been credited to your account. The remainder of your order will ship as usual. You should expect to receive your office supplies within 3 to 5 business days.

A customer service representative will contact you soon to discuss possible suitable replacement calendars. We at Supplies 4 Less appreciate your business and hope that you can find a calendar that meets your needs.

Sincerely,

<e-mail signature, including name, title, company and contact information>

Letter Containing Instructions for Returning Merchandise

Purpose

- To inform a customer of the process for returning unwanted merchandise

Alternative Purposes

- To answer a customer's request for return information
- To provide instructions on exchanging merchandise
- To clarify information on merchandise that has already been returned

January 30, 2008

Susan Neville
Office Manager
407 W. Morgan St., Suite 500
Tampa, FL 50021

Dear Ms. Neville:

Enclosed please find the software you ordered from us on January 15.

If for any reason you wish to return part or all of this shipment, you have 30 days to do so to receive a full refund. Simply package the items securely and ship them back to us using the enclosed shipping label.

Please note that to protect against software piracy, the manufacturer requires that all returned disks be in their sealed envelopes in order for a return to be accepted. Therefore, we ask that you inspect all packaging and instructions before you open the envelopes with the software to ensure that you have purchased the correct product.

We at Supplies 4 Less appreciate your ongoing business. If there is anything else you need, feel free to call our customer service department at 555.555.5555 or visit our Web site at **www.supplies4less.com**.

Sincerely,

Rodney Lewis
Customer Service Manager

If you are answering a customer's request for return information:

In response to your January 25 query regarding merchandise returns, Supplies 4 Less will provide full refunds for items returned within 30 days.

Your latest order included several software packages. Please note that in order ...

If you have already received returned merchandise:

This letter is in response to the software packages you returned to our warehouse earlier this month. Please note that we have received the items and your credit card has been credited with a full refund for the price and sales tax of the products. You will find a charge for $43.25 on your next bill, which is the cost of shipping the items.

If you are providing information about exchanging merchandise:

If for any reason you wish to return or exchange any of the items in this shipment, you have 30 days to do so. Simply package the items securely and ship them back to us using the enclosed shipping label. If you would like to exchange an item, fill out the enclosed Merchandise Exchange Form and include any additional difference in price. Your account will be credited if you are owed money for the exchange.

E-Mail

Dear Ms. Neville:

Your software order shipped today.

Once you receive the items, please note that if for any reason you wish to return part or all of your shipment, you have 30 days to do so to receive a full refund. Simply package the items securely and ship them back to us using the enclosed shipping label.

Please note that to protect against software piracy, the manufacturer requires that all returned disks be in their sealed envelopes in order for a return to be accepted. Therefore, we ask that you inspect all packaging and instructions before you open the envelopes with the software to ensure you have purchased the correct product.

We at Supplies 4 Less appreciate your ongoing business. If there is anything else you need, feel free to call our customer service department at 555.555.5555 or visit our Web site at **www.supplies4less.com**.

<e-mail signature, including name, title, company and contact information>

Letter Accompanying Product Shipment

Purpose

- To outline the contents of a shipment and review details

Alternative Purposes

- To identify a partial shipment
- To identify a difference between the order and items shipped
- To verify that an order shipped to a separate address

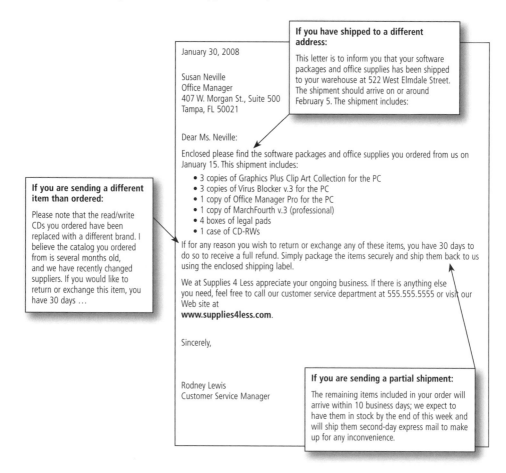

If you have shipped to a different address:

This letter is to inform you that your software packages and office supplies has been shipped to your warehouse at 522 West Elmdale Street. The shipment should arrive on or around February 5. The shipment includes:

January 30, 2008

Susan Neville
Office Manager
407 W. Morgan St., Suite 500
Tampa, FL 50021

Dear Ms. Neville:

Enclosed please find the software packages and office supplies you ordered from us on January 15. This shipment includes:

- 3 copies of Graphics Plus Clip Art Collection for the PC
- 3 copies of Virus Blocker v.3 for the PC
- 1 copy of Office Manager Pro for the PC
- 1 copy of MarchFourth v.3 (professional)
- 4 boxes of legal pads
- 1 case of CD-RWs

If you are sending a different item than ordered:

Please note that the read/write CDs you ordered have been replaced with a different brand. I believe the catalog you ordered from is several months old, and we have recently changed suppliers. If you would like to return or exchange this item, you have 30 days ...

If for any reason you wish to return or exchange any of these items, you have 30 days to do so to receive a full refund. Simply package the items securely and ship them back to us using the enclosed shipping label.

We at Supplies 4 Less appreciate your ongoing business. If there is anything else you need, feel free to call our customer service department at 555.555.5555 or visit our Web site at **www.supplies4less.com**.

Sincerely,

Rodney Lewis
Customer Service Manager

If you are sending a partial shipment:

The remaining items included in your order will arrive within 10 business days; we expect to have them in stock by the end of this week and will ship them second-day express mail to make up for any inconvenience.

E-Mail

Dear Ms. Neville:

Attached please find a condensed installation program for the software package you ordered.

We at Supplies 4 Less appreciate your ongoing business. If there is anything else you need, feel free to call our customer service department at 555.555.5555 or visit our Web site at **www.supplies4less.com**.

Sincerely,

<e-mail signature, including name, title, company and contact information>

Letter Announcing an Item Is out of Stock

Purpose

- To alert a customer that an item he or she has ordered is out of stock

Alternative Purposes

- To suggest a replacement for the out-of-stock item
- To offer a refund for the item
- To provide a refund

If you are recommending a replacement:

A new shipment of the calendars will arrive in early February. However, if you do not wish to wait until then, let me suggest a similar calendar that we have in supply. The Daily Desk Calendar has the same dimensions and many of the same features as the Minute-Minder brand and costs less. If you would like to receive the Daily Desk Calendars, I can ship them out today—just give me a call. We can credit your account for the difference in price and cancel your original order for the Minute-Minders.

January 20, 2008

Susan Neville
Office Manager
407 W. Morgan St., Suite 500
Tampa, FL 50021

Dear Ms. Neville:

I regret to inform you that the deluxe Minute-Minder calendars you ordered are currently out of stock. Demand for these calendars has exceeded our expectations and our inventory is depleted.

A new shipment of the calendars will arrive in early February; I will make sure that your order is filled from that shipment. If you need this order sooner, you may shop for a replacement calendar product on our Web site at **www.supplies4less.com**. We would be happy to substitute another style of calendar and ship that to you as soon as possible.

I am sorry for any inconvenience this may have caused and assure you that we at Supplies 4 Less will do whatever we can to resolve it to your satisfaction.

Sincerely,

Rodney Lewis
Customer Service Manager

If you are offering a refund:

A new shipment of the calendars will arrive in early February; I will make sure that your order is filled from that shipment. If you need calendars before then, simply call our toll-free customer service number to cancel the order. We will refund your payment in full.

If you are giving them a refund:

Because of the time-sensitive nature of this order, we feel the best solution is to issue a full refund of your payment. We hope that you will consider purchasing another brand or style of calendar from Supplies 4 Less.

E-Mail

Dear Ms. Neville:

I regret to inform you that the deluxe Minute-Minder calendars you ordered are currently out of stock. Demand for these calendars has exceeded our expectations and our inventory is depleted.

A new shipment of the calendars will arrive in early February; I will make sure that your order is filled from that shipment.

If you do not wish to wait until then to receive your calendars, you may shop for a replacement calendar product on our Web site at **www.supplies4less.com**.

I am sorry for any inconvenience this may have caused and assure you that we at Supplies 4 Less will do whatever we can to resolve it to your satisfaction.

Sincerely,

<e-mail signature, including name, title, company and contact information>

Letter Announcing a Change or Delay in Shipping

Purpose

- To alert a customer to a change in shipment of a current or future order

Alternative Purposes

- To alert a customer to a delay in his or her shipment
- To alert a customer to a change in shipping costs
- To alert a customer to a change in shipping carrier

If you are announcing a change in shipping costs:

This letter is to inform you of a change in shipping and handling fees for all Supplies 4 Less orders. Beginning immediately, all new orders will be subject to this new fee structure, which is outlined on the enclosed flyer. Please note that product pricing will remain the same.

January 20, 2008

Susan Neville
Office Manager
407 W. Morgan St., Suite 500
Tampa, FL 50021

Dear Ms. Neville:

If you are alerting a customer to a delay in his or her shipment:

This letter is to inform you that your order dated January 12 left our warehouse 2 days ago. However, as you are probably aware, our shipping company went on strike yesterday and your shipment will undoubtedly be delayed. We are doing everything we can to work around this strike, and if you need your items immediately, we are willing to send a duplicate order via another shipping company or via regular postal mail.

Please consider that all other shippers are overwhelmed with demand due to the strike, so we cannot guarantee delivery in less than 3 days. With that in mind, please let our customer service department know if you would like a duplicate order shipped.

This letter is to inform you that beginning with your order dated January 12, all Supplies 4 Less shipments must be delivered to an authorized employee or contractor, who must sign a receipt stating that he or she has taken possession of the shipment.

In the past, we have agreed to leave a shipment outside an unoccupied office or with a building receptionist or doorman. However, we have experienced several problems with stolen and damaged shipments recently and believe that this change in policy is necessary to protect our products and avoid additional costs to our company and our customers.

Let me assure you that this change will not impact the speed or quality of our shipments to you.

If you have any questions on this matter, please feel free to contact our customer service department at 555.555.5555.

Sincerely,

Rodney Lewis
Customer Service Manager

If you are announcing a change in shipping carrier:

This letter is to inform you that beginning immediately, all Supplies 4 Less orders will be shipped via SES shipping services rather than TriState Shipping. SES will also handle all merchandise returns; if you plan to return or exchange any merchandise you have received in the last 30 days, please contact us for a new SES return shipping label.

E-Mail

Dear Ms. Neville:

This message is to inform you that beginning with your order dated January 12, all Supplies 4 Less shipments must be delivered to an authorized employee or contractor who must sign a receipt stating that he or she has taken possession of the shipment.

In the past, we have agreed to leave a shipment outside an unoccupied office or with a building receptionist or doorman. However, we have experienced several problems with stolen and damaged shipments recently and believe that this change in policy is necessary to protect our products and avoid additional costs to our company and our customers.

Let me assure you that this change will not impact the speed or quality of our shipments to you.

If you have any questions on this matter, please feel free to respond to me directly.

Sincerely,

<e-mail signature, including name, title, company and contact information>

Letter Announcing a Pricing Change

Purpose

- To inform customers of a price change for an advertised item

Alternative Purposes

- To correct a previously quoted price
- To inform a customer of a price increase on his or her order
- To inform a customer of a price decrease on his or her order

---

January 20, 2008

Susan Neville
Office Manager
407 W. Morgan St., Suite 500
Tampa, FL 50021

Dear Ms. Neville:

You should have received a direct-mail package from Supplies 4 Less last week advertising our new Minute-Minder calendars. This letter is to let you know that there is an error in the price list in that direct-mail piece; the price per calendar is actually $4, not $14.

Please replace the original price list with the correct one enclosed to avoid any future confusion.

We apologize for this error but hope that this revised information will spark your interest in purchasing new calendars for your staff.

Sincerely,

Rodney Lewis
Customer Service Manager

If you are correcting a previously quoted price:

When you called our customer service department last week, I understand that our representative quoted you a price of $14 per Minute-Minder calendar. The actual price is $4 per calendar. Our department was given a product information sheet with a mistake in the price list.

If you are informing the customer of a price increase:

Your order for Minute-Minder calendars dated January 17 lists an out-of-date price for these products. The current price is $4 per calendar, not $2. I have enclosed our most recent catalog along with a new order form. If you would like to purchase the calendars at the correct price, you can either submit a new order form or call our toll-free number.

If you are informing the customer of a price decrease:

Your order for Minute-Minder calendars dated January 17 lists an out-of-date price for these products. The price has gone down to $4 per calendar, so you will pay less than you planned. However, we need your permission to process your order with the new pricing information. Please fill out the enclosed Change of Order form or call our toll-free number.

E-Mail

Dear Ms. Neville:

The e-mail message sent from Supplies 4 Less last week contained a pricing error. Our new Minute-Minder calendars are $4 per calendar, not $14.

Please replace the original price list with the attachment to avoid any future confusion.

We regret this error but hope that this revised information will spark your interest in purchasing new calendars for your staff.

Sincerely,

<e-mail signature, including name, title, company and contact information>

Letter Welcoming New Retail Customer

Purpose

- To initiate contact with a new customer and encourage future business

Alternative Purposes

- To offer a discount to encourage future business
- To send a catalog or brochure to encourage future business
- To send an application for a proprietary credit card

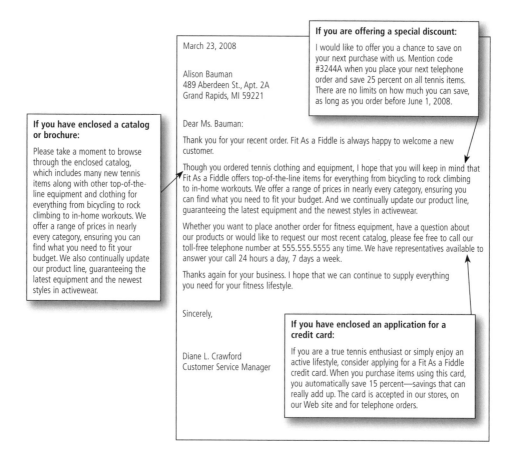

If you are offering a special discount:

I would like to offer you a chance to save on your next purchase with us. Mention code #3244A when you place your next telephone order and save 25 percent on all tennis items. There are no limits on how much you can save, as long as you order before June 1, 2008.

March 23, 2008

Alison Bauman
489 Aberdeen St., Apt. 2A
Grand Rapids, MI 59221

If you have enclosed a catalog or brochure:

Please take a moment to browse through the enclosed catalog, which includes many new tennis items along with other top-of-the-line equipment and clothing for everything from bicycling to rock climbing to in-home workouts. We offer a range of prices in nearly every category, ensuring you can find what you need to fit your budget. We also continually update our product line, guaranteeing the latest equipment and the newest styles in activewear.

Dear Ms. Bauman:

Thank you for your recent order. Fit As a Fiddle is always happy to welcome a new customer.

Though you ordered tennis clothing and equipment, I hope that you will keep in mind that Fit As a Fiddle offers top-of-the-line items for everything from bicycling to rock climbing to in-home workouts. We offer a range of prices in nearly every category, ensuring you can find what you need to fit your budget. And we continually update our product line, guaranteeing the latest equipment and the newest styles in activewear.

Whether you want to place another order for fitness equipment, have a question about our products or would like to request our most recent catalog, please fee free to call our toll-free telephone number at 555.555.5555 any time. We have representatives available to answer your call 24 hours a day, 7 days a week.

Thanks again for your business. I hope that we can continue to supply everything you need for your fitness lifestyle.

Sincerely,

Diane L. Crawford
Customer Service Manager

If you have enclosed an application for a credit card:

If you are a true tennis enthusiast or simply enjoy an active lifestyle, consider applying for a Fit As a Fiddle credit card. When you purchase items using this card, you automatically save 15 percent—savings that can really add up. The card is accepted in our stores, on our Web site and for telephone orders.

E-Mail

Dear Ms. Bauman:

Thank you for your recent order. Fit as a Fiddle is always happy to welcome a new customer.

Though you ordered tennis clothing and equipment, keep in mind that Fit As a Fiddle offers top-of-the-line items for everything from bicycling to rock climbing to in-home workouts. Click here to visit our Web site and see the current selection.

Thanks again for your business. I hope that we can continue to supply everything you need for your fitness lifestyle.

Sincerely,

<e-mail signature, including name, title, company and contact information>

Letter Welcoming a New Business-to-Business Customer

Purpose

- To initiate contact with a new customer and encourage future business

Alternative Purposes

- To offer a discount to encourage future business
- To send a catalog or brochure to encourage future business
- To offer a frequent-buyer program

March 23, 2008

Trisha Bagnall
Executive Assistant
Global Lighting Inc.
489 Aberdeen St., Suite 500
Grand Rapids, MI 59221

Dear Ms. Bagnall:

Thank you for your recent order. Supplies 4 Less is always happy to welcome a new customer.

Though you ordered general office supplies, I hope that you will keep in mind that Supplies 4 Less is also a licensed reseller of popular business software. If you check our catalog or our Web site, you will see that we offer low prices on everything from word processing applications to clip art packages. And whether you order software, office supplies or a combination of both, we offer free shipping on all orders over $100. That can add up to considerable savings.

When you are ready to replenish your office supplies or purchase other items from us, we offer two convenient ways to order: visit our Web site at **www.supplies4less.com** or call our toll-free telephone number at 555.555.5555. We have representatives available to answer your call 24 hours a day, 7 days a week.

Thank you again for your business. I hope that we can continue to help you keep your company well supplied with quality office products.

Sincerely,

Rodney Lewis
Customer Service Manager

If you are offering a special discount:

Though you ordered general office supplies, I hope that you will keep in mind that Supplies 4 Less is also a licensed reseller of popular business software. Because you are a new customer, I would like to offer you a chance to save 25 percent on the clip art package of your choice. Simply use discount code #3244A when you place your next order, and 25 percent will be deducted automatically. There are no limits on how much you can save, as long as you order before June 1, 2008.

If you have enclosed a catalog or brochure:

Though you ordered general office supplies, I hope that you will keep in mind that Supplies 4 Less is also a licensed reseller of popular business software. Please take a moment to browse the enclosed catalog, and you will see that we offer low prices on everything from Microsoft® Office to clip art packages. And whether you order software, office supplies or a combination of both, we offer free shipping on all orders over $100. That can add up to considerable savings.

If you are offering a frequent-buyers program:

Once you are convinced that Supplies 4 Less offers the best selection of office supplies and software at reasonable prices, consider joining our Frequent Buyers Club. Members in this club enjoy exclusive discounts. For more information and to sign up, see the enclosed brochure.

E-Mail

Dear Ms. Bagnall:

Thank you for your recent order. Supplies 4 Less is always happy to welcome a new customer.

Though you ordered general office supplies, I hope that you will keep in mind that Supplies 4 Less is also a licensed reseller of popular business software. Click here and you will see that we offer low prices on everything from Microsoft® Office to clip art packages.

And whether you order software, office supplies or a combination of both, we offer free shipping on all orders over $100. That can add up to considerable savings.

When you are ready to replenish your office supplies or purchase other items from us, we offer two convenient ways to order: visit our Web site or call our toll-free number at 555.555.5555 any time. We have representatives available to answer your call 24 hours a day, 7 days a week.

Thank you again for your business. I hope that we can continue to help you keep your company well supplied with quality office products.

Sincerely,

<e-mail signature, including name, title, company and contact information>

Letter Welcoming Back an Inactive Retail Customer

Purpose

- To renew contact with an inactive customer and encourage future business

Alternative Purposes

- To offer a discount to encourage future business
- To send a catalog or brochure to encourage future business
- To send an application for a proprietary credit card

If you are offering a special discount:

Just as you have obviously made a commitment to fitness, we at Fit as a Fiddle have made a commitment to pleasing our customers. That is why we would like to offer you the opportunity to save 25 percent on your next order from Fit as a Fiddle. Simply mention code #3244A. There are no limits on how much you can save, as long as you order before June 1, 2008.

March 23, 2008

Alison Bauman
489 Aberdeen St., Apt. 2A
Grand Rapids, MI 59221

Dear Ms. Bauman:

Thank you for your recent order. It has been several months since we heard from you here at Fit as a Fiddle, and we are happy to serve you again with quality fitness clothing and gear.

Just as you have obviously made a commitment to fitness, we at Fit as a Fiddle have made a commitment to pleasing our customers. As a long-time customer, you are probably familiar with our Quality Pledge to provide the best available items for everything from bicycling to rock climbing to in-home workouts. We also offer a range of prices in nearly every category, so you are sure to find what you need to fit your budget.

Whether you want to place another order for fitness equipment, have a question about our products or would like a copy of our most recent catalog, please feel free to call our toll-free number at 555.555.5555 any time. We have representatives available to answer your call 24 hours a day, 7 days a week.

Thank you again for your business; we look forward to supplying everything you need for your fitness lifestyle.

Sincerely,

Diane L. Crawford
Customer Service Manager

If you have enclosed an application for a credit card:

Just as you have obviously made a commitment to fitness, we at Fit as a Fiddle have made a commitment to pleasing our customers. That is why we would like to offer you the opportunity to apply for a Fit as a Fiddle credit card. When you purchase items using this card, you automatically save 15 percent. As you know, for active individuals such as yourself, these savings can really add up. The card is accepted in our stores, on our Web site and for telephone orders.

If you have enclosed a catalog or brochure:

Please take a moment to browse through the enclosed catalog, which includes many items that we have added since your previous order. You will find new tennis items along with top-of-the-line items for everything from bicycling to rock climbing to in-home workouts. We offer a range of prices in nearly every category, so you are sure to find what you need to fit your budget.

E-Mail

Dear Ms. Bauman:

Thank you for your recent order. It has been several months since we heard from you here at Fit as a Fiddle, and we are happy to serve you again with quality fitness clothing and gear.

Just as you have obviously made a commitment to fitness, we at Fit as a Fiddle have made a commitment to pleasing our customers. As a long-time customer, you are probably familiar with our Quality Pledge to provide the best available items for everything from bicycling to rock climbing to in-home workouts. Click here to visit our Web site and view our current selections.

Thank you again for your business; we look forward to continuing to supply everything you need for your fitness lifestyle.

Sincerely,

<e-mail signature, including name, title, company and contact information>

Letter Welcoming Back an Inactive Business-to-Business Customer

Purpose

- To renew contact with an inactive customer and encourage future business

Alternative Purposes

- To offer a discount to encourage future business
- To send a catalog or brochure to encourage future business
- To offer a frequent-buyer program

> **If you have enclosed a catalog or brochure:**
>
> A brief glance at your order history shows that you are primarily interested in basic office supplies. Did you know that Supplies 4 Less is also a licensed reseller of popular business software? Please take a moment to browse the enclosed catalog and check out our low prices on everything from word processing applications to clip art packages. And whether you are ordering software, office supplies or a combination of both, we offer free shipping on all orders over $100. That can add up to considerable savings.

> **If you are offering a special discount:**
>
> A brief glance at your order history shows that you are primarily interested in basic office supplies such as paper and pens. Did you know that Supplies 4 Less is also a licensed reseller of popular business software? Because of your continued business, I would like to offer you a chance to save 25 percent on the clip art package of your choice. Simply use discount code #3244A when you place your next order, and 25 percent will be automatically deducted. There are no limits on how much you can save, as long as you order before June 1, 2008.

March 23, 2008

Trisha Bagnall
Global Lighting Inc.
489 Aberdeen St., Suite 500
Grand Rapids, MI 59221

Dear Ms. Bagnall:

Thank you for your recent order. It has been several months since we heard from you here at Supplies 4 Less, and we are happy to fill your most recent order.

A brief glance at your order history shows that you are primarily interested in basic office supplies such as paper and pens. Did you know that Supplies 4 Less is also a licensed reseller of popular business software? If you check our catalog or Web site, you will see that we offer low prices on everything from word processing applications to clip art packages. And whether you are ordering software, office supplies or a combination of both, we offer free shipping on all orders over $100. That can add up to considerable savings.

When you are ready to replenish your office supplies or purchase other items from us, we offer two convenient ways to order: visit our Web site at **www.supplies4less.com** or call our toll-free number at 555.555.5555 any time. We have representatives available to answer your call 24 hours a day, 7 days a week.

Thank you again for your business; we look forward to continuing to help you keep your company well supplied with quality office products.

Sincerely,

Rodney Lewis
Customer Service Manager

> **If you are offering a frequent-buyers program:**
>
> A brief glance at your order history shows that you are primarily interested in basic office supplies such as paper and pens. For much-needed items such as these, the costs of replenishing supplies can really add up. One way to save money on these basics is to join the Supplies 4 Less Frequent Buyers Club. Members in this club enjoy exclusive discounts. For more information and to sign up, see the enclosed brochure.

E-Mail

Dear Ms. Bagnall:

Thank you for your recent order. It has been several months since we heard from you here at Supplies 4 Less, and we are happy to fill your most recent order.

A brief glance at your order history shows that you are primarily interested in basic office supplies such as paper and pens. Did you know that Supplies 4 Less is also a licensed reseller of popular business software? Click here and you will see that we offer low prices on everything from word processing applications to clip art packages.

And whether you are ordering software, office supplies or a combination of both, we offer free shipping on all orders over $100. That can add up to considerable savings.

When you are ready to replenish your office supplies or purchase other items from us, we offer two convenient ways to order: visit our Web site at **www.supplies4less.com** or call our toll-free telephone number at 555.555.5555 any time. We have representatives available to answer your call 24 hours a day, 7 days a week.

Thank you again for your business; we look forward to continuing to help you keep your company well supplied with quality office products.

Sincerely,

<e-mail signature, including name, title, company and contact information>

Apologetic Reply to a Letter of Complaint

Purpose

- To formally apologize in response to a complaint

Alternative Purposes

- To offer a refund in response to a complaint
- To offer a discount in response to a complaint
- To offer free product in response to a complaint

If you are offering a refund:

Our warehouse has shipped a complete set of hardware to your address, which you should have received by now. However, if you prefer to return the shelving package for a complete refund, we will certainly honor that request. If that is what you would like to do, simply follow the instructions enclosed in the original package. Given the circumstances, we would be happy to refund your return shipping costs.

If you are offering a discount:

Our warehouse has shipped a complete set of hardware to your address, which you should have received by now. I have also enclosed a check for 10 percent of your purchase and hope that this will help ease any inconvenience caused by the delay in receiving the correct hardware. You should be able to complete construction of the bookshelves with no further difficulty.

January 30, 2008

Samuel W. Pritchard
721 N. Chicago Ave.
Memphis, TN 49214

Dear Mr. Pritchard:

I would like to apologize personally for the defective set of bookshelves you purchased from Build-It Furniture. I understand your frustration at finding an incomplete package of hardware in the set and appreciate your drawing our attention to this error.

Our warehouse has shipped a complete set of hardware to your address, which you should have received by now. You should be able to complete construction of the bookshelves with no further difficulty. However, if you should run into problems with assembly, please feel free to call our customer service department at 555.555.5555; our representatives can walk you through any steps you may have difficulty with.

Once again, I apologize for any inconvenience caused by the incomplete shipment and assure you that this error is not typical of Build-It Furniture. I hope we can count on your continued business for all your future furniture needs.

Sincerely,

Josephine A. Tate
President and Founder

If you are offering free product:

Our warehouse has shipped a complete set of hardware to your address, which you should have received by now. To make up for the inconvenience caused by our error, I would also like to offer you a free wall shelf that matches the bookshelves you purchased. If you would like this shelf, just call our customer service department at 555.555.5555 and mention this letter. They will have the shelf shipped to you at no cost.

E-Mail

Dear Mr. Pritchard:

I would like to apologize personally for the defective set of bookshelves you purchased from Build-It Furniture. I appreciate your drawing our attention to this error.

Today our warehouse shipped a complete set of hardware to your address. You should be able to complete construction of the bookshelves with no further difficulty. However, if you should run into problems with assembly, please feel free to contact our customer service department; our representatives can walk you through any steps you may have difficulty with.

Once again, I apologize for any inconvenience caused by the incomplete shipment and assure you that this error is not typical of Build-It Furniture. I hope we can count on your continued business for all your future furniture needs.

Sincerely,

<e-mail signature, including name, title, company and contact information>

Explanatory Reply to a Letter of Complaint

Purpose

- To respond to a complaint and offer an explanation for the error or problem

Alternative Purposes

- To offer a refund in response to a complaint
- To offer a discount in response to a complaint
- To offer free product in response to a complaint

If you are offering free product:

Our warehouse has shipped a complete set of hardware to your address, which you should have received by now. To make up for the inconvenience caused by our error, I would also like to offer you a free wall shelf that matches the bookshelves you purchased. If you would like this shelf, just call our customer service department at 555.555.5555 and mention this letter. They will have the shelf shipped to you at no cost.

January 30, 2008

Samuel W. Pritchard
721 N. Chicago Ave.
Memphis, TN 49214

Dear Mr. Pritchard:

Thank you for your letter of January 25 in which you stated that you had received an incomplete kit of our Danish Modern bookshelves. I understand your frustration at finding an incomplete package of hardware in the set and appreciate your drawing our attention to this error.

When we received your letter, we immediately checked our inventory to ascertain how this problem happened. Our warehouse foreman discovered that the hardware packets for the Danish Modern style of shelving had been mixed in with packets for a similar style of shelving. Unfortunately, the wrong packet was sent with your order. Needless to say, we have sorted out the hardware so that this will not happen again.

Our warehouse has shipped a complete set of hardware to your address, which you should have received by now. You should be able to complete construction of the bookshelves with no further difficulty.

I apologize for any inconvenience caused by the incomplete shipment and assure you that this error is not typical of Build-It Furniture. I hope we can count on your continued business for all your future furniture needs.

Sincerely,

Josephine A. Tate
President and Founder

If you are offering a discount:

Our warehouse has shipped a complete set of hardware to your address, which you should have received by now. I have also enclosed a check for 10 percent of your purchase and hope that this will help ease any inconvenience caused by the delay in receiving the correct hardware. You should be able to complete construction of the bookshelves with no further difficulty.

If you are offering a refund:

Our warehouse has shipped a complete set of hardware to your address, which you should have received by now. However, if you prefer to return the shelving package for a complete refund, we will certainly honor that request. If that is what you would like to do, simply follow the instructions enclosed in the original package. Given the circumstances, we would be happy to refund your return shipping costs.

E-Mail

Dear Mr. Pritchard:

Thank you for your e-mail. I understand your frustration at finding an incomplete package of hardware in the set and appreciate your drawing our attention to this error.

When we received your message, we immediately checked our inventory to ascertain how this problem happened. Our warehouse foreman discovered that the hardware packets for the Danish Modern style of shelving had been mixed in with packets for a similar style of shelving. Unfortunately, the wrong packet was sent with your order. Needless to say, we have sorted out the hardware so that this will not happen again.

Our warehouse shipped a complete set of hardware to your address today. You should be able to complete construction of the bookshelves with no further difficulty.

I apologize for any inconvenience caused by the incomplete shipment and assure you that this error is not typical of Build-It Furniture. I hope we can count on your continued business for all your future furniture needs.

Sincerely,

<e-mail signature, including name, title, company and contact information>

Reply to a Letter of Complaint with Assurance of Action Taken

Purpose

- To respond to a complaint and assure the customer that action has been taken

Alternative Purposes

- To offer a refund in response to a complaint
- To offer a discount in response to a complaint
- To offer free product in response to a complaint

If you are offering a refund:

You should have received a complete set of hardware by now, enabling you to complete construction of the bookshelves with no further difficulty. However, if you prefer to return the shelving package for a complete refund, we will certainly honor that request. If that is what you would like to do, simply follow the instructions enclosed in the original package. Given the circumstances, we would be happy to refund your return shipping costs.

If you are offering a discount:

You should have received a complete set of hardware by now, enabling you to complete construction of the bookshelves with no further difficulty. I have also enclosed a check for 10 percent of your purchase and hope that this will help ease any inconvenience caused by the delay in receiving the correct hardware.

January 30, 2008

Samuel W. Pritchard
721 N. Chicago Ave.
Memphis, TN 49214

Dear Mr. Pritchard:

Thank you for your letter of January 25 in which you stated that you had received an incomplete kit of our Danish Modern bookshelves. I understand your frustration at finding an incomplete package of hardware in the set and appreciate your drawing our attention to this error.

You should have received a complete set of hardware by now, enabling you to complete construction of the bookshelves with no further difficulty.

You might be interested to know that we have determined that the error occurred because of a mistake in our warehouse assembly instructions. We have corrected and redistributed the packing lists for the Danish Modern series of furniture and have also double-checked the lists for all other products to ensure that everything is complete and correct.

I apologize for any inconvenience caused by the incomplete shipment. I hope we can count on your continued business for all your future furniture needs.

Sincerely,

Josephine A. Tate
President and Founder

If you are offering free product:

You should have received a complete set of hardware by now, enabling you to complete construction of the bookshelves with no further difficulty. To make up for the inconvenience caused by our error, I would also like to offer you a free wall shelf that matches the bookshelves you purchased. If you would like this shelf, just call our customer service department at 555.555.5555 and mention this letter. They will have the shelf shipped to you at no cost.

E-Mail

Dear Mr. Pritchard:

Thank you for your e-mail. I understand your frustration at finding an incomplete package of hardware in the set and appreciate your drawing our attention to this error.

You should have received a complete set of hardware by now, enabling you to complete construction of the bookshelves with no further difficulty.

You might be interested to know that we have determined that the error occurred because of a mistake in our warehouse assembly instructions. We have corrected and redistributed the packing lists for the Danish Modern series of furniture and have also double-checked the lists for all other products to ensure that everything is complete and correct.

I apologize for any inconvenience caused by the incomplete shipment. I hope we can count on your continued business for all your future furniture needs.

Sincerely,

<e-mail signature, including name, title, company and contact information>

Reply to a Letter of Complaint Requesting More Information

Purpose

- To respond to a complaint with a request for more information

Alternative Purposes

- To request more information and apologize for an error
- To request more information and assure the customer that no error was made
- To request more information and recommend returning the product

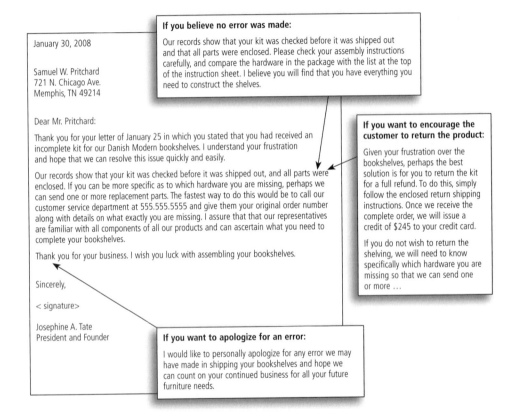

January 30, 2008

Samuel W. Pritchard
721 N. Chicago Ave.
Memphis, TN 49214

Dear Mr. Pritchard:

Thank you for your letter of January 25 in which you stated that you had received an incomplete kit for our Danish Modern bookshelves. I understand your frustration and hope that we can resolve this issue quickly and easily.

Our records show that your kit was checked before it was shipped out, and all parts were enclosed. If you can be more specific as to which hardware you are missing, perhaps we can send one or more replacement parts. The fastest way to do this would be to call our customer service department at 555.555.5555 and give them your original order number along with details on what exactly you are missing. I assure that that our representatives are familiar with all components of all our products and can ascertain what you need to complete your bookshelves.

Thank you for your business. I wish you luck with assembling your bookshelves.

Sincerely,

< signature>

Josephine A. Tate
President and Founder

If you believe no error was made:

Our records show that your kit was checked before it was shipped out and that all parts were enclosed. Please check your assembly instructions carefully, and compare the hardware in the package with the list at the top of the instruction sheet. I believe you will find that you have everything you need to construct the shelves.

If you want to encourage the customer to return the product:

Given your frustration over the bookshelves, perhaps the best solution is for you to return the kit for a full refund. To do this, simply follow the enclosed return shipping instructions. Once we receive the complete order, we will issue a credit of $245 to your credit card.

If you do not wish to return the shelving, we will need to know specifically which hardware you are missing so that we can send one or more ...

If you want to apologize for an error:

I would like to personally apologize for any error we may have made in shipping your bookshelves and hope we can count on your continued business for all your future furniture needs.

E-Mail

Dear Mr. Pritchard:

Thank you for your e-mail. I understand your frustration and hope that we can resolve this issue quickly and easily.

Our records show that your kit was checked before it was shipped out and that all parts were enclosed. If you can be more specific as to which hardware you are missing, perhaps we can send one or more replacement parts.

The fastest way to do this would be to call our customer service department at 555.555.5555 and give them your original order number along with details on what exactly you are missing.

Thank you for your business. I wish you luck with assembling your bookshelves.

Sincerely,

< e-mail signature including name, title, company and contact information>

Follow-Up Reply to a Letter of Complaint

Purpose

- To check back with a customer who has received your reply to his or her complaint

Alternative Purposes

- To offer a discount for a future purchase
- To enclose a catalog or brochure
- To offer an update on an explanation

If you are offering an update of your original explanation:

I certainly hope the answer to the above question is yes. As you know, we took measures not only to resolve the issue you had but to ensure that this error would not be repeated. I am happy to report that we instituted a new quality assurance procedure to check all assembly kits we ship, and we have not experienced a single error in shipping since that time.

If you are offering a discount:

I would like to offer you an exclusive discount on your next order from Build-It Furniture; simply use the discount code SWP when you order by phone, mail or Internet, and you will receive 25 percent off your next purchase. I hope this offer of personal savings will ensure your business in the future. I also hope that you will let me know if you have experienced further problems with your original order.

March 27, 2008

Samuel W. Pritchard
721 N. Chicago Ave.
Memphis, TN 49214

Dear Mr. Pritchard:

It has been nearly a month since I responded to your letter regarding a problem with your assembly kit for Danish Modern bookshelves. Since we have not heard back from you, can I assume that you received the additional hardware, your shelves are assembled and you are happy with the results?

I certainly hope the answer to the above question is yes. At Build-It Furniture, we work hard to ensure that our customers are satisfied with our products, and I was concerned to see you had a problem with the shipment you received. As you know, we took measures not only to resolve the issue you had but to ensure that this error would not be repeated.

I hope that we can count on your business in the future and that you will let me know personally if you have experienced any further problems with your original order.

Sincerely,

Josephine A. Tate
President and Founder

If you are enclosing a catalog or brochure:

I hope that we can count on your business in the future. The enclosed catalog features our new product line, which includes new pieces in the same Danish Modern style as your bookshelves. I also hope that you will let me know personally if you have experienced any further problems with your original order.

E-Mail

Dear Mr. Pritchard:

It has been nearly a month since I responded to your e-mail regarding a problem with your assembly kit for Danish Modern bookshelves. Since we have not heard back from you, can I assume that you received the additional hardware, your shelves are assembled and you are happy with the results?

At Build-It Furniture, we work hard to ensure that our customers are satisfied with our products, and I was concerned to see you had a problem with the shipment you received. As you know, we took measures not only to resolve the issue you had but to ensure that this error would not be repeated.

I hope that we can count on your business in the future and that you will let me know personally if you have experienced any further problems with your original order.

Sincerely,

<e-mail signature, including name, title, company and contact information>

Letter Acknowledging Compliment to an Employee

Purpose

- To formally acknowledge a written compliment to one of your employees

Alternative Purposes

- To acknowledge a written compliment about your products or services
- To acknowledge a written compliment about your business in general
- To acknowledge a written compliment about yourself

March 17, 2008

Kathleen Meijer
Office Manager
Harrison Accounting Services
5592 W. Harrison St.
Atlanta, GA 49210

Dear Ms. Meijer:

Thank you for your complimentary letter of March 10. It is always nice to hear praise—especially from one of our valued customers.

I am pleased to learn that you found Terry Shaw to be so helpful and pleasant. Everyone on our help desk team is trained to not only solve customers' technical issues but to be patient, friendly and clear in their explanations and directions. It is our goal to untangle your computer troubles and help you learn to solve similar problems in the future, if necessary. I am glad that Terry was able to do this for you, and I have passed your letter on to him with my own personal thanks.

Thank you again for taking the time to write. I hope that we can continue to earn your praise in our future dealings.

Sincerely,

Clarence T. Wilson
Director of Technical Support

If you are acknowledging a compliment to your product or service:

I am pleased to learn that you find our help desk services to be so helpful and pleasant. Everyone on our support team is trained to not only solve customers' technical issues but to be patient, friendly and clear in their explanations and directions. It is our goal to untangle your computer troubles and to help you learn to solve similar problems in the future, if necessary. I am glad that you have found this to be true.

If you are acknowledging a compliment to your business:

I am pleased to learn that you have had such positive experiences dealing with our company. We strive to help our customers with all kinds of technical issues and believe that our friendly attitude is an important part of the mix. It is our goal to not only untangle your computer troubles but to help you learn to solve similar problems in the future, if necessary.

If you are acknowledging a compliment to yourself:

I am pleased to learn that you have such a high opinion of my work with your company. I simply consider it my job to help people like you solve technical issues and, if possible, teach them to tackle similar problems in the future. For me, it is all part of doing business. I value the relationship we have built with Harrison Accounting and appreciate your kind words.

E-Mail

Dear Ms. Meijer:

Thank you for your complimentary e-mail message. It is always nice to hear praise—especially from one of our valued customers.

I am pleased to learn that you found Terry Shaw to be so helpful and pleasant. Everyone on our help desk team is trained to not only solve customers' technical issues but to be patient, friendly and clear in their explanations and directions.

It is our goal to untangle your computer troubles and to help you learn to solve similar problems in the future, if necessary. I am glad that Terry was able to do this for you. I have forwarded your message to him, along with my own personal thanks.

Thank you again for taking the time to write. I hope that we can continue to earn your praise in our future dealings.

Sincerely,

<e-mail signature, including name, title, company and contact information>

Letter Acknowledging a Suggestion for Change

Purpose

- To personally acknowledge a customer's formal suggestion for a change

Alternative Purposes

- To explain why the change cannot be implemented
- To outline how you plan to implement the change
- To offer a reward for his or her suggestion

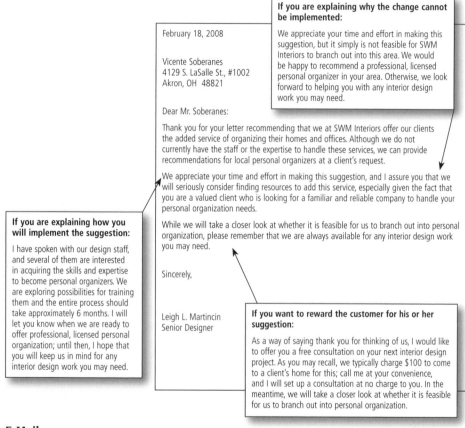

If you are explaining why the change cannot be implemented:

We appreciate your time and effort in making this suggestion, but it simply is not feasible for SWM Interiors to branch out into this area. We would be happy to recommend a professional, licensed personal organizer in your area. Otherwise, we look forward to helping you with any interior design work you may need.

February 18, 2008

Vicente Soberanes
4129 S. LaSalle St., #1002
Akron, OH 48821

Dear Mr. Soberanes:

Thank you for your letter recommending that we at SWM Interiors offer our clients the added service of organizing their homes and offices. Although we do not currently have the staff or the expertise to handle these services, we can provide recommendations for local personal organizers at a client's request.

We appreciate your time and effort in making this suggestion, and I assure you that we will seriously consider finding resources to add this service, especially given the fact that you are a valued client who is looking for a familiar and reliable company to handle your personal organization needs.

While we will take a closer look at whether it is feasible for us to branch out into personal organization, please remember that we are always available for any interior design work you may need.

Sincerely,

Leigh L. Martincin
Senior Designer

If you are explaining how you will implement the suggestion:

I have spoken with our design staff, and several of them are interested in acquiring the skills and expertise to become personal organizers. We are exploring possibilities for training them and the entire process should take approximately 6 months. I will let you know when we are ready to offer professional, licensed personal organization; until then, I hope that you will keep us in mind for any interior design work you may need.

If you want to reward the customer for his or her suggestion:

As a way of saying thank you for thinking of us, I would like to offer you a free consultation on your next interior design project. As you may recall, we typically charge $100 to come to a client's home for this; call me at your convenience, and I will set up a consultation at no charge to you. In the meantime, we will take a closer look at whether it is feasible for us to branch out into personal organization.

E-Mail

Dear Mr. Soberanes:

Thank you for recommending that we offer the added service of organizing clients' homes and offices. Although we do not currently have the staff or the expertise to handle these services, we can provide recommendations for local personal organizers at a client's request.

We appreciate your making this suggestion, and I assure you that we will seriously consider it, especially given the fact that you are a valued client who is looking for a familiar and reliable company to handle your personal organization needs.

While we will take a closer look at this possibility, please remember that we are always available for any interior design work you may need.

Sincerely,

<e-mail signature, including name, title, company and contact information>

Letter Requesting Customer Feedback

Purpose

- To formally ask for a customer's feedback or opinion on your company, products or services

Alternative Purposes

- To request a phone interview to get feedback
- To ask the customer to fill out an online survey
- To offer a reward for completing a questionnaire

March 27, 2008

Jill A. Sanders
4002 W. Rush St.
Indianapolis, IN 48821

Dear Ms. Sanders:

Every aspect of how Knit-Wits serves customers like you is regularly reviewed and carefully analyzed. One of the most important components of these reviews is gathering feedback directly from our customers.

It is because of suggestions and responses from our customers that we have made changes such as the following:

- offering more options for shipping carriers
- adding a line of children's apparel
- extending our hours for telephone ordering

As one of our valued customers, you can help us improve our service, our products and our overall way of doing business. Please take a few minutes to fill out the enclosed questionnaire on your experience dealing with Knit-Wits.

Thank you in advance for sharing your thoughts with us. We appreciate your time and effort in providing feedback to us.

Sincerely,

Tanya Ludovic
Director of Customer Relations

If you are requesting a phone interview:

As one of our valued customers, you can help us improve our service, our products and our overall way of doing business. We would like to ask you a few questions over the phone; this brief survey should take only a few minutes. Please call 555.555.5555 before April 10 to share your experience dealing with Knit-Wits.

If you want to send the customer to your Web site:

As one of our valued customers, you can help us improve our service, our products and our overall way of doing business. Please take a few minutes to fill out our online questionnaire at **www.knitwits.com**. You will also find exclusive online bargains on our Web site, so go online now!

If you are offering a reward for a completed survey:

I have enclosed a dollar bill as a thank you for sharing your thoughts with us. Your feedback is certainly worth more than a dollar, but I hope this small token of appreciation will help express the importance of your response.

E-Mail

Dear Ms. Sanders:

Every aspect of how Knit-Wits serves customers like you is regularly reviewed and carefully analyzed. One of the most important components of these reviews is gathering feedback directly from our customers.

It is because of suggestions and responses from our customers that we have made changes such as the following:

- offering more options for shipping carriers
- adding a line of children's apparel
- extending our hours for telephone ordering

As one of our valued customers, you can help us improve our service, our products and our overall way of doing business. Please take a few minutes to fill out our online questionnaire at **www.knitwits.com**. You will also find exclusive online bargains on our Web site, so visit **www.knitwits.com** now!

Thank you in advance for sharing your thoughts with us. We appreciate your time and effort in providing feedback to us.

Sincerely,

<e-mail signature, including name, title, company and contact information>

Thank You Letter for Customer Feedback

Purpose

- To personally thank a customer for providing requested feedback on your company, products or services

Alternative Purposes

- To thank a customer for a phone interview
- To thank a customer for participating in a focus group
- To offer a reward for completing a questionnaire

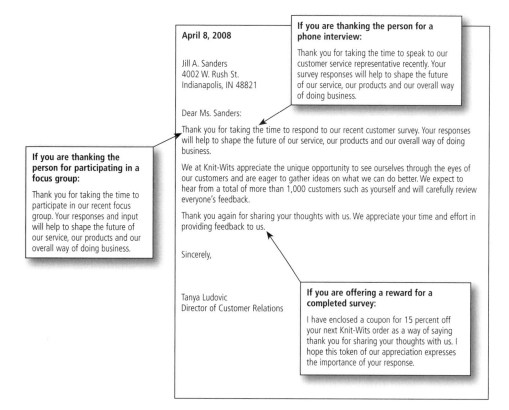

April 8, 2008

Jill A. Sanders
4002 W. Rush St.
Indianapolis, IN 48821

Dear Ms. Sanders:

Thank you for taking the time to respond to our recent customer survey. Your responses will help to shape the future of our service, our products and our overall way of doing business.

We at Knit-Wits appreciate the unique opportunity to see ourselves through the eyes of our customers and are eager to gather ideas on what we can do better. We expect to hear from a total of more than 1,000 customers such as yourself and will carefully review everyone's feedback.

Thank you again for sharing your thoughts with us. We appreciate your time and effort in providing feedback to us.

Sincerely,

Tanya Ludovic
Director of Customer Relations

If you are thanking the person for a phone interview:

Thank you for taking the time to speak to our customer service representative recently. Your survey responses will help to shape the future of our service, our products and our overall way of doing business.

If you are thanking the person for participating in a focus group:

Thank you for taking the time to participate in our recent focus group. Your responses and input will help to shape the future of our service, our products and our overall way of doing business.

If you are offering a reward for a completed survey:

I have enclosed a coupon for 15 percent off your next Knit-Wits order as a way of saying thank you for sharing your thoughts with us. I hope this token of our appreciation expresses the importance of your response.

E-Mail

Dear Ms. Sanders:

Thank you for taking the time to respond to our recent customer survey. Your responses will help to shape the future of our service, our products and our overall way of doing business.

We at Knit-Wits appreciate the unique opportunity to see ourselves through the eyes of our customers and are eager to gather ideas on what we can do better.

We appreciate your time and effort in providing feedback to us.

Sincerely,

<e-mail signature, including name, title, company and contact information>

Letter Reminding Customer to Visit Web Site

Purpose

- To remind a customer to visit your company's Web site to order, find information and communicate

Alternative Purposes

- To direct a customer to a specific section of the site
- To direct a customer to special Web pricing
- To direct a customer to sign up for e-mail updates

January 14, 2008

Henry Franklin
198 Stockton Dr.
Dayton, OH 58823

Dear Mr. Franklin:

It is impossible to beat the convenience of ordering apparel from a catalog . . . or is it?

If you have not visited Knit-Wits' Web site at **www.knitwits.com** lately, you should check it out. You can find all the shirts, sports apparel and outerwear we feature in our catalogs—and more. Even better, we regularly offer special Web-only discounts on selected items.

Perhaps you are not comfortable ordering and paying for items online. If that is the case, let me assure you that your information is 100 percent secure on **www.knitwits.com**. Your personal information, including your credit card number, is just as safe as if you were to send in a hard copy order form or speak with one of our telephone representatives.

We will continue to offer our customers a variety of ways to browse our products and place their orders. Once you see how quickly and easily you can shop on **www.knitwits.com**, I think you will agree: You cannot beat the convenience of ordering apparel online!

Sincerely,

Tanya Ludovic
Director of Customer Relations

If you are directing the customer to a specific section:

To browse our comprehensive selection of men's shirts, simply click on men's shirts on the left side of the home page. You can view any shirt in a variety of colors, see a close-up of a shirt and place shirts in your shopping cart for future consideration or purchase.

If you are directing the customer to special Web pricing:

This month we are offering Web-only savings on a selection of men's shirts. To see these bargains, visit **www.knitwits.com** and click on Today's Specials. Note that these prices apply only to Internet orders, and the items on sale will change beginning February 1.

You can save up to 40 percent on our monthly Web-only sales; visit **www.knitwits.com** today. Check it often to see how much you can save!

If you are asking the customer to sign up for e-mail updates:

You can stay up-to-date on special sales and new products; just sign up for Knit-Wits' monthly e-mail updates. We will send you a brief e-mail note no more than once a month, alerting you to new discounts, new products and other changes you should know about.

Sign up today. Simply to go to **www.knitwits.com** and click on E-Mail News. Provide your information and we will send you your first update in February.

E-Mail

Dear Mr. Franklin:

You cannot beat the convenience of ordering apparel from a catalog . . . or can you?

If you have not visited **www.knitwits.com** lately, you should. You can find all the shirts, sports apparel and outerwear we feature in our catalogs—and more. Even better, we regularly offer special Web-only discounts on selected items.

Perhaps you are not comfortable ordering and paying for items online. If that is the case, let me assure you that your information is 100 percent secure on **www.knitwits.com**. Your personal information, including your credit card number, is just as safe as if you were to send in a hard copy order form or speak with one of our telephone representatives.

Knit-Wits will continue to offer our customers a variety of ways to browse our products and place their orders. Once you see how quickly and easily you can shop on **www.knitwits.com**, I think you will agree: You cannot beat the convenience of ordering apparel online!

Sincerely,

<e-mail signature, including name, title, company and contact information>

Letter Notifying Customers of a Company Move

Purpose

- To formally notify your customers of an upcoming change of address

Alternative Purposes

- To notify customers of a move that has already occurred
- To notify customers of an upcoming interruption in service due to a move
- To notify customers of improvements/expansions to your location

If you are notifying customers of improvements or expansion of your offices:

Clean Sweepers is under construction. Beginning this week, we are adding on to our current space.

Though we have done everything we can to ensure that the construction does not pose any inconvenience to our customers, we may experience brief periods where our phone service is interrupted.

However, you can expect our usual attention to detail and prompt response from both our office staff and our janitorial staff before, during and after our expansion.

If you are notifying customers of an upcoming interruption in service:

We have done everything we can to ensure that this move does not pose any inconvenience to our customers.

However, please note that our offices will be closed on Friday, March 1. Any cleaning you have scheduled for that day will be completed, but there will be no office support available until the following weekend.

If you are notifying customers of a move that has already occurred:

Please note that Clean Sweepers has moved to a new address. On February 15, we moved to:

Clean Sweepers
6999 Montrose Ave.
Lincoln, NE 62922

Our e-mail addresses, telephone and fax numbers have not changed.

February 20, 2008

Renaldo Rivera
Office Manager
Eckhart Industries
582 S. Canal St.
Lincoln, NE 62904

Dear Mr. Rivera:

Please note that as of March 1, Clean Sweepers will have a new address. Beginning with that date, please send any correspondence, including payments to:

Clean Sweepers
6999 Montrose Ave.
Lincoln, NE 62922

Our e-mail addresses, telephone and fax numbers will not change.

We have done everything we can to ensure that this move does not pose any inconvenience to our customers. There will be no interruption in our telephone and fax service, our customer service or our Web site during the move. You can expect our usual attention to detail and prompt response from both our office staff and our janitorial staff before, during and after our move.

The fact is Clean Sweepers has outgrown our long-time location. Our new facility includes a warehouse space for supplies and equipment, so we can offer more janitorial services to more customers. This growth in our business means added services and more resources for current customers like you.

Sincerely,

James C. Cleverdon
Customer Service Coordinator

E-Mail

Dear Mr. Rivera:

Please note that as of March 1, Clean Sweepers will have a new address.

Beginning with that date, please send any correspondence, including payments to:

Clean Sweepers
6999 Montrose Ave.
Lincoln, NE 62922

Our e-mail addresses, telephone and fax numbers will not change.

There will be no interruption in our telephone and fax service, our customer service or our Web site during the move. You can expect our usual attention to detail and prompt response from both our office staff and our janitorial staff before, during and after our move.

The fact is, Clean Sweepers has outgrown our long-time location. Our new facility includes a warehouse space for supplies and equipment, so we can offer more janitorial services to more customers. This growth in our business means added services and more resources for current customers like you.

Sincerely,

<e-mail signature, including name, title, company and contact information>

Letter Notifying Customers of a Merger or Acquisition Involving Your Company

Purpose

- To officially announce your company's merger to your customers

Alternative Purposes

- To announce that your company has acquired another business
- To announce that your company has been acquired by another business
- To announce that your company has laid off employees

March 8, 2008

Renaldo Rivera
Office Manager
Eckhart Industries
582 S. Canal St.
Lincoln, NE 62904

Dear Mr. Rivera:

As a businessperson, you know how important it is for a company to change and grow in order to prosper. This is as true for your janitorial service as it is for your own organization.

Clean Sweepers is proud to announce that we have merged with Nebraska Housekeepers, a residential cleaning service based in Omaha. This friendly merger will double the size of our staff and enable us to consolidate some of our back office functions. The result: more resources and energy to spend on you, our customers.

Our company name, contact information and commitment to quality will remain the same. We will be making some changes to our billing processes within the next 2 months. Information on these changes will be enclosed in your April bill.

If you have any questions on this change in Clean Sweepers, please do not hesitate to call our toll-free number. Any of our customer service representatives will be happy to address any concerns you might have.

Sincerely,

James C. Cleverdon
Customer Service Coordinator

> **If you are announcing that your company has acquired another business:**
>
> Clean Sweepers is proud to announce that we have acquired an Omaha-based residential cleaning service called Nebraska Housekeepers. This acquisition will double the size of our staff and enable us to consolidate some of our back office functions with those of Nebraska Housekeepers. The result: more resources and energy to spend on you, our customers.

> **If you are announcing that your company has been acquired by another business:**
>
> This week, Clean Sweepers was acquired by Nebraska Housekeepers, a residential cleaning service based in Omaha. This acquisition will double the size of our staff and enable the two companies to consolidate some of our back office functions. The result: more resources and energy to spend on you, our customers.
>
> Beginning in April, we will officially be known as Nebraska Housekeepers. Our contact information and, more importantly, our commitment to quality will remain the same.

> **If you are announcing layoffs:**
>
> You may have seen news articles announcing layoffs at Clean Sweepers. It is true that we downsized some of our back office staff as well as some of our part-time janitorial staff. These changes allow us to focus more on providing quality service to you, our customers.

E-Mail

Dear Mr. Rivera:

As a businessperson, you know how important it is for a company to change and grow in order to prosper. This is as true for your janitorial service as it is for your own organization.

Clean Sweepers is proud to announce that we have merged with Nebraska Housekeepers, a residential cleaning service based in Omaha.

This friendly merger will double the size of our staff and enable us to consolidate some of our back office functions. The result: more resources and energy to spend on you, our customers.

Our company name, contact information and commitment to quality will remain the same. We will be making some changes to our billing processes within the next 2 months. Information on these changes will be enclosed in your April bill.

If you have any questions on this change in Clean Sweepers, please do not hesitate to contact me.

Sincerely,

<e-mail signature, including name, title, company and contact information>

Letter Notifying Customers of a Change in Business Hours

Purpose

- To officially inform customers of a reduction in business hours

Alternative Purposes

- To inform customers of an increase in business hours
- To inform customers of a shift in business hours
- To inform customers of alternate ways to contact your business

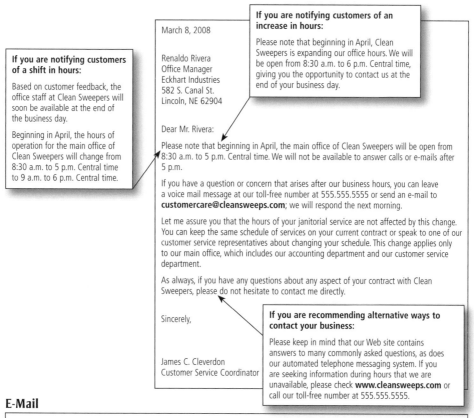

If you are notifying customers of an increase in hours:

Please note that beginning in April, Clean Sweepers is expanding our office hours. We will be open from 8:30 a.m. to 6 p.m. Central time, giving you the opportunity to contact us at the end of your business day.

If you are notifying customers of a shift in hours:

Based on customer feedback, the office staff at Clean Sweepers will soon be available at the end of the business day.

Beginning in April, the hours of operation for the main office of Clean Sweepers will change from 8:30 a.m. to 5 p.m. Central time to 9 a.m. to 6 p.m. Central time.

March 8, 2008

Renaldo Rivera
Office Manager
Eckhart Industries
582 S. Canal St.
Lincoln, NE 62904

Dear Mr. Rivera:

Please note that beginning in April, the main office of Clean Sweepers will be open from 8:30 a.m. to 5 p.m. Central time. We will not be available to answer calls or e-mails after 5 p.m.

If you have a question or concern that arises after our business hours, you can leave a voice mail message at our toll-free number at 555.555.5555 or send an e-mail to **customercare@cleansweeps.com**; we will respond the next morning.

Let me assure you that the hours of your janitorial service are not affected by this change. You can keep the same schedule of services on your current contract or speak to one of our customer service representatives about changing your schedule. This change applies only to our main office, which includes our accounting department and our customer service department.

As always, if you have any questions about any aspect of your contract with Clean Sweepers, please do not hesitate to contact me directly.

Sincerely,

James C. Cleverdon
Customer Service Coordinator

If you are recommending alternative ways to contact your business:

Please keep in mind that our Web site contains answers to many commonly asked questions, as does our automated telephone messaging system. If you are seeking information during hours that we are unavailable, please check **www.cleansweeps.com** or call our toll-free number at 555.555.5555.

E-Mail

Dear Mr. Rivera:

Please note that beginning in April, the main office of Clean Sweepers will be open from 8:30 a.m. to 5 p.m. Central time. We will not be available to answer calls or e-mails after 5 p.m.

If you have a question or concern that arises after our business hours, you may leave a voice mail message at our toll-free number at 555.555.5555 or send us an e-mail; we will respond the next morning.

Let me assure you that the hours of your janitorial service are not affected by this change. You can keep the same schedule of services on your current contract or speak to one of our customer service representatives about changing your schedule. This change only applies to our main office, which includes our accounting department and our customer service department.

As always, if you have any questions about any aspect of your contract with Clean Sweepers, please do not hesitate to contact me directly.

Sincerely,

<e-mail signature, including name, title, company and contact information>

Letter Notifying a Customer That His or Her Payment Method Will Expire Soon

Purpose

- To warn a customer that his or her payment method is about to expire

Alternative Purposes

- To notify a customer that his or her credit card was canceled and payment is due
- To alert a customer that his or her payment amount will change
- To alert the customer that you are suspending service until a new payment method is offered

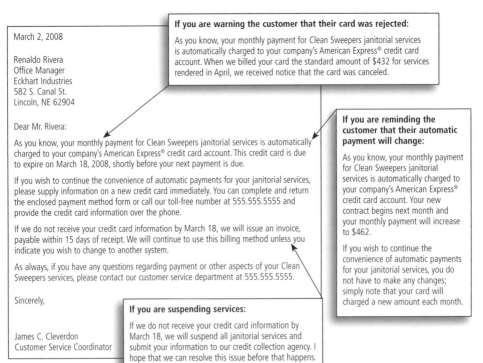

March 2, 2008

Renaldo Rivera
Office Manager
Eckhart Industries
582 S. Canal St.
Lincoln, NE 62904

Dear Mr. Rivera:

As you know, your monthly payment for Clean Sweepers janitorial services is automatically charged to your company's American Express® credit card account. This credit card is due to expire on March 18, 2008, shortly before your next payment is due.

If you wish to continue the convenience of automatic payments for your janitorial services, please supply information on a new credit card immediately. You can complete and return the enclosed payment method form or call our toll-free number at 555.555.5555 and provide the credit card information over the phone.

If we do not receive your credit card information by March 18, we will issue an invoice, payable within 15 days of receipt. We will continue to use this billing method unless you indicate you wish to change to another system.

As always, if you have any questions regarding payment or other aspects of your Clean Sweepers services, please contact our customer service department at 555.555.5555.

Sincerely,

James C. Cleverdon
Customer Service Coordinator

If you are warning the customer that their card was rejected:

As you know, your monthly payment for Clean Sweepers janitorial services is automatically charged to your company's American Express® credit card account. When we billed your card the standard amount of $432 for services rendered in April, we received notice that the card was canceled.

If you are reminding the customer that their automatic payment will change:

As you know, your monthly payment for Clean Sweepers janitorial services is automatically charged to your company's American Express® credit card account. Your new contract begins next month and your monthly payment will increase to $462.

If you wish to continue the convenience of automatic payments for your janitorial services, you do not have to make any changes; simply note that your card will charged a new amount each month.

If you are suspending services:

If we do not receive your credit card information by March 18, we will suspend all janitorial services and submit your information to our credit collection agency. I hope that we can resolve this issue before that happens.

E-Mail

Dear Mr. Rivera:

As you know, your monthly payment for Clean Sweepers janitorial services is automatically charged to your company's American Express® credit card account.

This credit card is due to expire on March 18, 2008, shortly before your next payment is due.

If you wish to continue the convenience of automatic payments for your janitorial services, please supply information on a new credit card immediately. The most secure way to do this is to call our customer service department at 555.555.5555 and provide the credit card information over the phone.

If we do not receive your credit card information by March 18, we will issue an invoice, payable within 15 days of receipt. We will continue to use this billing method unless you indicate you wish to change to another system.

Please respond to this e-mail if you have any questions regarding payment or other aspects of your Clean Sweepers services.

Sincerely,

<e-mail signature, including name, title, company and contact information>

Letter Asking Customers to Sign Up for Regular Updates

Purpose

- To encourage existing customers to accept updates on your business, products or services

Alternative Purposes

- To request opt-in permission to send an e-mail update or e-newsletter
- To request names and contact information for colleagues to send updates to
- To check for updates on current contact information

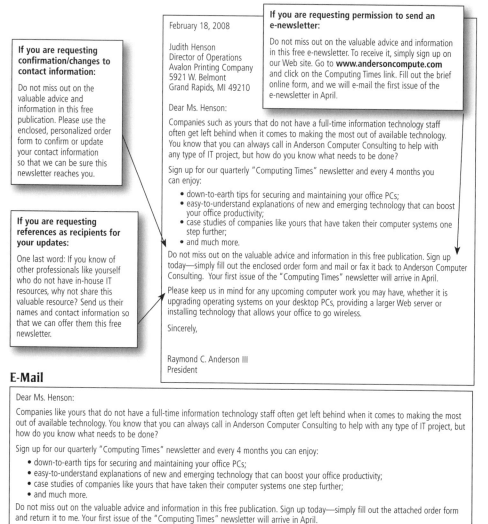

If you are requesting confirmation/changes to contact information:

Do not miss out on the valuable advice and information in this free publication. Please use the enclosed, personalized order form to confirm or update your contact information so that we can be sure this newsletter reaches you.

If you are requesting references as recipients for your updates:

One last word: If you know of other professionals like yourself who do not have in-house IT resources, why not share this valuable resource? Send us their names and contact information so that we can offer them this free newsletter.

If you are requesting permission to send an e-newsletter:

Do not miss out on the valuable advice and information in this free e-newsletter. To receive it, simply sign up on our Web site. Go to **www.andersoncompute.com** and click on the Computing Times link. Fill out the brief online form, and we will e-mail the first issue of the e-newsletter in April.

February 18, 2008

Judith Henson
Director of Operations
Avalon Printing Company
5921 W. Belmont
Grand Rapids, MI 49210

Dear Ms. Henson:

Companies such as yours that do not have a full-time information technology staff often get left behind when it comes to making the most out of available technology. You know that you can always call in Anderson Computer Consulting to help with any type of IT project, but how do you know what needs to be done?

Sign up for our quarterly "Computing Times" newsletter and every 4 months you can enjoy:

- down-to-earth tips for securing and maintaining your office PCs;
- easy-to-understand explanations of new and emerging technology that can boost your office productivity;
- case studies of companies like yours that have taken their computer systems one step further;
- and much more.

Do not miss out on the valuable advice and information in this free publication. Sign up today—simply fill out the enclosed order form and mail or fax it back to Anderson Computer Consulting. Your first issue of the "Computing Times" newsletter will arrive in April.

Please keep us in mind for any upcoming computer work you may have, whether it is upgrading operating systems on your desktop PCs, providing a larger Web server or installing technology that allows your office to go wireless.

Sincerely,

Raymond C. Anderson III
President

E-Mail

Dear Ms. Henson:

Companies like yours that do not have a full-time information technology staff often get left behind when it comes to making the most out of available technology. You know that you can always call in Anderson Computer Consulting to help with any type of IT project, but how do you know what needs to be done?

Sign up for our quarterly "Computing Times" newsletter and every 4 months you can enjoy:

- down-to-earth tips for securing and maintaining your office PCs;
- easy-to-understand explanations of new and emerging technology that can boost your office productivity;
- case studies of companies like yours that have taken their computer systems one step further;
- and much more.

Do not miss out on the valuable advice and information in this free publication. Sign up today—simply fill out the attached order form and return it to me. Your first issue of the "Computing Times" newsletter will arrive in April.

Please keep us in mind for any upcoming computer work you may have, whether it is upgrading operating systems on your desktop PCs, providing a larger Web server or installing technology that allows your office to go wireless.

Sincerely,

<e-mail signature, including name, title, company and contact information>

Letter Acknowledging That Customer Has Signed Up for Regular Updates

Purpose

- To confirm that a customer has agreed to accept updates on your business, products or services

Alternative Purposes

- To acknowledge opt-in permission to receive an e-mail update or e-newsletter
- To acknowledge receipt of names and contact information for colleagues
- To acknowledge receipt of changes to current contact information

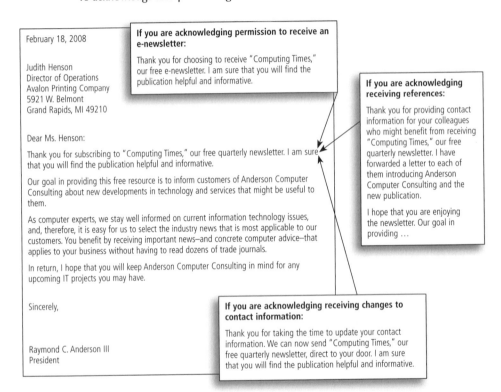

February 18, 2008

If you are acknowledging permission to receive an e-newsletter:

Thank you for choosing to receive "Computing Times," our free e-newsletter. I am sure that you will find the publication helpful and informative.

If you are acknowledging receiving references:

Thank you for providing contact information for your colleagues who might benefit from receiving "Computing Times," our free quarterly newsletter. I have forwarded a letter to each of them introducing Anderson Computer Consulting and the new publication.

I hope that you are enjoying the newsletter. Our goal in providing …

Judith Henson
Director of Operations
Avalon Printing Company
5921 W. Belmont
Grand Rapids, MI 49210

Dear Ms. Henson:

Thank you for subscribing to "Computing Times," our free quarterly newsletter. I am sure that you will find the publication helpful and informative.

Our goal in providing this free resource is to inform customers of Anderson Computer Consulting about new developments in technology and services that might be useful to them.

As computer experts, we stay well informed on current information technology issues, and, therefore, it is easy for us to select the industry news that is most applicable to our customers. You benefit by receiving important news—and concrete computer advice—that applies to your business without having to read dozens of trade journals.

In return, I hope that you will keep Anderson Computer Consulting in mind for any upcoming IT projects you may have.

If you are acknowledging receiving changes to contact information:

Thank you for taking the time to update your contact information. We can now send "Computing Times," our free quarterly newsletter, direct to your door. I am sure that you will find the publication helpful and informative.

Sincerely,

Raymond C. Anderson III
President

E-Mail

Dear Ms. Henson:

Thank you for subscribing to "Computing Times," our free quarterly newsletter. I am sure that you will find the publication helpful and informative.

Our goal in providing this free resource is to inform customers of Anderson Computer Consulting about new developments in technology and services that may prove useful in their businesses.

As computer experts, we stay well informed on current information technology issues, and, therefore, it is easy for us to select the industry news that is most applicable to our customers. You benefit by receiving important news—and concrete computer advice—that applies to your business without having to read dozens of trade journals. In return, I hope that you will keep Anderson Computer Consulting in mind for any upcoming IT projects you may have.

Sincerely,

<e-mail signature, including name, title, company and contact information>

Thank You Letter to Customers

Purpose

- To thank customers for their business

Alternative Purposes

- To thank a customer for a substantial order
- To thank a customer for an extended relationship
- To thank a customer for his or her business, despite problems

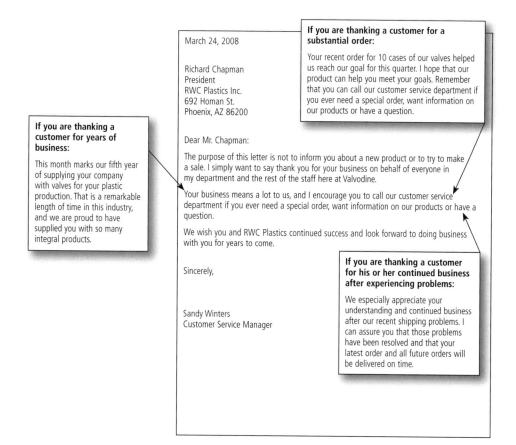

If you are thanking a customer for a substantial order:

Your recent order for 10 cases of our valves helped us reach our goal for this quarter. I hope that our product can help you meet your goals. Remember that you can call our customer service department if you ever need a special order, want information on our products or have a question.

March 24, 2008

Richard Chapman
President
RWC Plastics Inc.
692 Homan St.
Phoenix, AZ 86200

If you are thanking a customer for years of business:

This month marks our fifth year of supplying your company with valves for your plastic production. That is a remarkable length of time in this industry, and we are proud to have supplied you with so many integral products.

Dear Mr. Chapman:

The purpose of this letter is not to inform you about a new product or to try to make a sale. I simply want to say thank you for your business on behalf of everyone in my department and the rest of the staff here at Valvodine.

Your business means a lot to us, and I encourage you to call our customer service department if you ever need a special order, want information on our products or have a question.

We wish you and RWC Plastics continued success and look forward to doing business with you for years to come.

Sincerely,

Sandy Winters
Customer Service Manager

If you are thanking a customer for his or her continued business after experiencing problems:

We especially appreciate your understanding and continued business after our recent shipping problems. I can assure you that those problems have been resolved and that your latest order and all future orders will be delivered on time.

E-Mail

Dear Mr. Chapman:

The purpose of this e-mail is not to inform you about a new product or to try to make a sale. I simply want to say thank you for your business on behalf of everyone in my department and the rest of the staff here at Valvodine.

Your business means a lot to us, and I encourage you to call our customer service department if you ever need a special order, want information on our products or have a question.

We wish you and RWC Plastics continued success and look forward to doing business with you for years to come.

Sincerely,

<e-mail signature, including name, title, company and contact information>

Holiday Greetings to Customers

Purpose

- To extend holiday greetings to customers

Alternative Purposes

- To wish customers a happy new year
- To wish a customer happy birthday
- To offer customers a special discount

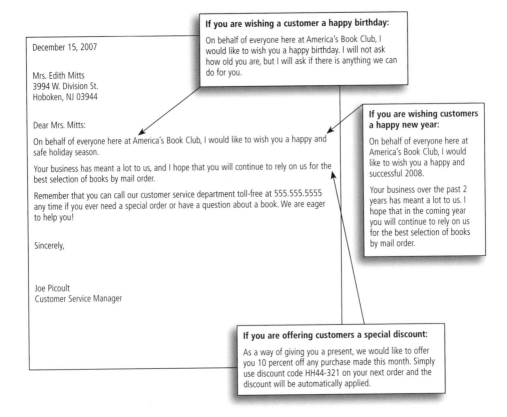

If you are wishing a customer a happy birthday:

On behalf of everyone here at America's Book Club, I would like to wish you a happy birthday. I will not ask how old you are, but I will ask if there is anything we can do for you.

December 15, 2007

Mrs. Edith Mitts
3994 W. Division St.
Hoboken, NJ 03944

Dear Mrs. Mitts:

On behalf of everyone here at America's Book Club, I would like to wish you a happy and safe holiday season.

Your business has meant a lot to us, and I hope that you will continue to rely on us for the best selection of books by mail order.

Remember that you can call our customer service department toll-free at 555.555.5555 any time if you ever need a special order or have a question about a book. We are eager to help you!

Sincerely,

Joe Picoult
Customer Service Manager

If you are wishing customers a happy new year:

On behalf of everyone here at America's Book Club, I would like to wish you a happy and successful 2008.

Your business over the past 2 years has meant a lot to us. I hope that in the coming year you will continue to rely on us for the best selection of books by mail order.

If you are offering customers a special discount:

As a way of giving you a present, we would like to offer you 10 percent off any purchase made this month. Simply use discount code HH44-321 on your next order and the discount will be automatically applied.

E-Mail

Dear Mrs. Mitts:

On behalf of everyone here at America's Book Club, I would like to wish you a happy and safe holiday season.

Your business has meant a lot to us, and I hope that you will continue to rely on us for the best selection of books by mail order.

Remember that you can contact our customer service department via e-mail if you ever need a special order or have a question about a book. We are eager to help you!

Sincerely,

<e-mail signature, including name, title, company and contact information>

Section Six

Essential Sales Letters

Cold-Call Letter Introducing Salesperson/Company to New Prospect
(straightforward version)

Purpose

- To begin communications with a prospective new customer

Alternative Purposes

- To introduce oneself to a prospective customer through a mutual acquaintance
- To offer a prospective customer a special offer
- To introduce one's company to a prospective customer with marketing collateral materials

---

If you were referred to the prospective customer:

Alice Baum, your former accounting manager, suggested I contact you about replacing your current payroll service with our firm, Payroll Plus. We have the size and scope ...

If you are offering a special deal to the prospective customer:

I would like to offer you and your accounting staff the opportunity to take advantage of the expertise at Payroll Plus. You can begin benefiting from our experience right away by attending a free, 1-hour, in-house seminar on how the new federal tax laws will impact payroll and other aspects of business accounting. I will call you during the week of March 24 to discuss scheduling the seminar at your convenience. I look forward to speaking with you soon.

March 12, 2008

Conrad Grant
Chief Financial Officer
Jamison International
542 State St. N.W., Suite 5300
San Jose, CA 90990

Dear Mr. Grant:

Let me introduce myself and my company, Payroll Plus, to you and outline how we can help you save money and time processing your payroll.

Payroll Plus has the size and scope necessary to provide Jamison International with the expertise and resources to meet federal, state and local payroll regulations. Like Jamison International, we have offices across the United States and clients in nearly every state, and we customize our products and services for each client.

No matter how complex your specific payroll needs, including employee withholding, information accessibility, or state-by-state or office-by-office customization, Payroll Plus can meet those needs. Our state-of-the-art, easy-to-use Web-based technology allows you to access and update your payroll information with ease. We also guarantee our services 100 percent and accept liability for any payroll-related penalties that may arise.

There are many other benefits to using Payroll Plus that I would like to discuss with you personally. I will call you during the week of March 24 to inquire about your specific payroll needs and whether your current service is meeting those needs. I look forward to speaking with you soon.

Sincerely,

Heidi Schiffle
Western Sales Manager

If you are sending a brochure or catalog:

The enclosed brochure outlines these and other benefits and includes customer testimonials and success stories. I will give you a call ...

E-Mail

Dear Mr. Grant:

Let me introduce myself and my company, Payroll Plus. We offer expert payroll services and tailor our services to the individual needs of each client. Jamison International could benefit from:

- our national size and scope, which provides the expertise your company needs to meet federal, state and local payroll regulations;
- customized employee withholding or state-by-state and office-by-office customization and more;
- state-of-the-art, easy-to-use Web-based technology, which allows you to access and update your payroll information; and
- the peace of mind we offer by guaranteeing our services 100 percent. We also accept liability for any payroll-related penalties that may arise.

There are many other benefits to using Payroll Plus. I will give you a call to talk about your specific payroll needs and whether your current service is meeting those needs. I look forward to speaking with you soon.

<e-mail signature, including name, title, company and contact information>

Cold-Call Letter Introducing Salesperson/Company to New Prospect
(hard-sell version)

Purpose

- To begin communications with a new prospective customer

Alternative Purposes

- To introduce oneself to a prospective customer through a mutual acquaintance
- To offer a prospective customer a special offer
- To introduce one's company to a prospective customer with marketing collateral materials

March 12, 2008

Conrad Grant
Chief Financial Officer
Jamison International
542 State St. N.W., Suite 5300
San Jose, CA 90990

If you were referred to the prospective customer:

Alice Baum, your former accounting manager, mentioned that you are using CHEX Inc. for your payroll services and that you are satisfied with their services. But I would like to ask you to consider this: How much are you getting for your monthly fees?

Dear Mr. Grant:

When it comes to your payroll service, what are you getting for your monthly fees? Does your service accept responsibility for its mistakes by paying any necessary penalties? Do they customize their services for you office by office or state by state? Can your employees check their pay stubs online at their convenience?

Payroll Plus will do all of this and more for Jamison International. Like your organization, we have offices across the United States and clients in nearly every state. Our size and scope gives Payroll Plus the expertise your company needs to meet federal, state and local payroll regulations. We also have the resources to tailor our products and services for each client.

Our state-of-the-art Web-based technology allows approved members of your accounting team to access and update payroll information with a click of the mouse. We guarantee the security of your information, both within our walls and on the Internet.

I am confident that Payroll Plus can improve on the quality and features of your current payroll service. I will call you shortly to talk about your specific payroll needs and discuss how we can meet, and even exceed, those needs. I look forward to speaking with you soon.

If you are sending a brochure or catalog:

I am sure Payroll Plus can improve on the quality and features of your current payroll service. Take a look at the enclosed brochure to find out more about the value-added features we offer. I will give you a call …

Sincerely,

If you are offering a special deal to the prospective customer:

You can start by taking advantage of the knowledge base at Payroll Plus. We are offering a free, 1-hour, in-house seminar on how the new federal tax laws will impact payroll and other aspects of business accounting. I will give you a call during the week of March 24 to discuss scheduling the seminar at your convenience.

Heidi Schiffle
Western Sales Manager

E-Mail

Dear Mr. Grant:

When it comes to your payroll service, what are you getting for your monthly fees? Does your service accept responsibility for its mistakes by paying any necessary penalties? Will they customize their services for you office by office or state by state? Can your employees check their pay stubs online at their convenience?

Payroll Plus is a national company with clients in nearly every state. Our size and scope gives us the expertise your company needs, whether it is meeting federal, state and local payroll regulations or providing the level of security you require for your sensitive information.

I am confident that Payroll Plus can improve on the quality and features of your current payroll service. I will call you shortly to discuss your specific payroll needs. I look forward to speaking with you soon.

<e-mail signature, including name, title, company and contact information>

Letter to Inactive Customer
(straightforward version)

Purpose

- To renew communication with an inactive customer

Alternative Purposes

- To attempt to schedule an appointment with an inactive customer
- To offer an incentive to an inactive customer
- To attempt to maintain regular communication with an inactive customer

---

If you are offering an incentive to spark interest:

The good news is that as a current customer of Payroll Plus, Richfield Lumber is entitled to choose one of these add-on services to your current contract at no additional charge—as long as you sign up for another year of our services in advance.

March 12, 2008

Kelly Bagnall
Accounting Manager
Richfield Lumber Co.
6437 Racine Ave.
Portland, OR 97531

Dear Ms. Bagnall:

I wanted to check in with you and see if you are satisfied with the Payroll Plus services your company has been using for the past 6 months. I also want to let you know about some additional features we have added recently.

You are already using our Web-based technology to view and update your payroll information, but did you know that you can now offer your employees the same convenience? We have updated our security features so that our clients can offer each employee unlimited password-protected views of his or her current and past pay stubs online.

In addition, we have enhanced our direct deposit acceptance. If an employee chooses, we can now split his or her monthly pay between two accounts. For example, an employee can choose to have 20 percent of every paycheck to go directly into a savings account and the remainder to a checking account, and that division can be automated by paycheck, month or quarter.

These are features that several of my other clients have added to their Payroll Plus services, and their employees view these additions as a value-added benefit. I am confident that your employees would too.

I will call you soon to see if you are interested in adding either or both of these new features to your Payroll Plus package. I look forward to speaking with you.

Sincerely,

Heidi Schiffle
Western Sales Manager

If you are scheduling an appointment:

I will be in Portland March 23-26 and will call you soon to see if I can schedule an appointment to stop by and discuss Richfield Lumber's current and future payroll needs. I look forward to seeing you again.

If you want to encourage regular contact:

You can sign up for our monthly e-newsletter "PayRoll News" to receive notifications of product upgrades, tax tips and other helpful information. I will call you soon to see if you are interested in signing up for this free e-publication and adding either or both of our new features to your Payroll Plus package.

E-Mail

Dear Ms. Bagnall:

I have not spoken with you for several months and wondered if you are still satisfied with Payroll Plus. I also want to let you know about some additional features we have added recently.

You are already using our Web-based technology to view and update your payroll information, but now you can offer your employees the same convenience. Our clients can offer their employees unlimited password-protected views of their current and past pay stubs online.

In addition, we have enhanced our direct deposit acceptance. If an employee chooses, we can now split his or her monthly pay between two accounts. For example, an employee can choose to have 20 percent of every paycheck to go directly into a savings account and the remainder to a checking account, and that division can be automated by paycheck, month or quarter.

I will call you soon to see if you are interested in adding either or both of these new features to your Payroll Plus package. I look forward to speaking with you.

<e-mail signature, including name, title, company and contact information>

Letter to Inactive Customer

(hard-sell version)

Purpose

- To renew communication with an inactive customer

Alternative Purposes

- To attempt to schedule an appointment with an inactive customer
- To offer an incentive to an inactive customer
- To attempt to maintain regular communication with an inactive customer

---

March 12, 2008

Kelly Bagnall
Accounting Manager
Richfield Lumber Co.
6437 Racine Ave.
Portland, OR 97531

Dear Ms. Bagnall:

You should be among the first to know: Payroll Plus is adding two exciting new features to our services.

I know that your accounting department appreciates the ease of our Web-based technology to view and update payroll information, but did you know that you can now offer your employees the same convenience? We have updated our security features so that our clients can offer each of their employees unlimited password-protected views of their current and past pay stubs online.

In addition, we have enhanced our direct deposit acceptance. If an employee chooses, we can now split his or her monthly pay between two accounts. For example, if an employee wants 20 percent of every paycheck to go directly into his or her savings account and the remainder into his or her checking account, that division can be automated by paycheck, month or quarter.

Our beta testers for these Payroll Plus features, including several Fortune 500 companies, were delighted with the convenience. This is a terrific way to provide more benefits to your employees at a minimal cost.

I will call you next week to discuss adding either or both of these new features to your Payroll Plus package. I look forward to speaking with you soon.

Sincerely,

Heidi Schiffle
Western Sales Manager

If you are offering an incentive to spark interest:

The good news is that as a current customer of Payroll Plus, Richfield Lumber is entitled to choose one of these add-on services to your current contract at no additional charge as long as you sign up for another year of our services in advance.

If you are scheduling an appointment:

I will be in Portland March 23-26 and will call you soon to see if I can schedule an appointment to discuss how much Richfield Lumber's employees would appreciate these added features. I look forward to seeing you again.

If you want to encourage regular contact:

You can sign up for our monthly e-newsletter "PayRoll News" to receive notifications of product upgrades, tax tips and other helpful information. I will call you next week to discuss this free e-publication as well as adding our new features to your Payroll Plus package.

E-Mail

Dear Ms. Bagnall:

You should be among the first to know: The convenience and cost-effective efficiency of Payroll Plus services have recently increased. We have two new features that can provide more benefits to your employees at a negligible cost:

1. We have updated our security features so that our clients can offer each of their employees unlimited password-protected views of their current and past pay stubs online.
2. We have enhanced our direct deposit acceptance. If an employee chooses, we can now split monthly paychecks between two accounts. For example, if an employee wants 20 percent of every paycheck to go directly into his or her savings account and the remainder into his or her checking account, that division can be automated by paycheck, month or quarter.

I will call you next week to discuss adding either or both of these new features to your Payroll Plus package. I look forward to speaking with you soon.

<e-mail signature, including name, title, company and contact information>

Letter Requesting Appointment with Prospective Customer

Purpose

- To attempt to set up a face-to-face sales meeting with a prospective customer

Alternative Purposes

- To schedule a phone interview with a prospective customer
- To invite a prospective customer to lunch or dinner
- To invite a prospective customer to your company

If you want to schedule a phone interview or conversation:

I would like to have 15 or 20 minutes of your time for a phone interview to determine your payroll needs and your level of satisfaction with your current service. I can provide ...

If you want to offer the person a tour or visit to your company:

Our Denver office is just a few miles from your headquarters. I would be delighted if you would come for a tour of our facilities and meet our regional team that handles services for so many of your neighbors.

February 8, 2008

Miriam Suarez, CPA
Director of Finances
White Mountain Trucking Co.
765 W. Jackson St.
Denver, CO 77965

Dear Ms. Suarez:

Many of your corporate neighbors in Denver enjoy payroll services that are convenient, customized and cost-effective compared with the competition. I know this because they are my customers.

Let me introduce myself and my company, Payroll Plus. Our national size and scope gives Payroll Plus the expertise your company needs to meet federal, state and local payroll regulations. We customize our products and services for each client. Whatever your specific payroll needs, including employee withholding, information accessibility or office-by-office customization, Payroll Plus can meet those needs.

We offer state-of-the-art, easy-to-use Web-based technology so you can control, view and update your payroll information as needed. Finally, we guarantee our services 100 percent and accept full liability for any payroll-related penalties that may arise.

I am frequently in Denver to meet with my clients and would like the opportunity to speak with you in person regarding your payroll needs and your level of satisfaction with your current service. I am confident that within 15 or 20 minutes I can provide a cost estimate for a customized service package that will meet or exceed all your payroll needs.

Please expect a phone call from me within the week. I will touch base with you to set up a mutually convenient time for us to meet. I look forward to speaking with you soon.

Sincerely,

Heidi Schiffle
Western Sales Manager

If you want to invite the person to lunch or dinner:

I am frequently in Denver to meet with my clients, and I would be delighted to take you out to lunch to discuss your payroll needs. I am confident that by the end of our conversation, I can provide ...

E-Mail

Dear Ms. Suarez:

Many of your corporate neighbors in Denver enjoy payroll services that are convenient, customized to their needs and cost-effective compared with the competition. I know this because they are my customers.

My company, Payroll Plus, offers many benefits that other payroll services cannot match.

- Our national size and scope provides the expertise your company needs to meet federal, state and local payroll regulations.
- We customize our products and services for each client. Whatever your payroll needs, including employee withholding, information accessibility or state-by-state or office-by-office customization, Payroll Plus can meet those needs.
- We offer state-of-the-art, easy-to-use Web-based technology so that you can access and update your payroll information.
- We guarantee our services 100 percent and will accept liability for any payroll-related penalties that may arise.

I am frequently in Denver to meet with my clients and would welcome a chance to speak with you in person regarding your payroll needs and your level of satisfaction with your current service.

Please let me know when would be a convenient time for us to meet.

<e-mail signature, including name, title, company and contact information>

Follow-Up Letter Requesting Appointment with Prospective Customer

Purpose

- To make a second attempt to set up a face-to-face sales meeting with a prospective customer

Alternative Purposes

- To follow up on attempt to schedule a phone interview with a prospective customer
- To follow up on attempt to invite a prospective customer to lunch or dinner
- To follow up on attempt to invite a prospective customer to your company

February 22, 2008

Miriam Suarez, CPA
Director of Finances
White Mountain Trucking Co.
765 W. Jackson St.
Denver, CO 77965

Dear Ms. Suarez:

White Mountain Trucking can benefit greatly from the customized payroll services my company offers in terms of convenience, value-added services and cost savings. After meeting with you to determine your company's specific payroll needs, I can provide a free estimate of costs and services that should leave no question in your mind that Payroll Plus offers more than your current payroll service for less money.

It is unfortunate that we were unable to meet during my last trip to Denver. My next visit is scheduled for the first week of March. I encourage you to spare just 15 minutes of your time to meet with me in person during that week.

I will be in touch shortly to set up a mutually convenient time to meet. I look forward to speaking with you soon.

Sincerely,

Heidi Schiffle
Western Sales Manager

If you want to schedule a phone interview or conversation:

It is unfortunate that we have been unable to speak by phone. I will try you again this week and encourage you to spare just 15 minutes of your time to speak with me.

If you want to invite the person to lunch or dinner:

It is unfortunate that we were unable to meet during my last trip to Denver. My next visit is scheduled for the first week of March. I would still like to take you out to lunch if convenient; if not, perhaps we can schedule a time to meet in your office for 15 or 20 minutes.

If you want to offer the person a tour or visit to your company:

It is unfortunate that we could not schedule a time for you to visit our headquarters office. I will try to reschedule this week. However, if you cannot spare the time away, perhaps we can meet briefly in your office to discuss your needs.

E-Mail

Dear Ms. Suarez:

White Mountain Trucking can benefit greatly from the customized payroll services my company offers in terms of convenience, value-added services and cost savings. After meeting with you to determine your company's specific payroll needs, I can provide a free estimate of costs and services that should leave no question in your mind that Payroll Plus offers more than your current payroll service for less money.

It is unfortunate that we were unable to meet during my last trip to Denver. My next visit is scheduled for the first week of March. I encourage you to spare just 15 minutes of your time to meet with me in person during that week.

Please let me know when would be a convenient time for you to meet with me.

<e-mail signature, including name, title, company and contact information>

Letter Requesting Appointment with Existing Customer

Purpose

- To attempt to set up a face-to-face sales meeting with a current customer

Alternative Purposes

- To schedule a phone interview with a current customer
- To invite a current customer to lunch or dinner
- To invite a current customer to your company

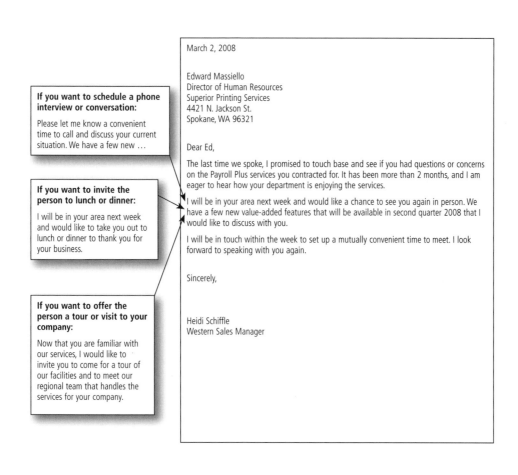

If you want to schedule a phone interview or conversation:

Please let me know a convenient time to call and discuss your current situation. We have a few new …

If you want to invite the person to lunch or dinner:

I will be in your area next week and would like to take you out to lunch or dinner to thank you for your business.

If you want to offer the person a tour or visit to your company:

Now that you are familiar with our services, I would like to invite you to come for a tour of our facilities and to meet our regional team that handles the services for your company.

March 2, 2008

Edward Massiello
Director of Human Resources
Superior Printing Services
4421 N. Jackson St.
Spokane, WA 96321

Dear Ed,

The last time we spoke, I promised to touch base and see if you had questions or concerns on the Payroll Plus services you contracted for. It has been more than 2 months, and I am eager to hear how your department is enjoying the services.

I will be in your area next week and would like a chance to see you again in person. We have a few new value-added features that will be available in second quarter 2008 that I would like to discuss with you.

I will be in touch within the week to set up a mutually convenient time to meet. I look forward to speaking with you again.

Sincerely,

Heidi Schiffle
Western Sales Manager

E-Mail

Dear Ed,

The last time I spoke with you, I promised to touch base and see if you had questions on your Payroll Plus services.

I will be in your area next week and would like a chance to see you again. We have a few new value-added features that will be available in second quarter 2008 that I would like to discuss with you.

I will be in touch shortly to set up a mutually convenient time to meet.

<e-mail signature, including name, title, company and contact information>

Follow-Up Letter Requesting Appointment with Existing Customer

Purpose

- To make a second attempt to set up a face-to-face sales meeting with a current customer

Alternative Purposes

- To follow up on attempt to schedule a phone interview with a current customer
- To follow up on attempt to invite a current customer to lunch or dinner
- To follow up on attempt to invite a current customer to your company

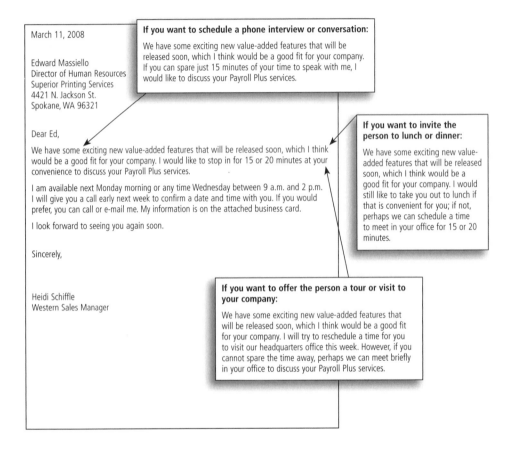

March 11, 2008

Edward Massiello
Director of Human Resources
Superior Printing Services
4421 N. Jackson St.
Spokane, WA 96321

Dear Ed,

We have some exciting new value-added features that will be released soon, which I think would be a good fit for your company. I would like to stop in for 15 or 20 minutes at your convenience to discuss your Payroll Plus services.

I am available next Monday morning or any time Wednesday between 9 a.m. and 2 p.m. I will give you a call early next week to confirm a date and time with you. If you would prefer, you can call or e-mail me. My information is on the attached business card.

I look forward to seeing you again soon.

Sincerely,

Heidi Schiffle
Western Sales Manager

If you want to schedule a phone interview or conversation:
We have some exciting new value-added features that will be released soon, which I think would be a good fit for your company. If you can spare just 15 minutes of your time to speak with me, I would like to discuss your Payroll Plus services.

If you want to invite the person to lunch or dinner:
We have some exciting new value-added features that will be released soon, which I think would be a good fit for your company. I would still like to take you out to lunch if that is convenient for you; if not, perhaps we can schedule a time to meet in your office for 15 or 20 minutes.

If you want to offer the person a tour or visit to your company:
We have some exciting new value-added features that will be released soon, which I think would be a good fit for your company. I will try to reschedule a time for you to visit our headquarters office this week. However, if you cannot spare the time away, perhaps we can meet briefly in your office to discuss your Payroll Plus services.

E-Mail

Dear Ed,

We have some exciting new value-added features that will be released soon, which I think would be a good fit for your company. I would still like to stop in for 15 or 20 minutes at your convenience to discuss your Payroll Plus services.

When would be a convenient time for us to meet? I look forward to seeing you again soon.

<e-mail signature, including name, title, company and contact information>

Letter Thanking Customer/Prospect for Appointment

Purpose

- To follow up a sales meeting with written correspondence that encourages contact

Alternative Purposes

- To follow up on a phone interview or consultation
- To follow up on lunch or dinner with a customer or prospect
- To follow up on a refusal to meet or speak

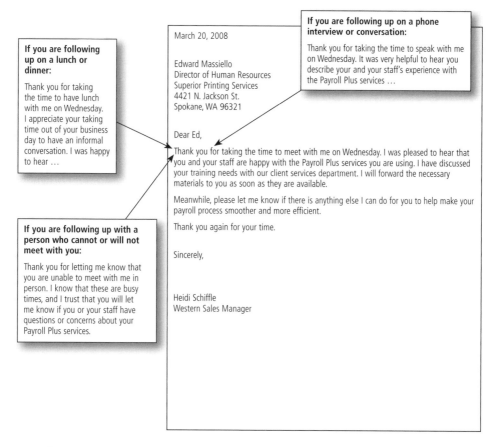

If you are following up on a lunch or dinner:

Thank you for taking the time to have lunch with me on Wednesday. I appreciate your taking time out of your business day to have an informal conversation. I was happy to hear …

If you are following up on a phone interview or conversation:

Thank you for taking the time to speak with me on Wednesday. It was very helpful to hear you describe your and your staff's experience with the Payroll Plus services …

If you are following up with a person who cannot or will not meet with you:

Thank you for letting me know that you are unable to meet with me in person. I know that these are busy times, and I trust that you will let me know if you or your staff have questions or concerns about your Payroll Plus services.

March 20, 2008

Edward Massiello
Director of Human Resources
Superior Printing Services
4421 N. Jackson St.
Spokane, WA 96321

Dear Ed,

Thank you for taking the time to meet with me on Wednesday. I was pleased to hear that you and your staff are happy with the Payroll Plus services you are using. I have discussed your training needs with our client services department. I will forward the necessary materials to you as soon as they are available.

Meanwhile, please let me know if there is anything else I can do for you to help make your payroll process smoother and more efficient.

Thank you again for your time.

Sincerely,

Heidi Schiffle
Western Sales Manager

E-Mail

Dear Ed,

Thank you for taking the time to meet with me on Wednesday. I was pleased to hear that you and your staff are happy with your Payroll Plus services.

I have discussed your training needs with our client services department. I will forward the necessary materials to you as soon as they are available.

Meanwhile, please let me know if there is anything else I can do for you to help make your payroll process smoother and more efficient.

Thanks again,

<e-mail signature, including name, title, company and contact information>

Letter Confirming Order

Purpose

- To confirm formally an order that has been placed and to verify the details

Alternative Purposes

- To correct information on a new order
- To question information on a new order
- To request additional information on a new order

If you are correcting information on the order:

Please note that though your order specified delivery of 10 cases of Mint Melody tea, this product was replaced this month and is now called FreshMint Tea. It is essentially the same tea, but the flavor has been improved and the packaging redesigned.

January 9, 2008

Amy T. Stull
Purchasing Agent
Foodstuff Inc.
33342 Commercial Drive, #203
Kansas City, MO 67787

Dear Ms. Stull:

Thank you for your order of 30 cases of Special Teas. As we discussed, you will receive 10 cases of green tea, 10 of chamomile tea and 10 of mint tea, for a total cost of $549.78.

Your customer account has been set up, so after this initial order, you will no longer have to pay in advance.

Please let me know if you have any questions regarding your order. I will contact you next week to make sure you received the product.

Thank you for your business. I look forward to speaking with you soon.

Sincerely,

Colleen Robinson
Sales Specialist

If you are questioning information on the order:

In your order, you specified that you need delivery on January 24. I am not sure if this date is firm or if you meant it as a no-later-than delivery date. If you would like to receive the shipment earlier than specified, please let me know.

If you are requesting additional information on the order:

Though you mentioned that your warehouse will need 2 hours' advance notice of the shipment, I do not have a contact name and number for the dock. Please forward that information to me via e-mail at your earliest convenience.

E-Mail

Dear Ms. Stull:

Thank you for your order. As we discussed, you will receive 10 cases of green tea, 10 of chamomile tea and 10 of mint tea, for a total cost of $549.78.

Your customer account has been set up, so after this initial order, you will no longer have to pay in advance.

Thank you for your business. I look forward to speaking with you soon.

<e-mail signature, including name, title, company and contact information>

Letter Accompanying Order Form or Contract

Purpose

- To encourage a customer to place an order

Alternative Purposes

- To encourage a customer to sign a contract
- To offer a completed order form for the customer to submit
- To customize an order form for a customer

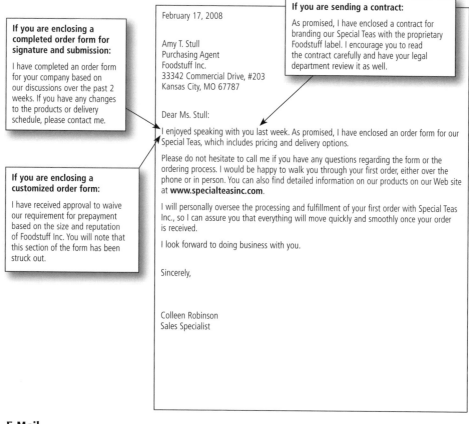

If you are enclosing a completed order form for signature and submission:

I have completed an order form for your company based on our discussions over the past 2 weeks. If you have any changes to the products or delivery schedule, please contact me.

If you are enclosing a customized order form:

I have received approval to waive our requirement for prepayment based on the size and reputation of Foodstuff Inc. You will note that this section of the form has been struck out.

If you are sending a contract:

As promised, I have enclosed a contract for branding our Special Teas with the proprietary Foodstuff label. I encourage you to read the contract carefully and have your legal department review it as well.

February 17, 2008

Amy T. Stull
Purchasing Agent
Foodstuff Inc.
33342 Commercial Drive, #203
Kansas City, MO 67787

Dear Ms. Stull:

I enjoyed speaking with you last week. As promised, I have enclosed an order form for our Special Teas, which includes pricing and delivery options.

Please do not hesitate to call me if you have any questions regarding the form or the ordering process. I would be happy to walk you through your first order, either over the phone or in person. You can also find detailed information on our products on our Web site at **www.specialteasinc.com**.

I will personally oversee the processing and fulfillment of your first order with Special Teas Inc., so I can assure you that everything will move quickly and smoothly once your order is received.

I look forward to doing business with you.

Sincerely,

Colleen Robinson
Sales Specialist

E-Mail

Dear Ms. Stull:

Thank you for speaking with me last week. As promised, I have attached a PDF of our order form.

Please do not hesitate to call me if you have any questions regarding the form or the ordering process. I would be happy to walk you through your first order, either over the phone or in person. You can also find detailed information on our products on our Web site at **www.specialteasinc.com**.

I will personally oversee the processing and fulfillment of your first order with Special Teas Inc., so I can assure you that everything will move quickly and smoothly once your order is received.

I look forward to doing business with you.

<e-mail signature, including name, title, company and contact information>

Letter Noting Change in Customer Order

Purpose

- To personally inform a customer of a change in an outstanding order

Alternative Purposes

- To inform a customer of a back-ordered item on his or her order
- To inform a customer of a change in pricing
- To inform a customer of a cancellation of his or her order

February 17, 2008

Amy T. Stull
Purchasing Agent
Foodstuff Inc.
33342 Commercial Drive, #203
Kansas City, MO 67787

Dear Ms. Stull:

I want to let you know that due to extremely rough weather in Asia, your February 13 order of 30 cases of Special Teas (order #44327-02) cannot be fulfilled as requested.

Unexpected storms on the coast of China have delayed the departure of the freighter carrying the latest batches of teas. We expect the teas to arrive at U.S. customs by the end of February and should be able to deliver your complete order by March 8 at the latest.

Unless I hear otherwise from you, I will assume that you wish the February 13 order to be fulfilled as you directed, with the earliest possible delivery.

I apologize for any inconvenience caused by this delay, and assure you that we at Special Teas Inc. will do everything within our power to expedite delivery of your shipment.

Sincerely,

Colleen Robinson
Sales Specialist

If an item is placed on back order:

Unexpected storms in China have destroyed the herbs needed to create our chamomile tea. We will be unable to fulfill any orders for chamomile until April. The remainder of your order will be delivered on time.

If the pricing on the order has changed:

Unexpected storms in China have destroyed the herbs needed to create our chamomile tea, creating a severe shortage of this particular product. Because of this shortage, we can no longer offer chamomile tea at the price listed on our order form previous to February 15. We can substitute another herbal tea for the chamomile you requested, or you can submit a new order. (I have enclosed a revised order form.)

If the order must be canceled:

Unexpected storms in China have destroyed the herbs needed to create our chamomile tea. Therefore, we will be unable to fulfill any orders for chamomile tea this year. I have canceled your order and am returning your payment.

E-Mail

Dear Ms. Stull:

I wanted to let you know as soon as possible that due to extremely rough weather in Asia, your February 13 order of 30 cases of Special Teas (order #44327-02) cannot be fulfilled as requested.

Unexpected storms have delayed shipment of the latest batches of teas. We expect to be able to deliver your complete order by March 8 at the latest.

Unless I hear otherwise from you, I will assume that you wish the February 13 order to be fulfilled as you directed, with the earliest possible delivery.

I apologize for any inconvenience caused by this delay, and assure you that we at Special Teas Inc. will do everything within our power to expedite delivery of your shipment.

<e-mail signature, including name, title, company and contact information>

Letter Thanking Customer for Completed Order

Purpose

- To personally thank a customer for his or her order and encourage future contact

Alternative Purposes

- To thank a customer for payment received
- To thank a customer for a communication regarding his or her order
- To thank a customer for doing business in general

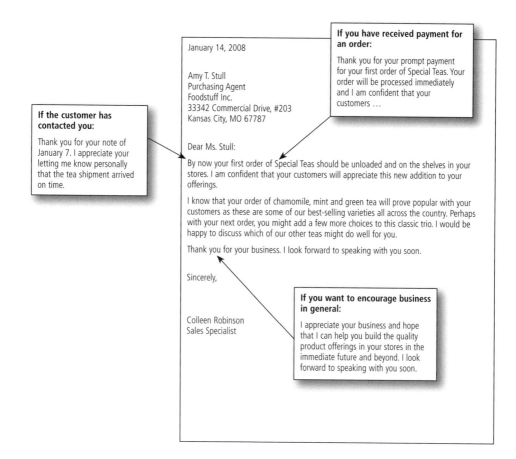

January 14, 2008

Amy T. Stull
Purchasing Agent
Foodstuff Inc.
33342 Commercial Drive, #203
Kansas City, MO 67787

Dear Ms. Stull:

By now your first order of Special Teas should be unloaded and on the shelves in your stores. I am confident that your customers will appreciate this new addition to your offerings.

I know that your order of chamomile, mint and green tea will prove popular with your customers as these are some of our best-selling varieties all across the country. Perhaps with your next order, you might add a few more choices to this classic trio. I would be happy to discuss which of our other teas might do well for you.

Thank you for your business. I look forward to speaking with you soon.

Sincerely,

Colleen Robinson
Sales Specialist

If you have received payment for an order:

Thank you for your prompt payment for your first order of Special Teas. Your order will be processed immediately and I am confident that your customers ...

If the customer has contacted you:

Thank you for your note of January 7. I appreciate your letting me know personally that the tea shipment arrived on time.

If you want to encourage business in general:

I appreciate your business and hope that I can help you build the quality product offerings in your stores in the immediate future and beyond. I look forward to speaking with you soon.

E-Mail

Dear Ms. Stull:

By now your first order of Special Teas should be unloaded and on the shelves in your stores.

I know that the chamomile, mint and green teas will prove popular with your customers as these are some of our best-selling varieties across the country. Perhaps with your next order, you might add a few more choices to this classic trio.

I would be happy to discuss which of our other teas might do well for you.

Thank you for your business.

<e-mail signature, including name, title, company and contact information>

Letter Requesting Renewal of Membership/Subscription

Purpose

- To personally ask a customer to renew a subscription to a publication

Alternative Purposes

- To ask a customer to renew membership in an association
- To ask a customer to renew a service contract or warranty
- To ask a customer to join a frequent buyers program

March 16, 2008

Michael J. Fredericks
Principal
Eagle Ridge Elementary School
443 Prairie Ave.
Eagle Ridge, KY 79245

Dear Mr. Fredericks:

Your school's subscription to Education Times Monthly will expire in May. The good news is that as a current subscriber, you are eligible for the lowest rate available. For just $49.95, you can renew your subscription for 2008-2009.

Please continue this valuable service for the sake of your teachers, your facility and your students. Simply complete the enclosed card and return it to me with payment and your service will continue uninterrupted.

Thank you for your continued business and best wishes for a productive school year.

Sincerely,

Jerry Schlautman
Educational Products Manager

P.S. If you have money in your budget to renew for 2 years, you can lock in the current rate.

If you are asking to renew membership:

Your membership in Elementary School Administrators of America (ESAA) will expire in May. I hope that you will decide to continue to take advantage of our member benefits, including our training seminars and newsletter.

If you are asking to renew a service contract:

Eagle Ridge Elementary School's contract for HVAC repair and maintenance will expire in May. If your budget allows you to renew the contract before it expires, I can guarantee that you will pay only a five percent increase for the new contract. This is a cost savings of $100 over what new customers pay.

If you are asking the person to join a frequent buyers program:

Sign up for the Schoolwide Savings Club and enjoy special savings on office supplies. As a member of the club, you are entitled to special savings and you earn points toward free gifts for your school.

E-Mail

Dear Mr. Fredericks:

Your school's subscription to Education Times Monthly will expire in May. The good news is that as a current subscriber, you are eligible for the lowest rate available. For just $49.95, you can renew your subscription for 2008-2009.

Please continue this valuable service for the sake of your teachers, your facility and your students. Simply complete our online form at **www.etm.com/renewal** and your service will continue uninterrupted.

Thank you for your continued business and best wishes for the remainder of the school year.

<e-mail signature, including name, title, company and contact information>

Annual/Biannual Letter to Customers

Purpose

- To personally maintain contact with each customer on a regular basis

Alternative Purposes

- To request a meeting with the customer
- To encourage feedback from the customer
- To invite the customer to lunch or dinner

If you want to meet with the customer:

I would like to speak with you about what these changes can mean for you and your print materials. I will call you next week to see if you have time for a 15- or 20-minute meeting.

January 17, 2008

Bernice Henson
Director of Marketing
SLT Communications
Dallas, TX 72105

If you would like to request feedback from the customer:

I would like to know how Paulson Graphics can better serve your needs. I will call you next week to discuss any ideas you might have for improving our service.

Dear Bernice,

It is the beginning of a new year, a time when I like to touch base with my most valued customers and check on their plans for printing in the coming months. This year, we are adding some new equipment that will enhance our capabilities, which may impact your plans.

I look forward to doing business with you in 2008 and trust that you will be able to take advantage of the options that our new equipment will provide.

Meanwhile, please do not hesitate to contact me if you have printing needs or questions. I would be happy to help you in any way I can.

Sincerely,

Taylor Mansfield
Sales Representative

If you are inviting the customer to lunch:

In order to show my appreciation for your business, I would like to take you to lunch at La Lumiere sometime this month. I will call you next week to set a date.

E-Mail

Dear Bernice,

It is the beginning of a new year, a time when I like to touch base with my most valued customers and check on their plans for printing in the coming months. This year, we are adding some new equipment that will enhance our capabilities, which may impact your plans.

I look forward to doing business with you in 2008 and trust that you will be able to take advantage of the options that our new equipment will provide.

Please do not hesitate to contact me if you have printing needs or questions. I would be happy to help you in any way I can.

<e-mail signature, including name, title, company and contact information>

Letter Thanking Customer for Business

Purpose

- To personally thank each customer

Alternative Purposes

- To encourage feedback from customers
- To suggest an annual or biannual meeting
- To send a thank you gift

January 17, 2008

Bernice Henson
Director of Marketing
SLT Communications
Dallas, TX 72105

Dear Bernice,

I want to let you know personally how much we at Paulson Graphics appreciate
your continued business.

I feel that our company has developed an excellent working relationship with SLT
Communications, and I hope that we can continue to help you produce print materials that
draw business. We constantly strive to improve the quality of our work, our service and our
pricing for customers like you.

Please do not hesitate to contact me if you having any printing needs or if you have print
production questions on a possible mailing. I would be happy to help you in any way I can.

Sincerely,

Taylor Mansfield
Sales Representative

If you are sending or enclosing a gift:

As a token of our appreciation for your business, I have
enclosed our 2008 wall calendar. I hope you find it useful.

If you would like to request feedback from the customer:

We would like to know
how we can better serve
your needs. I will call you
next week to discuss any
ideas you might have for
improving our service. I
look forward to speaking
with you.

If you want to meet with the customer:

I will contact you next week to see if you have time to
meet with me to discuss your future printing needs. I look
forward to speaking with you.

E-Mail

Dear Bernice,

I want to let you know personally how much we at Paulson Graphics appreciate your continued business. I hope that we can continue to
help you produce print materials that draw business. We constantly strive to improve the quality of our work, our service and our pricing
for customers like you.

Please do not hesitate to contact me if you having any printing needs or if you have print production questions on a possible mailing. I
would be happy to help you in any way I can.

<e-mail signature, including your name, title, company and contact information>

Letter Accompanying Unsolicited Sales Brochure or Catalog

Purpose

- To guide a prospective customer to look at the accompanying marketing materials

Alternative Purposes

- To guide a prospective customer to look at a Web site
- To introduce a new business or location
- To preface a sales telephone call

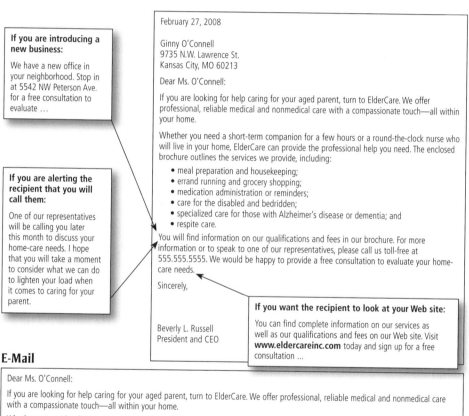

If you are introducing a new business:

We have a new office in your neighborhood. Stop in at 5542 NW Peterson Ave. for a free consultation to evaluate …

If you are alerting the recipient that you will call them:

One of our representatives will be calling you later this month to discuss your home-care needs. I hope that you will take a moment to consider what we can do to lighten your load when it comes to caring for your parent.

February 27, 2008

Ginny O'Connell
9735 N.W. Lawrence St.
Kansas City, MO 60213

Dear Ms. O'Connell:

If you are looking for help caring for your aged parent, turn to ElderCare. We offer professional, reliable medical and nonmedical care with a compassionate touch—all within your home.

Whether you need a short-term companion for a few hours or a round-the-clock nurse who will live in your home, ElderCare can provide the professional help you need. The enclosed brochure outlines the services we provide, including:

- meal preparation and housekeeping;
- errand running and grocery shopping;
- medication administration or reminders;
- care for the disabled and bedridden;
- specialized care for those with Alzheimer's disease or dementia; and
- respite care.

You will find information on our qualifications and fees in our brochure. For more information or to speak to one of our representatives, please call us toll-free at 555.555.5555. We would be happy to provide a free consultation to evaluate your home-care needs.

Sincerely,

Beverly L. Russell
President and CEO

If you want the recipient to look at your Web site:

You can find complete information on our services as well as our qualifications and fees on our Web site. Visit **www.eldercareinc.com** today and sign up for a free consultation …

E-Mail

Dear Ms. O'Connell:

If you are looking for help caring for your aged parent, turn to ElderCare. We offer professional, reliable medical and nonmedical care with a compassionate touch—all within your home.

Whether you need a short-term companion for a few hours or a round-the-clock nurse who will live in your home, ElderCare can provide the professional help you need.

The attached brochure outlines the services we provide, including:

- meal preparation and housekeeping;
- errand running and grocery shopping;
- medication administration or reminders;
- care for the disabled and bedridden;
- specialized care for those with Alzheimer's disease or dementia; and
- respite care.

To speak to one of our representatives, please call us toll-free at 555.555.5555. We would be happy to provide a free consultation to evaluate your home-care needs.

Sincerely,

<e-mail signature, including name, title, company and contact information>

Letter Accompanying Requested Sales Brochure or Catalog

Purpose

- To contact a qualified lead regarding a request for marketing materials

Alternative Purposes

- To encourage an order or sale
- To guide a prospective customer to look at a Web site
- To preface a sales telephone call

February 27, 2008

Ginny O'Connell
9735 N.W. Lawrence St.
Kansas City, MO 60213

Dear Ms. O'Connell:

Enclosed please find the brochure you requested on the in-home care services that ElderCare provides in your area. As you know from our newspaper ad, we offer professional, reliable medical and nonmedical care with a compassionate touch—all within your home.

Whether you need a short-term companion for a few hours or a round-the-clock nurse who will live in your home, ElderCare can provide the professional help you need. The brochure outlines the services we provide, including:

- meal preparation and housekeeping;
- errand running and grocery shopping;
- medication administration or reminders;
- care for the disabled and bedridden;
- specialized care for those with Alzheimer's disease or dementia; and
- respite care.

You will find information on our qualifications and fees in our brochure. For more information, please call us toll-free at 555.555.5555. We would be happy to provide a free consultation to evaluate your home-care needs.

Sincerely,

Beverly L. Russell
President and CEO

If you want to encourage a sale:

To sign up for customized in-home care, you can fill out the enclosed card and mail it in, fill out an online form at **www.eldercareinc.com** or call our toll-free number to speak with a representative. The sooner you contact us, the sooner we can help care for your parent.

If you want the recipient to visit your Web site:

You can find complete information on our services as well as our qualifications and fees on our Web site. Visit **www.eldercareinc.com** today and sign up for a free consultation ...

If you are alerting the recipient that you will call them:

One of our representatives will be calling you later this month to discuss your home-care needs. I hope that you will take a moment to consider what we can do to lighten your load when it comes to caring for your parent.

E-Mail

Dear Ms. O'Connell:

Attached please find a PDF of the brochure you requested on ElderCare's in-home care services. As you know from our newspaper ad, we offer professional, reliable medical and nonmedical care with a compassionate touch—all within your home.

Whether you need a short-term companion for a few hours or a round-the-clock nurse who will live in your home, ElderCare can provide the professional help you need. The brochure outlines the services we provide, including:

- meal preparation and housekeeping;
- errand running and grocery shopping;
- medication administration or reminders;
- care for the disabled and bedridden;
- specialized care for those with Alzheimer's disease or dementia; and
- respite care.

You will find information on our qualifications and fees in our brochure. Please call us toll-free at 555.555.5555 for a free consultation to evaluate your home-care needs.

Sincerely,

<e-mail signature, including name, title, company and contact information>

Letter Accompanying Customer Questionnaire

Purpose

- To ask a customer to provide feedback on an aspect of your business

Alternative Purposes

- To send a customer to your Web site to fill out an online survey
- To request a telephone interview to gather feedback
- To invite a customer to participate in a focus group

March 20, 2008

Ginny O'Connell
9735 N.W. Lawrence St.
Kansas City, MO 60213

Dear Ms. O'Connell:

Though we at ElderCare do our best to provide quality care, prompt service and reasonable pricing to our customers, we often wonder what things we could be doing better. And our best way of learning how to improve is to ask our customers to share their experiences with us.

Please take a moment to fill out the enclosed survey and mail it back to us in the stamped envelope provided. The survey is brief and should take only 3 to 4 minutes of your time.

Your feedback is important to us and will help shape the services we provide to you and to other families. Please take the time to share your thoughts and ideas on ElderCare.

Thank you in advance for helping us continue to improve our services.

Sincerely,

Beverly L. Russell
President and CEO

If you want the recipient to fill out an online survey:

Please take a moment to fill out our online survey at **www.eldercareinc.com/survey**. The survey is brief and should take only 3 to 4 minutes of your time.

If you are alerting the recipient to a telephone survey:

A representative from our marketing team will be calling you one evening next week to conduct a brief telephone survey. It would be very helpful to us if you can take a few minutes to answer our questions.

If you are inviting the recipient to participate in a focus group:

Because you are an important customer of ours, we would like you to take part in a focus group next month. Details on available locations and times can be found on the enclosed flyer.

E-Mail

Dear Ms. O'Connell:

Though we at ElderCare do our best to provide quality care, prompt service and reasonable pricing to our customers, we often wonder what things we could be doing better. And our best way of learning how to improve is to ask our customers to share their experiences with us.

Please take 3 to 4 minutes to fill out the attached survey and send it back to me. Your feedback is important and will help shape the services we provide to you and to other families.

Thank you in advance for helping us continue to improve our services.

Sincerely,

<e-mail signature, including name, title, company and contact information>

Follow-Up Letter on Sales Brochure or Catalog Already Sent

Purpose

- To follow up on a qualified lead regarding a previous request for marketing collateral materials

Alternative Purposes

- To encourage a qualified lead to visit your Web site
- To encourage a qualified lead to take your telephone call
- To request an appointment with a qualified lead

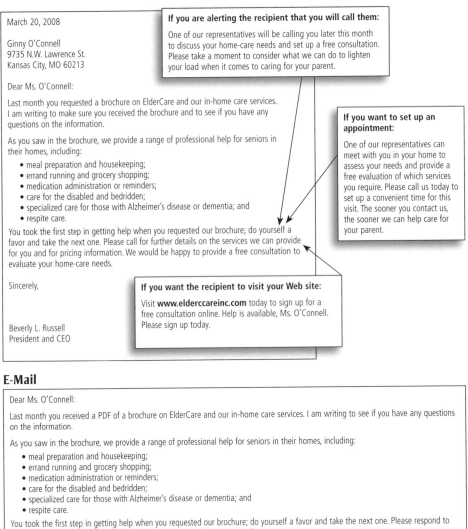

March 20, 2008

Ginny O'Connell
9735 N.W. Lawrence St.
Kansas City, MO 60213

Dear Ms. O'Connell:

Last month you requested a brochure on ElderCare and our in-home care services. I am writing to make sure you received the brochure and to see if you have any questions on the information.

As you saw in the brochure, we provide a range of professional help for seniors in their homes, including:

- meal preparation and housekeeping;
- errand running and grocery shopping;
- medication administration or reminders;
- care for the disabled and bedridden;
- specialized care for those with Alzheimer's disease or dementia; and
- respite care.

You took the first step in getting help when you requested our brochure; do yourself a favor and take the next one. Please call for further details on the services we can provide for you and for pricing information. We would be happy to provide a free consultation to evaluate your home-care needs.

Sincerely,

Beverly L. Russell
President and CEO

If you are alerting the recipient that you will call them:

One of our representatives will be calling you later this month to discuss your home-care needs and set up a free consultation. Please take a moment to consider what we can do to lighten your load when it comes to caring for your parent.

If you want to set up an appointment:

One of our representatives can meet with you in your home to assess your needs and provide a free evaluation of which services you require. Please call us today to set up a convenient time for this visit. The sooner you contact us, the sooner we can help care for your parent.

If you want the recipient to visit your Web site:

Visit **www.elderccareinc.com** today to sign up for a free consultation online. Help is available, Ms. O'Connell. Please sign up today.

E-Mail

Dear Ms. O'Connell:

Last month you received a PDF of a brochure on ElderCare and our in-home care services. I am writing to see if you have any questions on the information.

As you saw in the brochure, we provide a range of professional help for seniors in their homes, including:

- meal preparation and housekeeping;
- errand running and grocery shopping;
- medication administration or reminders;
- care for the disabled and bedridden;
- specialized care for those with Alzheimer's disease or dementia; and
- respite care.

You took the first step in getting help when you requested our brochure; do yourself a favor and take the next one. Please respond to this e-mail to receive a free consultation to evaluate your home-care needs.

Sincerely,

<e-mail signature, including name, title, company and contact information>

Invitation to Company-Sponsored Event

Purpose

- To invite customers to attend a nonwork function that your company is sponsoring or hosting

Alternative Purposes

- To invite customers to pay to attend a fund-raiser
- To invite customers to contribute to a fund-raiser
- To encourage customers to invite others to an event

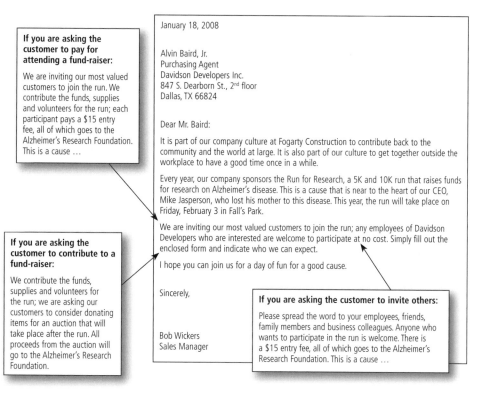

If you are asking the customer to pay for attending a fund-raiser:

We are inviting our most valued customers to join the run. We contribute the funds, supplies and volunteers for the run; each participant pays a $15 entry fee, all of which goes to the Alzheimer's Research Foundation. This is a cause …

If you are asking the customer to contribute to a fund-raiser:

We contribute the funds, supplies and volunteers for the run; we are asking our customers to consider donating items for an auction that will take place after the run. All proceeds from the auction will go to the Alzheimer's Research Foundation.

January 18, 2008

Alvin Baird, Jr.
Purchasing Agent
Davidson Developers Inc.
847 S. Dearborn St., 2nd floor
Dallas, TX 66824

Dear Mr. Baird:

It is part of our company culture at Fogarty Construction to contribute back to the community and the world at large. It is also part of our culture to get together outside the workplace to have a good time once in a while.

Every year, our company sponsors the Run for Research, a 5K and 10K run that raises funds for research on Alzheimer's disease. This is a cause that is near to the heart of our CEO, Mike Jasperson, who lost his mother to this disease. This year, the run will take place on Friday, February 3 in Fall's Park.

We are inviting our most valued customers to join the run; any employees of Davidson Developers who are interested are welcome to participate at no cost. Simply fill out the enclosed form and indicate who we can expect.

I hope you can join us for a day of fun for a good cause.

Sincerely,

Bob Wickers
Sales Manager

If you are asking the customer to invite others:

Please spread the word to your employees, friends, family members and business colleagues. Anyone who wants to participate in the run is welcome. There is a $15 entry fee, all of which goes to the Alzheimer's Research Foundation. This is a cause …

E-Mail

Dear Mr. Baird:

It is part of our company culture at Fogarty Construction to contribute back to the community and the world at large. It is also part of our culture to get together outside the workplace to have a good time once in a while.

Every year, our company sponsors the Run for Research, a 5K and 10K run that raises funds for research on Alzheimer's disease.

This year, the run will take place on Friday, February 3 in Fall's Park.

We are inviting our most valued customers to join the run; any employees of Davidson Developers who are interested are welcome to participate at no cost. Simply fill out the attached PDF and indicate who we can expect.

I hope you can join us for a day of fun for a good cause.

Sincerely,

<e-mail signature, including name, title, company and contact information>

Letter Announcing Special Sale or Incentive

Purpose

- To provide information to customers on a general, limited-time offer

Alternative Purposes

- To provide information to qualified leads on a general, limited-time offer
- To provide information to unqualified leads on a general, limited-time offer
- To provide information to inactive customers on a general, limited-time offer

February 23, 2008

Heidi Tabor
Office Manager
Klein & Saffer Inc.
332 Southport St., Suite 1500
Tampa, FL 69321

Dear Ms. Tabor:

You have experienced the convenience and ease of holding conference calls with an Internet component through Webinar Plus. We would like to thank you for your previous business by offering you a way to save on your Web-based meetings this year.

Now through March 30, we are offering two-for-one sessions. Order a Webinar Plus meeting during this time and you will be entitled to a second meeting any time during 2008. You pay nothing for the second meeting, as long as it does not exceed the number of participants in your first meeting.

Take advantage of this limited-time offer to:

- host visual, Web-based product demonstrations for your customers or prospects;
- hold national training sessions for your staff;
- offer walk-throughs of your annual report to board members or shareholders; or
- save money on travel by conducting sales meetings via Web and telephone.

This special offer is available only through the end of March. Call today to set up your first Web-based meeting or schedule it online at **www.webinarplusmeetings.com**.

Sincerely,

Gregg Wiles
President

If you are presenting an offer to a qualified lead:

From our previous conversations, I know that you have considered adding an Internet component to your company's conference calls. Now you have an opportunity to test this new technology at a substantial discount.

If you are presenting an offer to an unqualified lead:

Your company relies on conference calls to share information, replace face-to-face meetings and save money on travel. Now you can add an Internet component to those calls to provide a visual aspect—at substantial savings.

If you are presenting an offer to an inactive customer:

You have not ordered a Webinar Plus meeting since early last year. To encourage you to use our state-of-the art meeting technology once again, we would like to offer you a special discount.

E-Mail

Dear Ms. Tabor:

You have experienced the convenience and ease of holding conference calls with an Internet component through Webinar Plus. We would like to thank you for your previous business by offering you a way to save on your Web-based meetings this year.

Order a Webinar Plus meeting any time before March 30 and you will receive a second meeting any time during 2008. You pay nothing for the second meeting, as long as it does not exceed the number of participants in your first meeting.

Take advantage of this limited-time offer to:

- host visual, Web-based product demonstrations for your customers or prospects;
- hold national training sessions for your staff;
- offer walk-throughs of your annual report to board members or shareholders; or
- save money on travel by conducting sales meetings via Web and telephone.

Please respond to this e-mail to set up your first Web-based meeting, or visit **www.webinarplusmeetings.com** to schedule it.

<e-mail signature, including name, title, company and contact information>

Letter Announcing New Product or Service

Purpose

- To provide information to customers on a new product or service

Alternative Purposes

- To provide information to qualified leads on a new product or service
- To provide information to unqualified leads on a new product or service
- To provide information to inactive customers on a new product or service

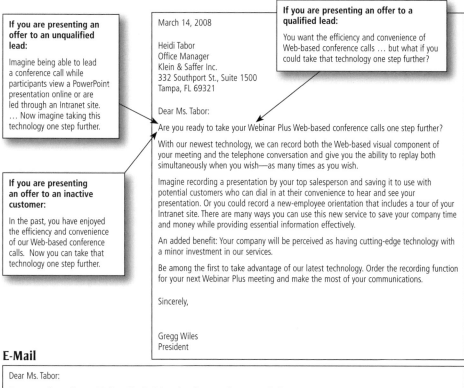

If you are presenting an offer to an unqualified lead:

Imagine being able to lead a conference call while participants view a PowerPoint presentation online or are led through an Intranet site. … Now imagine taking this technology one step further.

If you are presenting an offer to an inactive customer:

In the past, you have enjoyed the efficiency and convenience of our Web-based conference calls. Now you can take that technology one step further.

If you are presenting an offer to a qualified lead:

You want the efficiency and convenience of Web-based conference calls … but what if you could take that technology one step further?

March 14, 2008

Heidi Tabor
Office Manager
Klein & Saffer Inc.
332 Southport St., Suite 1500
Tampa, FL 69321

Dear Ms. Tabor:

Are you ready to take your Webinar Plus Web-based conference calls one step further?

With our newest technology, we can record both the Web-based visual component of your meeting and the telephone conversation and give you the ability to replay both simultaneously when you wish—as many times as you wish.

Imagine recording a presentation by your top salesperson and saving it to use with potential customers who can dial in at their convenience to hear and see your presentation. Or you could record a new-employee orientation that includes a tour of your Intranet site. There are many ways you can use this new service to save your company time and money while providing essential information effectively.

An added benefit: Your company will be perceived as having cutting-edge technology with a minor investment in our services.

Be among the first to take advantage of our latest technology. Order the recording function for your next Webinar Plus meeting and make the most of your communications.

Sincerely,

Gregg Wiles
President

E-Mail

Dear Ms. Tabor:

Are you ready to take your Webinar Plus Web-based conference calls one step further?

With our newest technology, we can record both the Web-based visual component of your meeting and the telephone conversation and give you the ability to replay both simultaneously when you wish—as many times as you wish.

Imagine these scenarios:

- You can record a presentation by your top salesperson and save it to use with potential customers who can dial in at their convenience to hear and see your presentation.
- You can record a new-employee orientation that includes a tour of your Intranet site.
- You can record a training session for employees and roll it out department by department.

There are many ways you can use this new service to save your company time and money while providing essential information effectively.

Be among the first to take advantage of our latest technology. Order the recording function for your next Webinar Plus meeting and make the most of your communications.

Sincerely,

<e-mail signature, including name, title, company and contact information>

Letter Announcing a Change in Pricing

Purpose

- To alert customers to an increase in pricing

Alternative Purposes

- To alert customers to a decrease in pricing
- To alert customers to a change in pricing structure
- To alert customers to a change in pricing policy

January 12, 2008

Heidi Tabor
Office Manager
Klein & Saffer Inc.
332 Southport St., Suite 1500
Tampa, FL 69321

Dear Ms. Tabor:

Changes are taking place at Webinar Plus. We are still offering the same state-of-the-art services for Web-based conference calls and the same prompt service and tech support. However, due to rising costs in the technology we depend on, the fees for all of our conferencing services will increase 10 percent beginning March 1, 2008. The enclosed brochure outlines the new pricing structure.

Even with this increase in pricing, you will find the fees for using Webinar Plus services are reasonable and competitive. Also, our value-added customer service ensures you get more for your money when you use Webinar Plus.

Please do not hesitate to contact your customer service representative if you have any questions on the change in pricing.

Sincerely,

Gregg Wiles
President

If you are introducing a decrease in pricing:

Better still, we are lowering the fees for these services due to advances in technology and less expensive bandwidth. You can now enjoy top-of-the-line conferencing at fees as low as $100 per meeting. The enclosed brochure outlines the new prices for each of our services.

If you are introducing a change in pricing structure:

However, due to changes in our scheduling, we will require all clients to purchase a minimum of three meetings. We can no longer support purchases of single meetings. Beginning March 1, if you want to schedule a Webinar Plus conference call, you must commit to at least three meetings, which you can schedule any time during 2008.

If you are introducing a change in pricing policy:

However, due to changes in our accounting procedures, we will require our clients to provide a credit card or bank account information so that meetings can be individually prepaid. The attached form includes specific payment information. Please complete it and return it to our accounting department.

E-Mail

Dear Ms. Tabor:

Changes are taking place at Webinar Plus. We are still offering the same state-of-the-art services for Web-based conference calls and the same prompt service and tech support. However, due to rising costs in the technology we depend on, the fees for all of our conferencing services will increase 10 percent beginning March 1, 2008. The attached PDF outlines our new pricing structure.

Even with this increase in pricing, you will find the fees for using Webinar Plus services are reasonable and competitive. Also, our value-added customer service ensures you get more for your money when you use Webinar Plus.

Please do not hesitate to contact your customer service representative if you have any questions on the change in pricing.

Sincerely,

<e-mail signature, including name, title, company and contact information>

Letter with Special Offer for Recipient

Purpose

- To offer a specific customer specific savings

Alternative Purposes

- To offer a specific customer a specific opportunity
- To offer a specific customer a specific contract
- To offer a specific customer specific special treatment

If you are offering a specific contract:

Because of the volume of conference calls you use, I am offering you an unusual option: The enclosed contract offers unlimited conference calls for a set annual fee. As one of our best customers, you should be able to save hundreds if not thousands of dollars by signing this contract. In return, we will enjoy your continued business.

If you are offering special treatment:

Because of the volume of conference calls you use, Klein & Saffer deserves special consideration. That is why I have assigned Robert Torrez to act as your customer service contact. Robert will handle all your scheduling, tech support and questions. I hope that you will take full advantage of his expertise and organizational skills.

If you are offering a specific opportunity:

Because of the volume of conference calls you use, I am offering you a unique opportunity: We would like to make Klein & Saffer a beta test site for our new technology. If you agree, you will have a chance to try the latest developments at no additional charge, with no obligation to buy.

March 8, 2008

Heidi Tabor
Office Manager
Klein & Saffer Inc.
332 Southport St., Suite 1500
Tampa, FL 69321

Dear Ms. Tabor:

Klein & Saffer is a valued customer of ours and we would like to show our appreciation for your business.

Because of the volume of conference calls you use, we are pleased to offer you a one-of-a-kind opportunity: Your company can enjoy an unlimited number of Webinar Plus conference calls in 2008 for just $5,000. You will be able to schedule as many Webinar Plus calls as you like, when you like, all for that one-time charge.

This is a terrific opportunity for a company like Klein & Saffer, which held more than 200 Webinar Plus conference calls last year. To take advantage of this offer, simply mention this letter to Janice Thrice, your customer service representative, when you are ready to begin scheduling your next call.

I look forward to your continued business in 2008.

Sincerely,

Gregg Wiles
President

E-Mail

Dear Ms. Tabor:

Klein & Saffer is a valued customer of ours. We would like to show our appreciation for your business with a one-of-a-kind deal: Your company can enjoy an unlimited number of Webinar Plus conference calls in 2008 for just $5,000. You will be able to schedule as many Webinar Plus calls as you like, when you like, all for that one-time charge.

This is a terrific opportunity for a company like Klein & Saffer, which held more than 200 Webinar Plus conference calls last year.

To take advantage of this offer, simply mention this e-mail to your customer service representative.

We look forward to your continued business in 2008.

Sincerely,

<e-mail signature, including name, title, company and contact information>

Letter Announcing Trade Show Participation

Purpose

- To notify customers that your company will be exhibiting at an industry trade show

Alternative Purposes

- To notify prospects that your company will be exhibiting at an industry trade show
- To notify customers that you will be attending an industry trade show
- To notify customers that your company will be presenting an industry conference

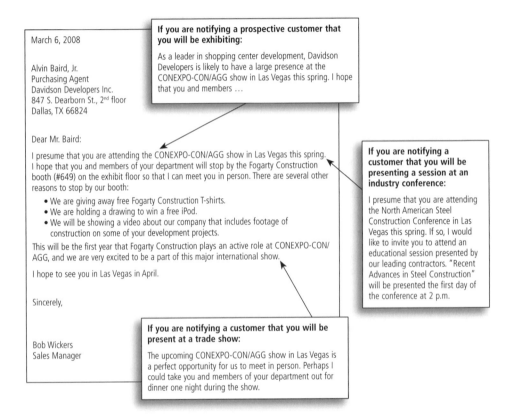

March 6, 2008

Alvin Baird, Jr.
Purchasing Agent
Davidson Developers Inc.
847 S. Dearborn St., 2nd floor
Dallas, TX 66824

Dear Mr. Baird:

I presume that you are attending the CONEXPO-CON/AGG show in Las Vegas this spring. I hope that you and members of your department will stop by the Fogarty Construction booth (#649) on the exhibit floor so that I can meet you in person. There are several other reasons to stop by our booth:

- We are giving away free Fogarty Construction T-shirts.
- We are holding a drawing to win a free iPod.
- We will be showing a video about our company that includes footage of construction on some of your development projects.

This will be the first year that Fogarty Construction plays an active role at CONEXPO-CON/AGG, and we are very excited to be a part of this major international show.

I hope to see you in Las Vegas in April.

Sincerely,

Bob Wickers
Sales Manager

If you are notifying a prospective customer that you will be exhibiting:

As a leader in shopping center development, Davidson Developers is likely to have a large presence at the CONEXPO-CON/AGG show in Las Vegas this spring. I hope that you and members …

If you are notifying a customer that you will be presenting a session at an industry conference:

I presume that you are attending the North American Steel Construction Conference in Las Vegas this spring. If so, I would like to invite you to attend an educational session presented by our leading contractors. "Recent Advances in Steel Construction" will be presented the first day of the conference at 2 p.m.

If you are notifying a customer that you will be present at a trade show:

The upcoming CONEXPO-CON/AGG show in Las Vegas is a perfect opportunity for us to meet in person. Perhaps I could take you and members of your department out for dinner one night during the show.

E-Mail

Dear Mr. Baird:

I presume that you are attending the CONEXPO-CON/AGG show in Las Vegas this spring. I hope that you and members of your department will stop by the Fogarty Construction booth (#649) on the exhibit floor so that I can meet you in person.

There are several other reasons to stop by our booth:

- We are giving away free Fogarty Construction T-shirts.
- We are holding a drawing to win a free iPod.
- We will be showing a video about our company that includes footage of construction on some of your development projects.

I hope to see you in Las Vegas in April.

Sincerely,

<e-mail signature, including name, title, company and contact information>

Letter Announcing Media Attention for Company/Products

Purpose

- To alert customers to recent media coverage of your company

Alternative Purposes

- To alert customers to recent media coverage of a product or service
- To alert customers to recent media coverage of an officer or management
- To alert customers to an award that your company has won

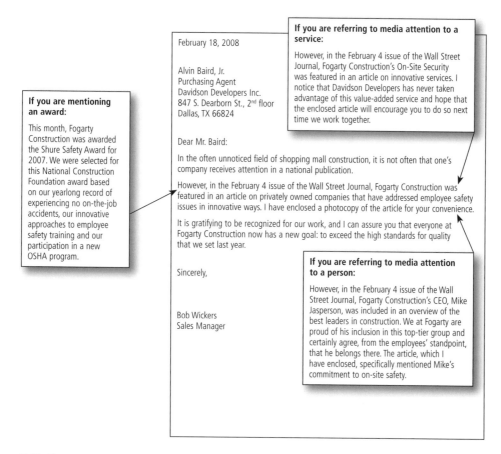

If you are referring to media attention to a service:

However, in the February 4 issue of the Wall Street Journal, Fogarty Construction's On-Site Security was featured in an article on innovative services. I notice that Davidson Developers has never taken advantage of this value-added service and hope that the enclosed article will encourage you to do so next time we work together.

If you are mentioning an award:

This month, Fogarty Construction was awarded the Shure Safety Award for 2007. We were selected for this National Construction Foundation award based on our yearlong record of experiencing no on-the-job accidents, our innovative approaches to employee safety training and our participation in a new OSHA program.

February 18, 2008

Alvin Baird, Jr.
Purchasing Agent
Davidson Developers Inc.
847 S. Dearborn St., 2nd floor
Dallas, TX 66824

Dear Mr. Baird:

In the often unnoticed field of shopping mall construction, it is not often that one's company receives attention in a national publication.

However, in the February 4 issue of the Wall Street Journal, Fogarty Construction was featured in an article on privately owned companies that have addressed employee safety issues in innovative ways. I have enclosed a photocopy of the article for your convenience.

It is gratifying to be recognized for our work, and I can assure you that everyone at Fogarty Construction now has a new goal: to exceed the high standards for quality that we set last year.

Sincerely,

Bob Wickers
Sales Manager

If you are referring to media attention to a person:

However, in the February 4 issue of the Wall Street Journal, Fogarty Construction's CEO, Mike Jasperson, was included in an overview of the best leaders in construction. We at Fogarty are proud of his inclusion in this top-tier group and certainly agree, from the employees' standpoint, that he belongs there. The article, which I have enclosed, specifically mentioned Mike's commitment to on-site safety.

E-Mail

Dear Mr. Baird:

In the often unnoticed field of shopping mall construction, it is not often that one's company receives attention in a national publication.

However, in the February 4 issue of the Wall Street Journal, Fogarty Construction was featured in an article on privately owned companies that have addressed employee safety issues in innovative ways. I have attached a PDF of the article for your convenience.

It is gratifying to be recognized for our work, and I can assure you that everyone at Fogarty Construction now has a new goal: to exceed the high standards for quality that we set last year.

Sincerely,

<e-mail signature, including name, title, company and contact information>

Letter Requesting Updated Demographic Information

Purpose

- To ask a customer to provide confirmation or corrections to contact information and other important demographic information

Alternative Purposes

- To ask for clarification on the customer's identity or individuality
- To alert a customer to a telephone call to check his or her contact information
- To ask a customer to confirm that he or she wants to continue receiving information

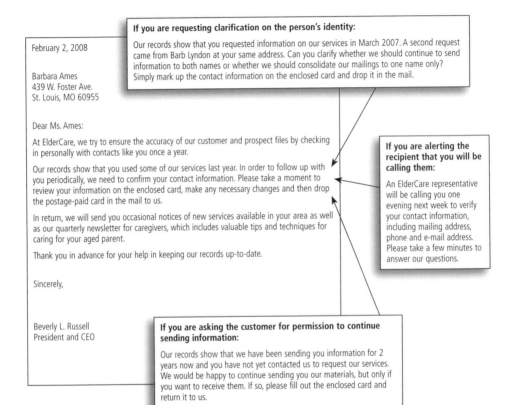

February 2, 2008

Barbara Ames
439 W. Foster Ave.
St. Louis, MO 60955

Dear Ms. Ames:

At ElderCare, we try to ensure the accuracy of our customer and prospect files by checking in personally with contacts like you once a year.

Our records show that you used some of our services last year. In order to follow up with you periodically, we need to confirm your contact information. Please take a moment to review your information on the enclosed card, make any necessary changes and then drop the postage-paid card in the mail to us.

In return, we will send you occasional notices of new services available in your area as well as our quarterly newsletter for caregivers, which includes valuable tips and techniques for caring for your aged parent.

Thank you in advance for your help in keeping our records up-to-date.

Sincerely,

Beverly L. Russell
President and CEO

If you are requesting clarification on the person's identity:

Our records show that you requested information on our services in March 2007. A second request came from Barb Lyndon at your same address. Can you clarify whether we should continue to send information to both names or whether we should consolidate our mailings to one name only? Simply mark up the contact information on the enclosed card and drop it in the mail.

If you are alerting the recipient that you will be calling them:

An ElderCare representative will be calling you one evening next week to verify your contact information, including mailing address, phone and e-mail address. Please take a few minutes to answer our questions.

If you are asking the customer for permission to continue sending information:

Our records show that we have been sending you information for 2 years now and you have not yet contacted us to request our services. We would be happy to continue sending you our materials, but only if you want to receive them. If so, please fill out the enclosed card and return it to us.

E-Mail

Dear Ms. Ames:

At ElderCare, we try to ensure the accuracy of our customer and prospect files by checking in personally with contacts like you once a year.

Our records show that you used some of our services last year. In order to follow up with you periodically, we need to confirm your contact information. Please take a moment to review your information below and respond to me with any changes.

In return, we will send you occasional notices of new services available in your area, as well as our quarterly newsletter for caregivers, which includes valuable tips and techniques for caring for your aged parent.

Thank you in advance for your help in keeping our records up-to-date.

Sincerely,

<e-mail signature, including name, title, company and contact information>

General Direct Mail Letter (Version 1)

Purpose

- To sell a product or service to consumers via a letter or mail package

Alternative Purposes

- To initiate contact with a prospective customer via a letter
- To drive a prospective customer to your Web site
- To drive a prospective customer to your store or office

If you want to drive the recipient to your Web site:

Now you can purchase Special Teas online. Simply visit **www.specialteasinc.com** to browse our selection and place your order. It is convenient, enrollment is easy and you will receive a shipment of fresh tea within days. So visit our Web site today.

March 19, 2008

Jennifer Shepard
342N 982E Windsor Rd.
Mt. Prospect, IL 62118

Dear Ms. Shepard:

If you are initiating contact:

Please take a moment to look over the enclosed catalog of Special Teas. I think you will find that the selection and quality of our teas cannot be found at any store in your town.

The good news is that now you can stock your tea selection …

A good cup of tea can calm you down after a hard day or perk you up with a much-needed energy boost. But sadly, most American grocery stores do not carry top-quality teas that make preparing and enjoying this drink such a pleasure. These mass-processed teas only hint at the full flavor and effects of a true tea.

Stock your tea selection with fresh, top-quality teas from Special Teas Inc. and enjoy carefully prepared, hand-processed teas fresh from their country of origin. Impress your visitors with the diverse selection and full flavor of your Special Teas. Try new flavors that are not available in grocery stores.

Now, when you sign up for our Teas by Mail program, you can sample some of the best teas from around the world without leaving your home. You will automatically receive a new package of exotic tea in the mail each month. It is convenient, enrollment is simple and you will always have plenty of tea on hand. So sign up today and receive your first packet of tea in April.

Sincerely,

If you want to drive the recipient to your store or office:

Now you can purchase Special Teas in our new Mt. Prospect store. We are located in the heart of downtown, at State Street and Jackson Avenue. Stop in soon and take advantage of the tea tastings we are offering through the end of March.

Conrad Phelps
Tea Specialist

E-Mail

Dear Ms. Shepard:

A good cup of tea can calm you down after a hard day or perk you up with a much-needed energy boost. But sadly, most American grocery stores do not carry top-quality teas that make preparing and enjoying this drink such a pleasure. These mass-processed teas only hint at the full flavor and effects of a true tea.

Stock your tea selection with fresh, top-quality teas from Special Teas Inc. You will:

- enjoy carefully prepared, hand-processed teas fresh from their country of origin;
- impress your visitors with the diverse selection and full flavor of your Special Teas; and
- try new flavors that are not available in grocery stores.

Now, when you sign up for our Teas by Mail program, you can sample some of the best teas from around the world without leaving your home. You will automatically receive a new package of exotic tea in the mail each month. It is convenient, enrollment is simple and you will always have plenty of tea on hand.

So sign up today and receive your first packet of tea in April.

Sincerely,

<e-mail signature, including name, title, company and contact information>

General Direct Mail Letter (Version 2)

Purpose

- To sell a product or service to businesses via a letter or mail package

Alternative Purposes

- To initiate contact with a prospective customer via a letter
- To drive a prospective customer to your Web site
- To drive a prospective customer to your store or office

March 19, 2008

Angela Mueller
Office Manager
Hardesty Construction
63 S. Fulton St., Suite 340
Mt. Prospect, IL 62118

Dear Ms. Mueller:

Most offices the size of Hardesty Construction spend too much on ink cartridges for printers, copiers and fax machines. This can become a major expense, as employees often have little regard for saving ink when they are printing or copying.

But you can save money on this line item by contracting with Business Ink to supply all your ink cartridge needs. We offer the lowest prices available on all brands and models of ink cartridges for businesses of all sizes.

Here are a few of the benefits of buying your ink cartridges from Business Ink:

- Save 20 to 40 percent on your ink cartridges when you sign a year's contract.
- Get the ink cartridges you need when you need them—delivered right to your door.
- Stop searching for hard-to-find cartridges. We stock most brands and models and guarantee that we can find anything we do not carry.

To reap these benefits, simply fill out the enclosed contract form and mail it back in the stamped envelope. One of our sales representatives will call you to confirm your needs and begin the service.

Do not miss out on these substantial savings! Sign up with Business Ink today.

Sincerely,

Terry Chin
Director of Marketing

If you want to drive the recipient to your store or office:

Now you can find the cartridges you need in your own neighborhood. Our store is located in the heart of downtown, at State Street and Jackson Avenue. Stop in and find savings of 20 to 40 percent on all types of ink cartridges.

If you are initiating contact:

Please take a moment to look over the enclosed brochure. I think you will find that the convenience and cost savings of buying cartridges through Business Ink makes us the obvious choice for your purchasing needs.

If you want to drive the recipient to your Web site:

To reap these benefits, visit our Web site at **www.businessinkcartridges.com** and fill out our online application. You will find a list of all the cartridges we offer, our business terms and more.

E-Mail

Dear Ms. Mueller:

Most offices the size of Hardesty Construction spend too much on ink cartridges for printers, copiers and fax machines.

But you can save money on this line item by contracting with Business Ink to supply all your ink cartridges. We offer the lowest prices available on all brands and models of ink cartridges.

Here are a few of the benefits of buying your ink cartridges from Business Ink:

- Save 20 to 40 percent on your ink cartridges when you sign a year's contract.
- Get the ink cartridges you need when you need them—delivered right to your door.
- Stop searching for hard-to-find cartridges. We stock most brands and models and guarantee that we can find anything we do not carry.

To reap these benefits, simply fill out the attached contract form and return it to me. One of our sales representatives will call you to confirm your needs and begin the service.

Do not miss out on these substantial savings! Sign up with Business Ink today.

Sincerely,

<e-mail signature, including name, title, company and contact information>

Letter Thanking Customer for Business

Purpose

- To express appreciation for continued business

Alternative Purposes

- To express appreciation for new business
- To express appreciation for a sizeable order
- To express appreciation for a referral

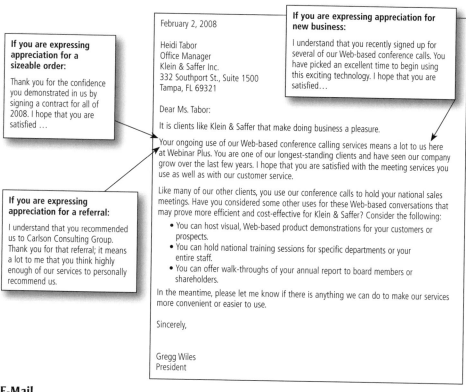

If you are expressing appreciation for a sizeable order:

Thank you for the confidence you demonstrated in us by signing a contract for all of 2008. I hope that you are satisfied ...

If you are expressing appreciation for a referral:

I understand that you recommended us to Carlson Consulting Group. Thank you for that referral; it means a lot to me that you think highly enough of our services to personally recommend us.

If you are expressing appreciation for new business:

I understand that you recently signed up for several of our Web-based conference calls. You have picked an excellent time to begin using this exciting technology. I hope that you are satisfied...

February 2, 2008

Heidi Tabor
Office Manager
Klein & Saffer Inc.
332 Southport St., Suite 1500
Tampa, FL 69321

Dear Ms. Tabor:

It is clients like Klein & Saffer that make doing business a pleasure.

Your ongoing use of our Web-based conference calling services means a lot to us here at Webinar Plus. You are one of our longest-standing clients and have seen our company grow over the last few years. I hope that you are satisfied with the meeting services you use as well as with our customer service.

Like many of our other clients, you use our conference calls to hold your national sales meetings. Have you considered some other uses for these Web-based conversations that may prove more efficient and cost-effective for Klein & Saffer? Consider the following:

- You can host visual, Web-based product demonstrations for your customers or prospects.
- You can hold national training sessions for specific departments or your entire staff.
- You can offer walk-throughs of your annual report to board members or shareholders.

In the meantime, please let me know if there is anything we can do to make our services more convenient or easier to use.

Sincerely,

Gregg Wiles
President

E-Mail

Dear Ms. Tabor:

It is clients like Klein & Saffer that make doing business a pleasure.

Your ongoing use of our Web-based conference calling services means a lot to us here at Webinar Plus. You are one of our longest-standing clients and have seen our company grow over the last few years.

Like many of our other clients, you use our conference calls to hold your national sales meetings. Have you considered some other uses for these Web-based conversations that may prove more efficient and cost-effective for Klein & Saffer? Consider the following:

- You can host visual, Web-based product demonstrations for your customers or prospects.
- You can hold national training sessions for specific departments or your entire staff.
- You can offer walk-throughs of your annual report to board members or shareholders.

In the meantime, please let me know if there is anything we can do to make our services more convenient or easier to use.

Sincerely,

<e-mail signature, including name, title, company and contact information>

Section Seven

.....

Essential Personal
Letters

Letter of Condolence on the Death of an Employee

Purpose

- To convey your personal sympathy to a family member of an employee who has passed away

Alternative Purposes

- To convey sympathy on behalf of the entire company or department
- To convey sympathy to a family member of a former employee who has passed away
- To convey sympathy to a family member of a business colleague who has passed away

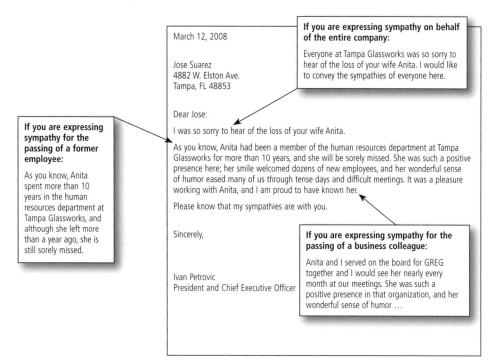

March 12, 2008

Jose Suarez
4882 W. Elston Ave.
Tampa, FL 48853

Dear Jose:

I was so sorry to hear of the loss of your wife Anita.

As you know, Anita had been a member of the human resources department at Tampa Glassworks for more than 10 years, and she will be sorely missed. She was such a positive presence here; her smile welcomed dozens of new employees, and her wonderful sense of humor eased many of us through tense days and difficult meetings. It was a pleasure working with Anita, and I am proud to have known her.

Please know that my sympathies are with you.

Sincerely,

Ivan Petrovic
President and Chief Executive Officer

If you are expressing sympathy on behalf of the entire company:

Everyone at Tampa Glassworks was so sorry to hear of the loss of your wife Anita. I would like to convey the sympathies of everyone here.

If you are expressing sympathy for the passing of a former employee:

As you know, Anita spent more than 10 years in the human resources department at Tampa Glassworks, and although she left more than a year ago, she is still sorely missed.

If you are expressing sympathy for the passing of a business colleague:

Anita and I served on the board for GREG together and I would see her nearly every month at our meetings. She was such a positive presence in that organization, and her wonderful sense of humor …

E-Mail

Dear Jose:

I was so sorry to hear of the loss of your wife Anita.

As you know, Anita had been a member of the human resources department at Tampa Glassworks for more than 10 years, and she will be sorely missed.

She was such a positive presence here; her smile welcomed dozens of new employees, and her wonderful sense of humor eased many of us through tense days and difficult meetings.

It was a pleasure working with Anita, and I am proud to have known her.

Please know that my sympathies are with you.

Sincerely,

<e-mail signature, including name, title, company and contact information>

Letter of Condolence to an Employee Regarding the Death of a Family Member

Purpose

- To convey your personal sympathy to an employee for a death in the family

Alternative Purposes

- To convey sympathy on behalf of the entire company or department
- To convey sympathy to an employee on the death of a child
- To convey sympathy to an employee on the death of a parent

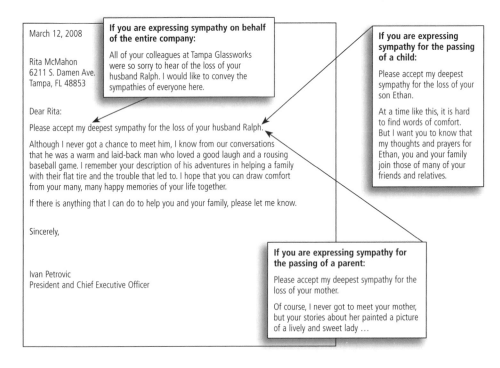

March 12, 2008

Rita McMahon
6211 S. Damen Ave.
Tampa, FL 48853

Dear Rita:

Please accept my deepest sympathy for the loss of your husband Ralph.

Although I never got a chance to meet him, I know from our conversations that he was a warm and laid-back man who loved a good laugh and a rousing baseball game. I remember your description of his adventures in helping a family with their flat tire and the trouble that led to. I hope that you can draw comfort from your many, many happy memories of your life together.

If there is anything that I can do to help you and your family, please let me know.

Sincerely,

Ivan Petrovic
President and Chief Executive Officer

If you are expressing sympathy on behalf of the entire company:

All of your colleagues at Tampa Glassworks were so sorry to hear of the loss of your husband Ralph. I would like to convey the sympathies of everyone here.

If you are expressing sympathy for the passing of a child:

Please accept my deepest sympathy for the loss of your son Ethan.

At a time like this, it is hard to find words of comfort. But I want you to know that my thoughts and prayers for Ethan, you and your family join those of many of your friends and relatives.

If you are expressing sympathy for the passing of a parent:

Please accept my deepest sympathy for the loss of your mother.

Of course, I never got to meet your mother, but your stories about her painted a picture of a lively and sweet lady …

E-Mail

Dear Rita:

Please accept my deepest sympathy for the loss of your husband Ralph.

Although I never got a chance to meet him, I know from our conversations that he was a warm and laid-back man who loved a good laugh and a rousing baseball game. I remember your description of his adventures in helping a family with their flat tire and the trouble that led to.

I hope that you can draw comfort from your many, many happy memories of your life together.

If there is anything that I can do to help you and your family, please let me know.

Sincerely,

<e-mail signature, including name, title, company and contact information>

Letter of Sympathy for an Illness or Misfortune

Purpose

- To convey your personal sympathy to an employee for his or her illness

Alternative Purposes

- To convey sympathy to a colleague for his or her illness
- To convey sympathy to an employee for a misfortune
- To convey sympathy on behalf of the entire company

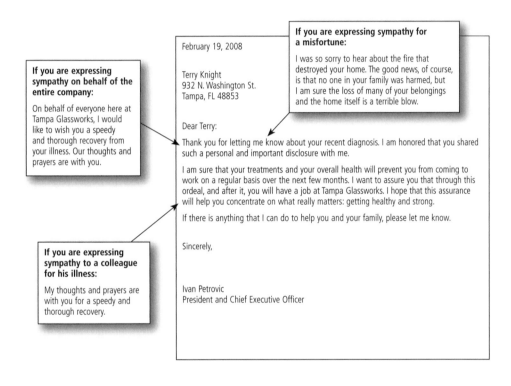

If you are expressing sympathy for a misfortune:

I was so sorry to hear about the fire that destroyed your home. The good news, of course, is that no one in your family was harmed, but I am sure the loss of many of your belongings and the home itself is a terrible blow.

If you are expressing sympathy on behalf of the entire company:

On behalf of everyone here at Tampa Glassworks, I would like to wish you a speedy and thorough recovery from your illness. Our thoughts and prayers are with you.

If you are expressing sympathy to a colleague for his illness:

My thoughts and prayers are with you for a speedy and thorough recovery.

February 19, 2008

Terry Knight
932 N. Washington St.
Tampa, FL 48853

Dear Terry:

Thank you for letting me know about your recent diagnosis. I am honored that you shared such a personal and important disclosure with me.

I am sure that your treatments and your overall health will prevent you from coming to work on a regular basis over the next few months. I want to assure you that through this ordeal, and after it, you will have a job at Tampa Glassworks. I hope that this assurance will help you concentrate on what really matters: getting healthy and strong.

If there is anything that I can do to help you and your family, please let me know.

Sincerely,

Ivan Petrovic
President and Chief Executive Officer

E-Mail

Dear Terry:

Thank you for letting me know about your recent diagnosis. I am honored that you shared such a personal and important disclosure with me.

I understand that your treatments will prevent you from coming to work on a regular basis over the next few months. I want to assure you that through this ordeal, and after it, you will have a job at Tampa Glassworks.

I hope that this assurance will help you concentrate on what really matters: getting healthy and strong.

If there is anything that I can do to help you and your family, please let me know.

Sincerely,

<e-mail signature, including name, title, company and contact information>

Thank You Letter in Response to Condolences or Sympathy

Purpose

- To thank a business colleague for his or her written condolences

Alternative Purposes

- To thank an employee for his or her written condolences
- To thank a business colleague for his or her personal condolences
- To thank an employee for his or her personal condolences

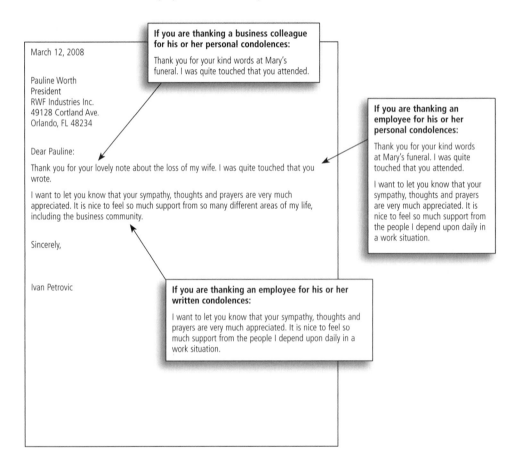

March 12, 2008

Pauline Worth
President
RWF Industries Inc.
49128 Cortland Ave.
Orlando, FL 48234

Dear Pauline:

Thank you for your lovely note about the loss of my wife. I was quite touched that you wrote.

I want to let you know that your sympathy, thoughts and prayers are very much appreciated. It is nice to feel so much support from so many different areas of my life, including the business community.

Sincerely,

Ivan Petrovic

If you are thanking a business colleague for his or her personal condolences:

Thank you for your kind words at Mary's funeral. I was quite touched that you attended.

If you are thanking an employee for his or her personal condolences:

Thank you for your kind words at Mary's funeral. I was quite touched that you attended.

I want to let you know that your sympathy, thoughts and prayers are very much appreciated. It is nice to feel so much support from the people I depend upon daily in a work situation.

If you are thanking an employee for his or her written condolences:

I want to let you know that your sympathy, thoughts and prayers are very much appreciated. It is nice to feel so much support from the people I depend upon daily in a work situation.

E-Mail

Dear Pauline:

Thank you for the lovely note you sent. I was quite touched that you wrote.

I want to let you know that your sympathy, thoughts and prayers are very much appreciated.

It is nice to feel so much support from so many different areas of my life, including the business community.

Sincerely,

<e-mail signature, including name, title, company and contact information>

Letter of Congratulations on the Retirement of an Employee

Purpose

- To personally congratulate an employee on his or her retirement

Alternative Purposes

- To congratulate an employee on his or her early retirement
- To congratulate a business colleague on his or her retirement
- To congratulate an employee on starting a new career

February 19, 2008

Richard Garibaldi
5932 S. Congress Parkway
Tampa, FL 48853

Dear Rich:

I want to personally congratulate you on your retirement from Tampa Glassworks. It was an honor to have worked with you for so many years.

It will be quite an adjustment for all of us not to see your smiling face here nearly every day. You will certainly be missed, not only for your encyclopedic knowledge of our products and processes, but also for your nonstop puns and jokes.

I hope that you will stay in touch; I would like to hear about your new life of leisure!

Sincerely,

Ivan Petrovic
President and Chief Executive Officer

> **If you are congratulating an employee on his or her early retirement:**
>
> I want to personally congratulate you on your early retirement from Tampa Glassworks. It was an honor to have worked with you, and we are sorry to see you leave. However, I am sure you will enjoy your early retirement.

> **If you are congratulating a business colleague on his or her retirement:**
>
> I want to personally congratulate you on your retirement. It was an honor to have worked with you.
>
> The glass industry will not seem the same without you, and we will all miss your encyclopedic knowledge of glass.

> **If you are congratulating an employee on starting a new career:**
>
> I hope that you will stay in touch; I would like to hear how your new restaurant fares. Please let me know if there is anything I can do to help you get started in this new venture.

E-Mail

Dear Rich:

I want to personally congratulate you on your retirement from Tampa Glassworks.

It was an honor to have worked with you for so many years.

It will be quite an adjustment for all of us not to see your smiling face here nearly every day. You will certainly be missed, not only for your encyclopedic knowledge of our products and processes, but also for your nonstop puns and jokes.

I hope that you will stay in touch; I would like to hear about your new life of leisure!

Sincerely,

<e-mail signature, including name, title, company and contact information>

General Letter of Congratulations for a Business Achievement

Purpose

- To congratulate a colleague on a specific business achievement

Alternative Purposes

- To congratulate a colleague on his or her promotion
- To congratulate an employee on a business achievement
- To congratulate an employee on his or her promotion

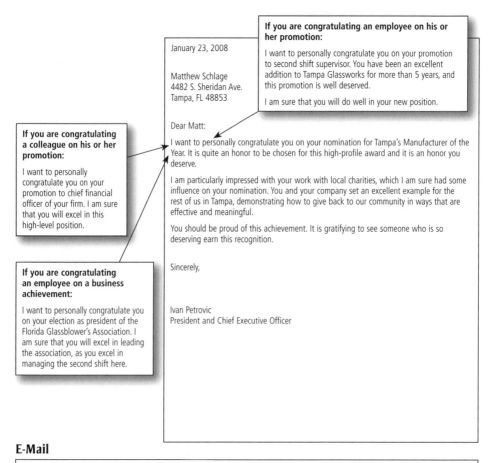

If you are congratulating an employee on his or her promotion:

I want to personally congratulate you on your promotion to second shift supervisor. You have been an excellent addition to Tampa Glassworks for more than 5 years, and this promotion is well deserved.

I am sure that you will do well in your new position.

January 23, 2008

Matthew Schlage
4482 S. Sheridan Ave.
Tampa, FL 48853

Dear Matt:

I want to personally congratulate you on your nomination for Tampa's Manufacturer of the Year. It is quite an honor to be chosen for this high-profile award and it is an honor you deserve.

I am particularly impressed with your work with local charities, which I am sure had some influence on your nomination. You and your company set an excellent example for the rest of us in Tampa, demonstrating how to give back to our community in ways that are effective and meaningful.

You should be proud of this achievement. It is gratifying to see someone who is so deserving earn this recognition.

Sincerely,

Ivan Petrovic
President and Chief Executive Officer

If you are congratulating a colleague on his or her promotion:

I want to personally congratulate you on your promotion to chief financial officer of your firm. I am sure that you will excel in this high-level position.

If you are congratulating an employee on a business achievement:

I want to personally congratulate you on your election as president of the Florida Glassblower's Association. I am sure that you will excel in leading the association, as you excel in managing the second shift here.

E-Mail

Dear Matt:

I want to personally congratulate you on your nomination for Tampa's Manufacturer of the Year.

It is quite an honor to be chosen for this high-profile award and it is an honor you deserve.

I am particularly impressed with your work with local charities, which I am sure had some influence on your nomination. You and your company set an excellent example for the rest of us in Tampa, demonstrating how to give back to our community in ways that are effective and meaningful.

It is gratifying to see someone who is so deserving earn this recognition.

Sincerely,

<e-mail signature, including name, title, company and contact information>

General Letter of Congratulations on a Personal or Social Achievement

Purpose

- To congratulate a colleague on a specific personal achievement

Alternative Purposes

- To congratulate a colleague on a social achievement
- To congratulate an employee on a personal achievement
- To congratulate an employee on a social achievement

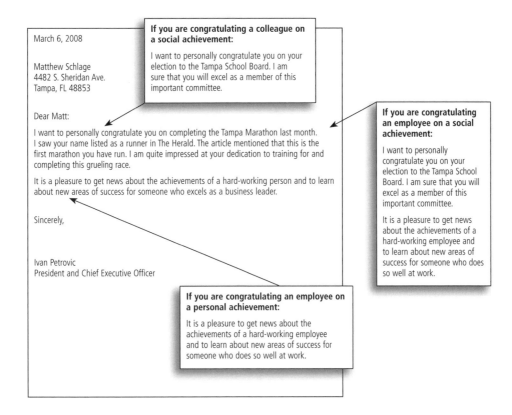

March 6, 2008

Matthew Schlage
4482 S. Sheridan Ave.
Tampa, FL 48853

Dear Matt:

I want to personally congratulate you on completing the Tampa Marathon last month. I saw your name listed as a runner in The Herald. The article mentioned that this is the first marathon you have run. I am quite impressed at your dedication to training for and completing this grueling race.

It is a pleasure to get news about the achievements of a hard-working person and to learn about new areas of success for someone who excels as a business leader.

Sincerely,

Ivan Petrovic
President and Chief Executive Officer

If you are congratulating a colleague on a social achievement:

I want to personally congratulate you on your election to the Tampa School Board. I am sure that you will excel as a member of this important committee.

If you are congratulating an employee on a social achievement:

I want to personally congratulate you on your election to the Tampa School Board. I am sure that you will excel as a member of this important committee.

It is a pleasure to get news about the achievements of a hard-working employee and to learn about new areas of success for someone who does so well at work.

If you are congratulating an employee on a personal achievement:

It is a pleasure to get news about the achievements of a hard-working employee and to learn about new areas of success for someone who does so well at work.

E-Mail

Dear Matt:

I want to personally congratulate you on completing the Tampa Marathon last month.

I saw your name listed as a runner in The Herald. The article mentioned that this is the first marathon you have run.

I am quite impressed at your dedication to training for and completing this grueling race.

It is a pleasure to get news about the achievements of a hard-working person and to learn about new areas of success for someone who excels as a business leader.

Sincerely,

<e-mail signature, including name, title, company and contact information>

Letter Accompanying an Article or Photo

Purpose

- To highlight an article or photo that is of professional interest to a colleague

Alternative Purposes

- To highlight an article that is of personal interest to a colleague
- To highlight an article regarding your colleague's company
- To highlight an article regarding your own company

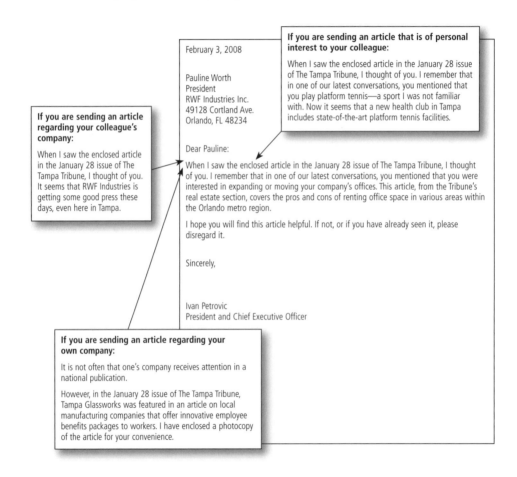

If you are sending an article that is of personal interest to your colleague:

When I saw the enclosed article in the January 28 issue of The Tampa Tribune, I thought of you. I remember that in one of our latest conversations, you mentioned that you play platform tennis—a sport I was not familiar with. Now it seems that a new health club in Tampa includes state-of-the-art platform tennis facilities.

If you are sending an article regarding your colleague's company:

When I saw the enclosed article in the January 28 issue of The Tampa Tribune, I thought of you. It seems that RWF Industries is getting some good press these days, even here in Tampa.

February 3, 2008

Pauline Worth
President
RWF Industries Inc.
49128 Cortland Ave.
Orlando, FL 48234

Dear Pauline:

When I saw the enclosed article in the January 28 issue of The Tampa Tribune, I thought of you. I remember that in one of our latest conversations, you mentioned that you were interested in expanding or moving your company's offices. This article, from the Tribune's real estate section, covers the pros and cons of renting office space in various areas within the Orlando metro region.

I hope you will find this article helpful. If not, or if you have already seen it, please disregard it.

Sincerely,

Ivan Petrovic
President and Chief Executive Officer

If you are sending an article regarding your own company:

It is not often that one's company receives attention in a national publication.

However, in the January 28 issue of The Tampa Tribune, Tampa Glassworks was featured in an article on local manufacturing companies that offer innovative employee benefits packages to workers. I have enclosed a photocopy of the article for your convenience.

E-Mail

Dear Pauline:

When I saw an article in The Tampa Tribune, I thought of you. I remember that in one of our latest conversations, you mentioned that you were interested in expanding or moving your company's offices. This article, available at **www.tampatribune/012808/realestate/orlandoffice.html**, covers the pros and cons of renting office space in various areas within the Orlando metro region.

I hope you will find this article helpful.

Sincerely,

<e-mail signature, including name, title, company and contact information>

Letter of Apology Regarding Business Circumstances

Purpose

- To personally apologize to a business colleague for an event or misunderstanding

Alternative Purposes

- To apologize for missing an appointment
- To apologize for something you said
- To apologize for an error or delay in your work

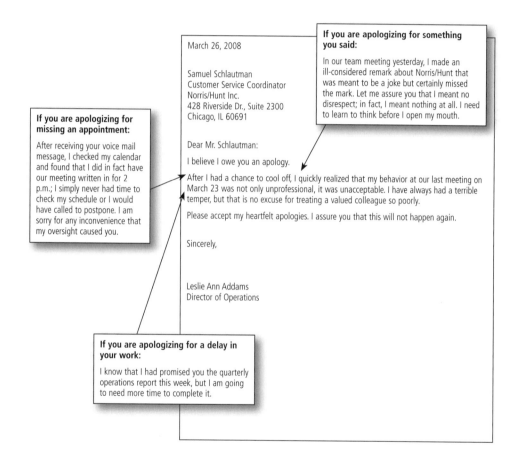

If you are apologizing for something you said:

In our team meeting yesterday, I made an ill-considered remark about Norris/Hunt that was meant to be a joke but certainly missed the mark. Let me assure you that I meant no disrespect; in fact, I meant nothing at all. I need to learn to think before I open my mouth.

March 26, 2008

Samuel Schlautman
Customer Service Coordinator
Norris/Hunt Inc.
428 Riverside Dr., Suite 2300
Chicago, IL 60691

If you are apologizing for missing an appointment:

After receiving your voice mail message, I checked my calendar and found that I did in fact have our meeting written in for 2 p.m.; I simply never had time to check my schedule or I would have called to postpone. I am sorry for any inconvenience that my oversight caused you.

Dear Mr. Schlautman:

I believe I owe you an apology.

After I had a chance to cool off, I quickly realized that my behavior at our last meeting on March 23 was not only unprofessional, it was unacceptable. I have always had a terrible temper, but that is no excuse for treating a valued colleague so poorly.

Please accept my heartfelt apologies. I assure you that this will not happen again.

Sincerely,

Leslie Ann Addams
Director of Operations

If you are apologizing for a delay in your work:

I know that I had promised you the quarterly operations report this week, but I am going to need more time to complete it.

E-Mail

Dear Mr. Schlautman:

I believe I owe you an apology for my behavior at our meeting on March 23.

After I had a chance to cool off, I quickly realized that my comments and attitude were not only unprofessional, they were unacceptable. I have always had a terrible temper, but that is no excuse for treating a valued colleague so poorly.

Please accept my heartfelt apologies. I assure you that this will not happen again.

Sincerely,

<e-mail signature, including name, title, company and contact information>

Letter of Apology Regarding Personal or Social Circumstances

Purpose

- To apologize to a business colleague for an event or misunderstanding unrelated to business

Alternative Purposes

- To apologize for missing a social obligation
- To apologize for something you said
- To apologize for the inability to do a favor

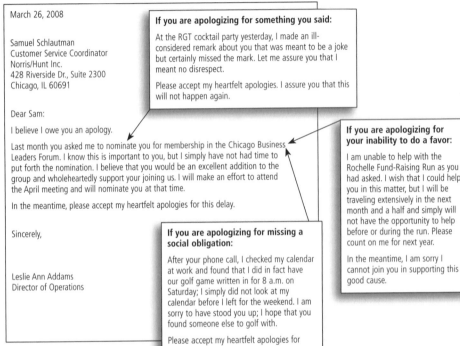

March 26, 2008

Samuel Schlautman
Customer Service Coordinator
Norris/Hunt Inc.
428 Riverside Dr., Suite 2300
Chicago, IL 60691

Dear Sam:

I believe I owe you an apology.

Last month you asked me to nominate you for membership in the Chicago Business Leaders Forum. I know this is important to you, but I simply have not had time to put forth the nomination. I believe that you would be an excellent addition to the group and wholeheartedly support your joining us. I will make an effort to attend the April meeting and will nominate you at that time.

In the meantime, please accept my heartfelt apologies for this delay.

Sincerely,

Leslie Ann Addams
Director of Operations

If you are apologizing for something you said:

At the RGT cocktail party yesterday, I made an ill-considered remark about you that was meant to be a joke but certainly missed the mark. Let me assure you that I meant no disrespect.

Please accept my heartfelt apologies. I assure you that this will not happen again.

If you are apologizing for your inability to do a favor:

I am unable to help with the Rochelle Fund-Raising Run as you had asked. I wish that I could help you in this matter, but I will be traveling extensively in the next month and a half and simply will not have the opportunity to help before or during the run. Please count on me for next year.

In the meantime, I am sorry I cannot join you in supporting this good cause.

If you are apologizing for missing a social obligation:

After your phone call, I checked my calendar at work and found that I did in fact have our golf game written in for 8 a.m. on Saturday; I simply did not look at my calendar before I left for the weekend. I am sorry to have stood you up; I hope that you found someone else to golf with.

Please accept my heartfelt apologies for missing our game.

E-Mail

Dear Sam:

I believe I owe you an apology.

I have not forgotten that you asked me to nominate you for membership in the Chicago Business Leaders Forum.

I know this is important to you, but I simply have not had time to put forth the nomination.

I believe that you would be an excellent addition to the group, and I wholeheartedly support your joining us. I will make an effort to attend the April meeting and will nominate you at that time.

In the meantime, please accept my heartfelt apologies for this delay.

Sincerely,

<e-mail signature, including name, title, company and contact information>

Response to Letter of Apology

Purpose

- To recognize and accept a business colleague's written apology

Alternative Purposes

- To accept an apology for rude behavior or remarks
- To accept an apology for a missed appointment
- To accept an apology for an error or delay in work

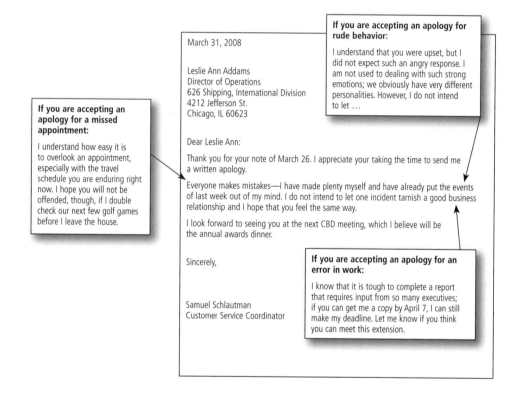

If you are accepting an apology for rude behavior:

I understand that you were upset, but I did not expect such an angry response. I am not used to dealing with such strong emotions; we obviously have very different personalities. However, I do not intend to let ...

March 31, 2008

Leslie Ann Addams
Director of Operations
626 Shipping, International Division
4212 Jefferson St.
Chicago, IL 60623

If you are accepting an apology for a missed appointment:

I understand how easy it is to overlook an appointment, especially with the travel schedule you are enduring right now. I hope you will not be offended, though, if I double check our next few golf games before I leave the house.

Dear Leslie Ann:

Thank you for your note of March 26. I appreciate your taking the time to send me a written apology.

Everyone makes mistakes—I have made plenty myself and have already put the events of last week out of my mind. I do not intend to let one incident tarnish a good business relationship and I hope that you feel the same way.

I look forward to seeing you at the next CBD meeting, which I believe will be the annual awards dinner.

Sincerely,

Samuel Schlautman
Customer Service Coordinator

If you are accepting an apology for an error in work:

I know that it is tough to complete a report that requires input from so many executives; if you can get me a copy by April 7, I can still make my deadline. Let me know if you think you can meet this extension.

E-Mail

Dear Leslie Ann:

Thank you for your note. I appreciate your taking the time to send me a written apology.

Everyone makes mistakes—I have made plenty myself and have already put the events of last week out of my mind. I do not intend to let one incident tarnish a good business relationship and I hope that you feel the same way.

I look forward to seeing you at the next CBD meeting, which I believe will be the annual awards dinner.

Sincerely,

<e-mail signature, including name, title, company and contact information>

Request to a Colleague for Information

Purpose

- To personally ask a business colleague for a specific piece of information

Alternative Purposes

- To ask a colleague to forward written information
- To ask a colleague for a source of information
- To ask a colleague for confidential information

March 1, 2007

Jason Sykes
Chief Financial Officer
Yellowtab Development Company Inc.
8871 W. Jarvis St.
Grand Rapids, MI 48832

Dear Jason:

When we met to discuss the South Street strip mall project last month, something you brought up during lunch stuck in my mind.

You mentioned that you had found a new corporate lawyer. You seemed very pleased with this lawyer's expertise in dealing with construction issues. I would love to find a different lawyer, as our current attorney is very hard to reach. Can you forward me the name and contact information for this new attorney you mentioned, along with any other information I might use?

I would like to thank you in advance for your help with this. Let me know if I can ever return the favor.

Sincerely,

Diane M. Baez
President and Founder

If you are asking a colleague to forward some written information:

You mentioned that you had an interesting article on the future of strip malls. I would be very interested to see that, especially before RTG Construction's board meeting later this month. Can you have a copy of that faxed or mailed to me? My fax number is 555.555.5555.

If you are asking a colleague for confidential information:

You mentioned that you are on the board of directors for the Michigan Builders Association (MBA). It occurred to me that you are privy to the winners of the MBA Awards, which are to be announced next month. Would you consider letting me know if my company has won as soon as you find out the final decisions? I am planning several out-of-town meetings in April and want to schedule around the awards ceremony if RTG Construction is among the winners.

If you are asking a colleague for a source of information:

You mentioned that you had learned about a new material for paving parking lots that is currently being tested in the South. I have been looking for information on this material and cannot find mention of it. Can you let me know where you learned about this?

E-Mail

Dear Jason:

When we broke for lunch during our meeting about the South Street strip mall project last month, you mentioned that you had found a new corporate lawyer.

You seemed very pleased with this lawyer's expertise in dealing with construction issues. I would love to find a different lawyer, as our current attorney is very hard to reach. Can you forward me the name and contact information for this new attorney you mentioned, along with any other information I might use?

I would like to thank you in advance for your help with this. Let me know if I can ever return the favor.

Sincerely,

<e-mail signature, including name, title, company and contact information>

Request to a Colleague for a Personal Favor

Purpose

- To personally ask a business colleague for a favor

Alternative Purposes

- To ask a colleague to nominate or recommend you for an award
- To ask a colleague to share financial information
- To ask a colleague to recommend you to a potential employer

---

If you are asking a colleague to nominate you for an award:

Therefore, I am writing to ask you for a favor. The Michigan Builders Association awards are coming up again, and a nomination for RTG Construction would be a feather in our cap. I am not even thinking about winning an award; being listed as a nominee is attention enough.

Would you consider putting in a nomination for us? I would be happy to provide any information you need for the application. I ask this because we could use a higher level of exposure right now, and a nomination from you would go a long way toward getting us noticed.

If you are asking a colleague to share financial information:

Therefore, I am writing to ask you for a favor. I know that you have used the consulting services of Theo French in the past. We are considering hiring him to help us plan a big project coming up, but his bid seems too high. Would you be willing to tell me what rate he has charged you in the recent past? I could use some bargaining power to bring his quote down, though of course I would never mention that I got inside information from you.

If you are asking a colleague to recommend you to a potential employer:

Therefore, I am writing to ask you for a favor, but first I must ask you to keep this information confidential. I am considering leaving RTG Construction to take a position with a more established company. Specifically, I am interviewing with Grand Rapids Builders, which I know is a large customer of yours.

Would you consider providing a personal recommendation for me? If you could give your contact at Grand Rapids Builders a call and mention that you know me, have worked with me and believe I am a good candidate for vice president of operations, it would be a tremendous help.

March 19, 2007

Jason Sykes
Chief Financial Officer
Yellowtab Development Co. Inc.
8871 W. Jarvis St.
Grand Rapids, MI 48832

Dear Jason:

We have worked together in one capacity or another for more than 6 years now, and we have seen our share of ups and downs in this business. I believe we have a good professional relationship, one that can be relied on for help from time to time.

Therefore, I am writing to ask you for a favor. RTG Construction is in the process of bidding on a job for Tyree Department Stores. They are planning a store in the South Street Mall, and we want to build it for them. I know that you have worked with Tyree in the past and believe that a personal recommendation from you would really help us win this contract.

Would you consider giving your contact at Tyree a call sometime this month and mentioning our record of success and reliability? I only ask this because I know we are up against some tough competition and could really use a personal endorsement from a source that Tyree trusts.

I hope that you will consider helping me with this matter. Please know that I will not hesitate to return the favor if you should ever need a similar recommendation.

Sincerely,

Diane M. Baez
President and Founder

E-Mail

Dear Jason:

I am writing to ask you for a favor.

RTG Construction is in the process of bidding on a job for Tyree Department Stores. They are planning a store in the South Street Mall, and we want to build it for them. I know that you have worked with Tyree in the past and believe that a personal recommendation from you would really help us win this contract.

Would you consider giving your contact at Tyree a call sometime this month and mentioning our record of success and reliability?

I only ask this because I know we are up against some tough competition and could really use a personal endorsement from a source that Tyree trusts.

Please know that I will not hesitate to return the favor if you should ever need a similar recommendation.

Sincerely,

<e-mail signature, including name, title, company and contact information>

Positive Response to a Colleague's Request for a Personal Favor

Purpose

- To agree to do a favor for a business colleague at his or her request

Alternative Purposes

- To agree to provide information to a colleague
- To agree to nominate someone for an award
- To agree to do a favor and to ask for a favor in return

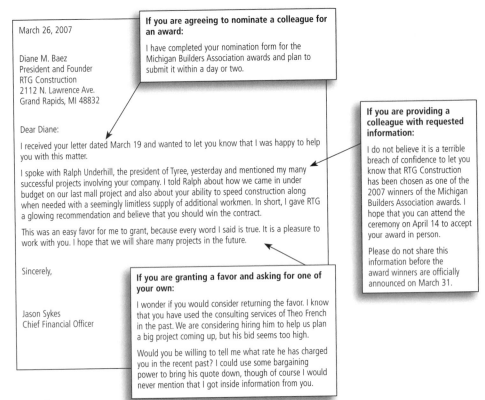

March 26, 2007

Diane M. Baez
President and Founder
RTG Construction
2112 N. Lawrence Ave.
Grand Rapids, MI 48832

Dear Diane:

I received your letter dated March 19 and wanted to let you know that I was happy to help you with this matter.

I spoke with Ralph Underhill, the president of Tyree, yesterday and mentioned my many successful projects involving your company. I told Ralph about how we came in under budget on our last mall project and also about your ability to speed construction along when needed with a seemingly limitless supply of additional workmen. In short, I gave RTG a glowing recommendation and believe that you should win the contract.

This was an easy favor for me to grant, because every word I said is true. It is a pleasure to work with you. I hope that we will share many projects in the future.

Sincerely,

Jason Sykes
Chief Financial Officer

If you are agreeing to nominate a colleague for an award:

I have completed your nomination form for the Michigan Builders Association awards and plan to submit it within a day or two.

If you are providing a colleague with requested information:

I do not believe it is a terrible breach of confidence to let you know that RTG Construction has been chosen as one of the 2007 winners of the Michigan Builders Association awards. I hope that you can attend the ceremony on April 14 to accept your award in person.

Please do not share this information before the award winners are officially announced on March 31.

If you are granting a favor and asking for one of your own:

I wonder if you would consider returning the favor. I know that you have used the consulting services of Theo French in the past. We are considering hiring him to help us plan a big project coming up, but his bid seems too high.

Would you be willing to tell me what rate he has charged you in the recent past? I could use some bargaining power to bring his quote down, though of course I would never mention that I got inside information from you.

E-Mail

Dear Diane:

I am happy to help you with this matter.

In fact, I spoke with Ralph Underhill, the president of Tyree, yesterday and mentioned my many successful projects involving your company.

I told Ralph about how we came in under budget on our last mall project and also about your ability to speed construction along when needed with a seemingly limitless supply of additional workmen.

In short, I gave RTG a glowing recommendation and believe that you should win the contract.

This was an easy favor for me to grant, because every word I said is true. It is a pleasure to work with you. I hope that we will share many projects in the future.

Sincerely,

<e-mail signature, including name, title, company and contact information>

Negative Response to a Colleague's Request for a Personal Favor

Purpose

- To decline to do a favor requested by a business colleague

Alternative Purposes

- To decline due to ethical or moral reasons
- To decline due to a company or personal policy
- To decline without providing a reason

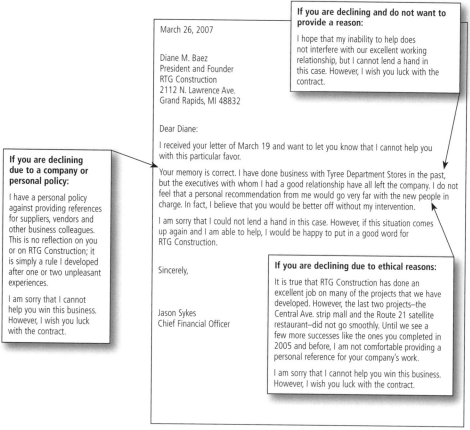

If you are declining and do not want to provide a reason:

I hope that my inability to help does not interfere with our excellent working relationship, but I cannot lend a hand in this case. However, I wish you luck with the contract.

March 26, 2007

Diane M. Baez
President and Founder
RTG Construction
2112 N. Lawrence Ave.
Grand Rapids, MI 48832

Dear Diane:

I received your letter of March 19 and want to let you know that I cannot help you with this particular favor.

Your memory is correct. I have done business with Tyree Department Stores in the past, but the executives with whom I had a good relationship have all left the company. I do not feel that a personal recommendation from me would go very far with the new people in charge. In fact, I believe that you would be better off without my intervention.

I am sorry that I could not lend a hand in this case. However, if this situation comes up again and I am able to help, I would be happy to put in a good word for RTG Construction.

Sincerely,

Jason Sykes
Chief Financial Officer

If you are declining due to a company or personal policy:

I have a personal policy against providing references for suppliers, vendors and other business colleagues. This is no reflection on you or on RTG Construction; it is simply a rule I developed after one or two unpleasant experiences.

I am sorry that I cannot help you win this business. However, I wish you luck with the contract.

If you are declining due to ethical reasons:

It is true that RTG Construction has done an excellent job on many of the projects that we have developed. However, the last two projects—the Central Ave. strip mall and the Route 21 satellite restaurant—did not go smoothly. Until we see a few more successes like the ones you completed in 2005 and before, I am not comfortable providing a personal reference for your company's work.

I am sorry that I cannot help you win this business. However, I wish you luck with the contract.

E-Mail

Dear Diane:

I want to let you know that I cannot help you with this particular favor.

Your memory is correct. I have done business with Tyree Department Stores in the past, but the executives with whom I had a good relationship have all left the company. I do not feel that a personal recommendation from me would go very far with the new people in charge. In fact, I believe that you would be better off without my intervention.

I am sorry that I could not lend a hand in this case. However, if this situation comes up again and I am able to help, I would be happy to put in a good word for RTG Construction.

Sincerely,

<e-mail signature, including name, title, company and contact information>

Letter Inviting Someone to a Business Event

Purpose

- To personally invite a business colleague to attend a business event

Alternative Purposes

- To invite a colleague to a business event that you are hosting
- To invite a colleague to a business event at which you will be honored
- To invite a colleague to a personal or social event for business reasons

If you are inviting a colleague to a social event for business reasons:

Wednesday, March 3 is the 12th Annual Trenton Black and White Ball. I attend this party every year and find it to be an excellent venue for meeting potential customers. I think that you would find it equally valuable.

February 20, 2008

Jean-Robert Sullivan
President
Unified Marketing Inc.
3288 Grand Ave., Suite 200
Trenton, NJ 02732

Dear Jean-Robert:

On Wednesday, March 3, the New Jersey chapter of the American Association of Television Marketers is hosting their first awards dinner.

I have reserved a table for 10 and would like to invite you and your wife to join me for the evening. The event promises to be entertaining, with a celebrity keynote speaker, as well as an excellent networking opportunity, since most of Trenton's largest businesses will be represented there.

The event will be held at the downtown Hilton, with cocktails at 7 p.m. and dinner at 8 p.m.

Please let me know if you and Emma can attend; I would love to have you both at the table.

Sincerely,

John T. Halbert
Manager, Sales and Marketing

If you are inviting a colleague to an event that you are hosting:

On Wednesday, March 3, my company will host a fund-raising banquet to help prevent domestic abuse in Trenton. I am not writing to ask you for a contribution; rather, I am inviting you to attend as my guest.

If you are inviting a colleague to an event at which you will be honored:

Because I will be recognized that evening for some of the campaign work I did in 2007, I have been able to reserve a table for 10 guests. I would like to invite you and your wife to join me for the evening. The event promises to be entertaining, with a celebrity keynote speaker, as well as an excellent networking opportunity, since most of Trenton's largest businesses will be represented there.

E-Mail

Dear Jean-Robert:

On Wednesday, March 3, the New Jersey chapter of the American Association of Television Marketers (AATM) is hosting their first awards dinner.

I have reserved a table for 10 and would like to invite you and your wife to join me for the evening.

The awards presentation promises to be entertaining, with a celebrity keynote speaker, as well as an excellent networking opportunity, since most of Trenton's largest businesses will be represented there.

The event will be held at the downtown Hilton, with cocktails at 7 p.m. and dinner at 8 p.m. Details on the event are on the AATM Web site.

Please let me know if you and Emma can attend; I would love to have you both at the table.

Sincerely,

<e-mail signature, including name, title, company and contact information>

Letter Accepting an Invitation to a Business Event

Purpose

- To accept a business colleague's written invitation to a business event

Alternative Purposes

- To accept an invitation to a business event that a colleague is hosting
- To accept an invitation to a business event at which a colleague will be honored
- To accept an invitation to a personal or social event for business reasons

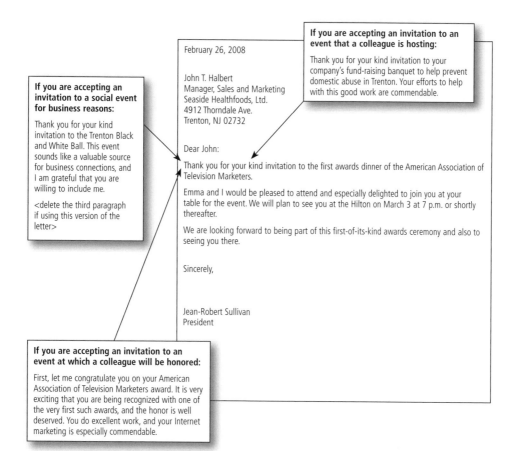

If you are accepting an invitation to an event that a colleague is hosting:

Thank you for your kind invitation to your company's fund-raising banquet to help prevent domestic abuse in Trenton. Your efforts to help with this good work are commendable.

If you are accepting an invitation to a social event for business reasons:

Thank you for your kind invitation to the Trenton Black and White Ball. This event sounds like a valuable source for business connections, and I am grateful that you are willing to include me.

<delete the third paragraph if using this version of the letter>

February 26, 2008

John T. Halbert
Manager, Sales and Marketing
Seaside Healthfoods, Ltd.
4912 Thorndale Ave.
Trenton, NJ 02732

Dear John:

Thank you for your kind invitation to the first awards dinner of the American Association of Television Marketers.

Emma and I would be pleased to attend and especially delighted to join you at your table for the event. We will plan to see you at the Hilton on March 3 at 7 p.m. or shortly thereafter.

We are looking forward to being part of this first-of-its-kind awards ceremony and also to seeing you there.

Sincerely,

Jean-Robert Sullivan
President

If you are accepting an invitation to an event at which a colleague will be honored:

First, let me congratulate you on your American Association of Television Marketers award. It is very exciting that you are being recognized with one of the very first such awards, and the honor is well deserved. You do excellent work, and your Internet marketing is especially commendable.

E-Mail

Dear John:

Thank you so much for your invitation to the first awards dinner of the American Association of Television Marketers.

Emma and I would be pleased to attend the event and especially delighted to join you at your table.

We are looking forward to being part of this first-of-its-kind awards ceremony and also to spending some time with you.

We will see you at the Hilton on March 3 at 7 p.m. or shortly thereafter.

Sincerely,

<e-mail signature, including name, title, company and contact information>

Letter Declining an Invitation to a Business Event

Purpose

- To decline a business colleague's written invitation to a business event

Alternative Purposes

- To decline an invitation to a business event that a colleague is hosting
- To decline an invitation to a business event at which a colleague will be honored
- To decline an invitation to a personal or social event for business reasons

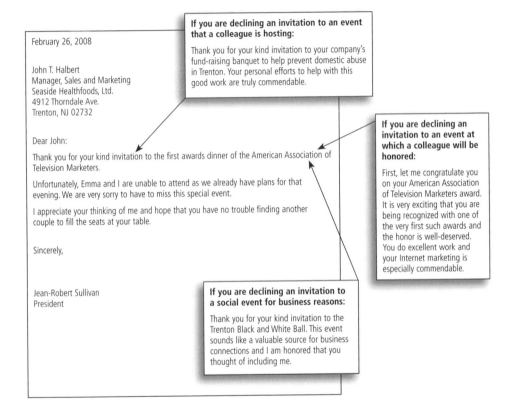

February 26, 2008

John T. Halbert
Manager, Sales and Marketing
Seaside Healthfoods, Ltd.
4912 Thorndale Ave.
Trenton, NJ 02732

Dear John:

Thank you for your kind invitation to the first awards dinner of the American Association of Television Marketers.

Unfortunately, Emma and I are unable to attend as we already have plans for that evening. We are very sorry to have to miss this special event.

I appreciate your thinking of me and hope that you have no trouble finding another couple to fill the seats at your table.

Sincerely,

Jean-Robert Sullivan
President

If you are declining an invitation to an event that a colleague is hosting:

Thank you for your kind invitation to your company's fund-raising banquet to help prevent domestic abuse in Trenton. Your personal efforts to help with this good work are truly commendable.

If you are declining an invitation to an event at which a colleague will be honored:

First, let me congratulate you on your American Association of Television Marketers award. It is very exciting that you are being recognized with one of the very first such awards and the honor is well-deserved. You do excellent work and your Internet marketing is especially commendable.

If you are declining an invitation to a social event for business reasons:

Thank you for your kind invitation to the Trenton Black and White Ball. This event sounds like a valuable source for business connections and I am honored that you thought of including me.

E-Mail

Dear John:

Thank you for your kind invitation to the first awards dinner of the American Association of Television Marketers.

Unfortunately, Emma and I are unable to attend as we already have plans for that evening. We are very sorry to have to miss this special event.

I appreciate your thinking of me and hope that you have no trouble finding another couple to fill the seats at your table.

Sincerely,

<e-mail signature, including name, title, company and contact information>

Request to a Colleague to Act as a Reference

Purpose

- To personally request that a business colleague act as your reference

Alternative Purposes

- To request that a colleague act as a personal reference
- To request that a colleague act as a financial or credit reference for your company
- To request that a colleague provide a written reference

If you are requesting that a colleague act as your personal reference:

I have applied for a corporate loan for our company in order to build up an Internet marketing division. I would like to list you as one of my personal references on the loan application. Would you be willing to answer some questions about our professional history and my overall reliability? If so, I would greatly appreciate it.

If you are requesting that a colleague act as your company's financial reference:

I have applied for a corporate loan for our company in order to build up an Internet marketing division. This addition will effectively double the size of our marketing department. Our forecasts show that it will increase our business by 65 percent in the first year.

I would like to list you as one of my credit references on the loan application. Would you be willing to answer some questions about our professional relationship over the years and about the current relationship of our organizations, including recent payment history? If so, I would greatly appreciate it.

February 12, 2007

Jean-Robert Sullivan
President
Unified Marketing Inc.
3288 Grand Ave., Suite 200
Trenton, NJ 02732

Dear Jean-Robert:

We have a long history together as marketing professionals, going back to the days in 2001 when I was a consultant for your department at RJM Steel. We have both come a long way in the past 5 or 6 years and I am about to make another change. But in order to do so, I need your help.

I have applied for a corporate loan for our company in order to build up an Internet marketing division.

I would like to list you as one of my business references on the loan application. Would you be willing to answer some questions about our professional history and my qualifications for this loan? If so, I would greatly appreciate it.

Please let me know whether I can give the lender, Trenton First National Bank, your name and phone number. I would like to submit the paperwork for this sometime next week.

Thank you in advance for considering this favor. Let me assure you that I will happily do the same for you if the need should ever arise.

Sincerely,

John T. Halbert

If you are requesting that a colleague provide a written reference:

I would like to have you act as one of my business references for the loan. Would you be willing to write a letter of recommendation for my company about our professional history and our qualifications for this loan? If so, I would greatly appreciate it.

Please let me know if you can help. I would like to submit the paperwork for this sometime next week.

E-Mail

Dear Jean-Robert:

I am writing to ask you for a favor.

We have a long history together as marketing professionals, going back to the days in 2001 when I was a consultant for your department at RJM Steel. We have both come a long way in the past 5 or 6 years and I am about to make another change. But in order to do so, I need your help.

I have applied for a corporate loan for our company in order to build up an Internet marketing division.

I would like to list you as one of my business references on the loan application. Would you be willing to answer some questions about our professional history and my qualifications for this loan? If so, I would greatly appreciate it.

Please let me know whether I can give the lender, Trenton First National Bank, your name and phone number. I would like to submit the paperwork for this sometime next week.

Thank you in advance for considering this favor. Let me assure you that I will happily do the same for you if the need should ever arise.

Sincerely,

<e-mail signature including name, title, company and contact information>

Positive Response to a Colleague's Request to Act as a Reference

Purpose

- To agree to provide a reference for a business colleague

Alternative Purposes

- To agree to act as a personal reference
- To agree to act as a financial or credit reference
- To agree to provide a written reference

February 17, 2007

John T. Halbert
Manager, Sales and Marketing
HRD Consulting
4877 Lincoln Ave.
Trenton, NJ 02732

Dear John:

Congratulations on the expansion of your marketing division; I wish you luck with adding the Internet component.

Of course I would be happy to act as a business reference for you and HRD Consulting. I am confident that you will execute a carefully thought-out plan for growth and would be happy to tell your lender about my confidence.

Please ask the bank to call my assistant, Nancy Johannsen, at 555.555.5555 and she will either find me or schedule a time for a phone interview.

Let me know how your project turns out; I may consider following your lead on this.

Sincerely,

Jean-Robert Sullivan
President

If you are agreeing to act as a personal reference:

Of course I would be happy to act as a personal reference for you. I am confident that with your personality and experience, you will execute a carefully thought-out plan for growth and I would be happy to tell your lender about my confidence.

If you are agreeing to act as a financial reference:

Of course I would be happy to act as a financial reference for HRD Consulting. Our experience in doing business with you over the past 2 years has been nothing but positive. I am confident that you will execute a carefully thought-out plan for growth and would be happy to tell your lender about my confidence.

If you are agreeing to provide a written reference:

Of course I would be happy to provide a letter of reference for you and HRD Consulting. I believe that I have the contact information I need and I will send a letter out within the week.

E-Mail

Dear John:

Congratulations on the expansion of your marketing division. I wish you luck with adding the Internet component.

Of course I would be happy to act as a business reference for you and HRD Consulting. I am confident that you will execute a carefully thought-out plan for growth and would be happy to tell your lender about my confidence.

Please ask the bank to call my assistant, Nancy Johannsen, at 555.555.5555 and she will either find me or schedule a time for a phone interview.

Let me know how your project turns out; I may consider following your lead on this.

Sincerely,

<e-mail signature, including name, title, company and contact information>

Negative Response to a Colleague's Request to Act as a Reference

Purpose

- To decline to provide a reference for a business colleague

Alternative Purposes

- To decline due to unsatisfactory history or performance
- To decline due to insufficient knowledge
- To decline due to insufficient information

If you are declining due to unsatisfactory performance:

I am sorry to say that I must decline your request. It is true that we have known each other for several years and that our company has used your consulting services in the past. However, the last time we hired you, we found your firm to be unorganized, unresponsive and generally unprofessional. In good conscience, based on that experience, I cannot provide a business reference for HRD Consulting.

February 17, 2007

John T. Halbert
Manager, Sales and Marketing
HRD Consulting
4877 Lincoln Ave.
Trenton, NJ 02732

Dear John:

This letter is in response to your request that I provide a business reference for HRD Consulting's application for a loan.

If you are declining due to insufficient knowledge:

I am sorry to say that I must decline your request. Although I have enjoyed a long and satisfactory business relationship with you in your previous role of independent consultant, I know nothing of HRD Consulting or its financial state. If it would be of any value in this situation, I would be happy to provide a personal reference for you, but I cannot vouch for your new company.

I am sorry to say that I must decline your request. Due to some legal problems I had in the past regarding companies for which I provided references, I have made it a personal policy not to put my name to any personal or business reference for anyone, no matter how well I know them or how positive my opinion of them is.

I am sorry that I cannot help you in this matter, but I am sure you will have no trouble finding someone else to provide a reference.

Sincerely,

Jean-Robert Sullivan
President

If you are declining due to insufficient information:

I am sorry to say that I cannot provide a reference without more details on what information I need to supply. I would be happy to confirm the details of business transactions between our companies, but if you are asking me to personally recommend HRD Consulting for a sizable loan, I cannot do that.

E-Mail

Dear John:

I am sorry to say that I must decline your request that I provide a business reference for HRD Consulting.

Due to some legal problems I had in the past regarding companies for which I provided references, I have made it a personal policy not to put my name to any personal or business reference for anyone, no matter how well I know them or how positive my opinion of them is.

I am sorry that I cannot help you in this matter, but I am sure you will have no trouble finding someone else to provide a reference.

Sincerely,

<e-mail signature, including name, title, company and contact information>

Letter Extending Holiday Greetings

Purpose

- To personally wish a business colleague well during the holidays

Alternative Purposes

- To invite a colleague to lunch or dinner to mark the holidays
- To enclose a gift for the holidays
- To let a colleague know that you have donated to a charity in his or her name

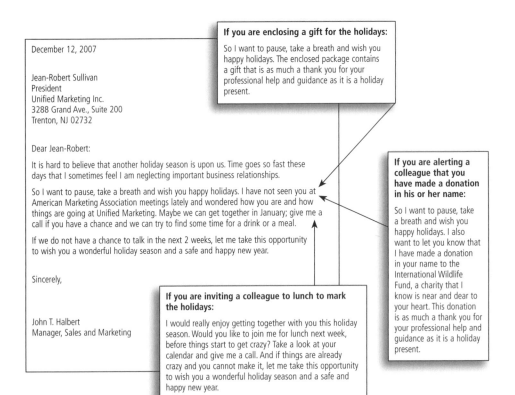

December 12, 2007

Jean-Robert Sullivan
President
Unified Marketing Inc.
3288 Grand Ave., Suite 200
Trenton, NJ 02732

Dear Jean-Robert:

It is hard to believe that another holiday season is upon us. Time goes so fast these days that I sometimes feel I am neglecting important business relationships.

So I want to pause, take a breath and wish you happy holidays. I have not seen you at American Marketing Association meetings lately and wondered how you are and how things are going at Unified Marketing. Maybe we can get together in January; give me a call if you have a chance and we can try to find some time for a drink or a meal.

If we do not have a chance to talk in the next 2 weeks, let me take this opportunity to wish you a wonderful holiday season and a safe and happy new year.

Sincerely,

John T. Halbert
Manager, Sales and Marketing

If you are enclosing a gift for the holidays:

So I want to pause, take a breath and wish you happy holidays. The enclosed package contains a gift that is as much a thank you for your professional help and guidance as it is a holiday present.

If you are alerting a colleague that you have made a donation in his or her name:

So I want to pause, take a breath and wish you happy holidays. I also want to let you know that I have made a donation in your name to the International Wildlife Fund, a charity that I know is near and dear to your heart. This donation is as much a thank you for your professional help and guidance as it is a holiday present.

If you are inviting a colleague to lunch to mark the holidays:

I would really enjoy getting together with you this holiday season. Would you like to join me for lunch next week, before things start to get crazy? Take a look at your calendar and give me a call. And if things are already crazy and you cannot make it, let me take this opportunity to wish you a wonderful holiday season and a safe and happy new year.

E-Mail

Dear Jean-Robert:

It is hard to believe that another holiday season is upon us. Time goes so fast these days that I sometimes feel I am neglecting important business relationships.

So I want to pause, take a breath and wish you happy holidays.

I have not seen you at American Marketing Association meetings lately and wondered how you are and how things are going at Unified Marketing. Maybe we can get together in January; let me know if you have a chance and we can try to find some time for a drink or a meal.

If we do not have a chance to talk in the next 2 weeks, let me take this opportunity to wish you a wonderful holiday season and a safe and happy new year.

Sincerely,

<e-mail signature, including name, title, company and contact information>

Letter Extending Birthday Greetings

Purpose

- To personally wish a business colleague a happy birthday

Alternative Purposes

- To invite a colleague to lunch or dinner to mark the occasion
- To enclose a birthday gift
- To extend a belated wish for a happy birthday

If you are extending belated birthday wishes:

Better late than never, they say. So, a bit past your birthday, here is a little opinion on aging for you: American author Donald R. Perry Marquis said, "Of middle age, the best that can be said is that a middle-aged person has likely learned how to have a little fun in spite of his troubles."

I hope that you did something special for your birthday that was more than a little fun. I also hope that things are going well for you and for Unified Marketing.

March 13, 2007

Jean-Robert Sullivan
President
Unified Marketing Inc.
3288 Grand Ave., Suite 200
Trenton, NJ 02732

If you are enclosing a birthday gift:

I hope that you have something special planned for your birthday that is more than a little fun. To help you celebrate and forget your troubles, I have enclosed a small birthday gift.

Dear Jean-Robert:

On the occasion of your birthday, here is a little opinion on aging for you: American author Donald R. Perry Marquis said, "Of middle age, the best that can be said is that a middle-aged person has likely learned how to have a little fun in spite of his troubles."

I hope that you have something special planned for your birthday that is more than a little fun. I also hope that things are going well for you and for Unified Marketing.

Maybe we can get together in the next few weeks; give me a call if you have a chance and we can try to find some time for a drink or a meal.

Sincerely,

John T. Halbert
Manager, Sales and Marketing

If you are inviting a colleague to lunch to mark the occasion:

I would like to help you celebrate in a smaller way. Would you like to join me for lunch next week? Take a look at your calendar; I will give you a call in a few days to see if we can find a day.

E-Mail

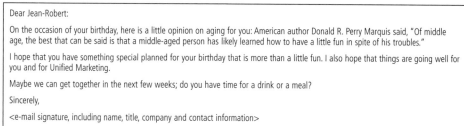

Dear Jean-Robert:

On the occasion of your birthday, here is a little opinion on aging for you: American author Donald R. Perry Marquis said, "Of middle age, the best that can be said is that a middle-aged person has likely learned how to have a little fun in spite of his troubles."

I hope that you have something special planned for your birthday that is more than a little fun. I also hope that things are going well for you and for Unified Marketing.

Maybe we can get together in the next few weeks; do you have time for a drink or a meal?

Sincerely,

<e-mail signature, including name, title, company and contact information>

Section Eight

.....

Essential Supply
Chain Letters

Letter Accompanying Product Shipment (Version 1)

Purpose

- To outline what is included in a shipment

Alternative Purposes

- To note that the shipment is one of several
- To note that the shipment fills a partial order
- To note that the shipment completes an order

If the shipment completes an order:

This letter accompanies a shipment of Frank's most recent order from Kleen-All Products. The shipment, based on your purchase order #KAP2390, dated January 15, 2008, includes the following items from your order:

<list of items>

Please note that this shipment completes your order.

If the shipment is one of several:

This letter accompanies a shipment of Frank's most recent order from Kleen-All Products. The shipment, based on your purchase order #KAP2390, dated January 15, 2008, includes the following items from your order:

<list of items>

The remainder of the shipment is on a second truck, which will arrive within 24 hours, per your delivery guidelines.

Please note that all pallets …

If the shipment does not include the complete order:

This letter accompanies a shipment of Frank's most recent order from Kleen-All Products. The shipment, based on your purchase order #KAP2390, dated January 15, 2008, includes the following items from your order:

<list of items>

Due to delays in receiving our packaging, we cannot ship the remainder of your order until next week. I will contact you with an exact arrival time by February 3 at the latest.

January 30, 2008

Warehouse Manager
Receivables Department
Frank's Finer Food Stores Warehouse
49002 Commercial Drive
Pittsburgh, PA 49284

Dear Warehouse Manager:

This letter accompanies a shipment of Frank's most recent order from Kleen-All Products. The shipment, based on your purchase order #KAP2390, dated January 15, 2008, includes all items from your order:

- 30 cases of Kleen-All all-purpose cleaner, 10 oz. (item #448359)
- 27 cases of Kleen-All laundry detergent, 3 lb. (item #448343)
- 24 cases of Kleen-All dish soap, 6 oz. (item #4483632)
- 24 cases of Kleen-All heavy-duty cleaner, 2 lb. (item #4483649)
- 24 cases of Kleen-All window washing solution, 8 oz. (item #4483618)

Please note that all pallets are labeled in accordance with your Supply Chain Guide, including RFID tags. For information on payment terms and merchandise returns procedures, please see the enclosed documents.

If you have any questions on the contents of this shipment, please contact me immediately at 555.555.5555 or at **jtdrummond@kleen-all.com.**

Sincerely,

J.T. Drummond
Director, Customer Service & Operations

E-Mail

Dear Warehouse Manager:

This afternoon you will receive shipment of Frank's most recent order from Kleen-All Products. The shipment, based on your purchase order #KAP2390, dated January 15, 2008, includes all items from your order:

30 cases of Kleen-All all-purpose cleaner, 10 oz. (item #448359)
27 cases of Kleen-All laundry detergent, 3 lb. (item #448343)
24 cases of Kleen-All dish soap, 6 oz. (item #4483632)
24 cases of Kleen-All heavy-duty cleaner, 2 lb. (item #4483649)
24 cases of Kleen-All window washing solution, 8 oz. (item #4483618)

Please note that all pallets are labeled in accordance with your Supply Chain Guide, including RFID tags. For information on payment terms and merchandise returns procedures, please see the attached documents.

If you have any questions on the contents of this shipment, please contact me immediately.

Sincerely,

<e-mail signature, including name, title, company and contact information>

Letter Accompanying Product Shipment (Version 2)

Purpose

- To announce ordered item is out of stock

Alternative Purposes

- To warn the customer of unknown delivery date
- To offer a refund until the item is available
- To place the entire order on hold

January 17, 2008

David Morelli
Purchasing Agent
Frank's Finer Food Stores Warehouse
49002 Commercial Drive
Pittsburgh, PA 49284

Dear Mr. Morelli:

This letter is in response to your company's recent order for Kleen-All Products.

Your purchase order #KAP2390, dated January 15, 2008, includes 24 cases of Kleen-All heavy-duty cleaner (item #4483649). We are currently out of stock on this item but expect to have enough available to fill your order by February 15.

Unless I hear otherwise from you, I will plan to ship the remaining items in your order immediately and send the heavy-duty cleaner as soon as possible. I will contact you when we receive stock to schedule the additional delivery.

If you have any questions on the fulfillment of this order or wish to make other arrangements for receiving any part of it, please contact me immediately at 555.555.5555 or at **jtdrummond@kleen-all.com**.

Sincerely,

J.T. Drummond
Director, Customer Service & Operations

If you do not have an estimated date for the out-of-stock item:

Your purchase order #KAP2390, dated January 15, 2008, includes 24 cases of Kleen-All heavy-duty cleaner (item #4483649). We are out of stock on this item due to problems clearing customs. I cannot yet estimate a date when we will be able to ship those 24 cases.

However, I will plan to ship the remaining items in your order immediately and send the heavy-duty cleaner as soon as possible. I will contact you when we receive stock to schedule the additional delivery.

If you plan to place the entire order on hold:

Your purchase order #KAP2390, dated January 15, 2008, includes 24 cases of Kleen-All heavy-duty cleaner (item #4483649). We are out of stock on this item due to problems clearing customs. I cannot yet estimate a date when we will be able to ship those 24 cases.

I know that Frank's Finer Foods prefers not to accept partial shipments, so I am placing this order on hold until we can fulfill the entire request. Please contact me if you would like any or all of the other products shipped.

If you are offering a partial refund:

Your purchase order #KAP2390, dated January 15, 2008, includes 24 cases of Kleen-All heavy-duty cleaner (item #4483649). We are out of stock on this item due to problems clearing customs. I cannot yet estimate a date when we will be able to ship those 24 cases.

We will process the remainder of your order and credit you with a refund for $960, the cost of the heavy-duty cleaner. When the stock arrives at our warehouse, I will let you know it is available.

E-Mail

Dear Mr. Morelli:

This e-mail is in response to your recent order for Kleen-All Products.

Your purchase order #KAP2390, dated January 15, 2008, includes 24 cases of Kleen-All heavy-duty cleaner (item #4483649).

We are currently out of stock on this item but expect to have enough available to fill your order by February 15.

Unless I hear otherwise from you, I will plan to ship the remaining items in your order immediately and send the heavy-duty cleaner as soon as possible. I will contact you when we receive stock to schedule the additional delivery.

If you have any questions on the fulfillment of this order or wish to make other arrangements for receiving any part of it, please contact me immediately.

Sincerely,

<e-mail signature, including name, title, company and contact information>

Letter Announcing Change or Delay in Shipping

Purpose

- To alert a customer to a change in shipping his or her order

Alternative Purposes

- To alert a customer to a delay in shipping his or her order
- To alert a customer to problems with his or her receivables
- To alert a customer to a change in delivery personnel

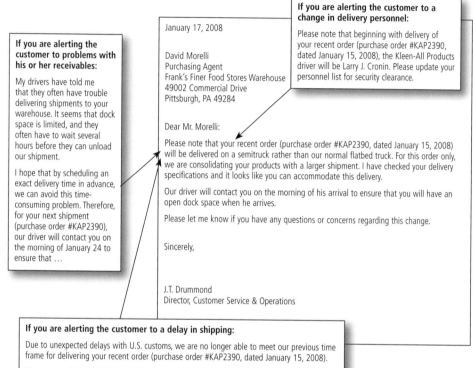

If you are alerting the customer to a change in delivery personnel:

Please note that beginning with delivery of your recent order (purchase order #KAP2390, dated January 15, 2008), the Kleen-All Products driver will be Larry J. Cronin. Please update your personnel list for security clearance.

If you are alerting the customer to problems with his or her receivables:

My drivers have told me that they often have trouble delivering shipments to your warehouse. It seems that dock space is limited, and they often have to wait several hours before they can unload our shipment.

I hope that by scheduling an exact delivery time in advance, we can avoid this time-consuming problem. Therefore, for your next shipment (purchase order #KAP2390), our driver will contact you on the morning of January 24 to ensure that …

January 17, 2008

David Morelli
Purchasing Agent
Frank's Finer Food Stores Warehouse
49002 Commercial Drive
Pittsburgh, PA 49284

Dear Mr. Morelli:

Please note that your recent order (purchase order #KAP2390, dated January 15, 2008) will be delivered on a semitruck rather than our normal flatbed truck. For this order only, we are consolidating your products with a larger shipment. I have checked your delivery specifications and it looks like you can accommodate this delivery.

Our driver will contact you on the morning of his arrival to ensure that you will have an open dock space when he arrives.

Please let me know if you have any questions or concerns regarding this change.

Sincerely,

J.T. Drummond
Director, Customer Service & Operations

If you are alerting the customer to a delay in shipping:

Due to unexpected delays with U.S. customs, we are no longer able to meet our previous time frame for delivering your recent order (purchase order #KAP2390, dated January 15, 2008).

We estimate that the shipment will arrive at your warehouse sometime during the week of February 24, rather than the originally stated date of February 2. As soon as our materials are released by customs, I will contact you with a specific delivery date.

E-Mail

Dear Mr. Morelli:

Please note that your recent order (purchase order #KAP2390, dated January 15, 2008) will be delivered on a semitruck rather than our normal flatbed truck. For this order only, we are consolidating your products with a larger shipment.

I have checked your delivery specifications and it looks as though you can accommodate this delivery.

Our driver will contact you on the morning of his arrival to ensure that you will have an open dock space when he arrives.

Please let me know if you have any questions or concerns regarding this change.

Sincerely,

<e-mail signature, including name, title, company and contact information>

Letter Announcing Change in Delivery Procedures

Purpose

- To alert customers to a change in your delivery procedures

Alternative Purposes

- To alert a customer that you are conforming to his or her change in delivery specifications
- To alert customers to a temporary change in delivery procedures
- To ask the customer's permission to change your delivery procedures

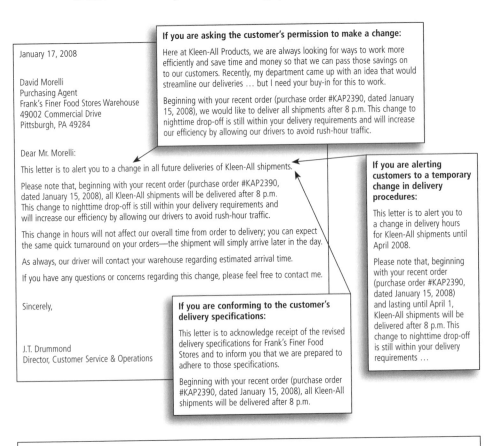

January 17, 2008

David Morelli
Purchasing Agent
Frank's Finer Food Stores Warehouse
49002 Commercial Drive
Pittsburgh, PA 49284

Dear Mr. Morelli:

This letter is to alert you to a change in all future deliveries of Kleen-All shipments.

Please note that, beginning with your recent order (purchase order #KAP2390, dated January 15, 2008), all Kleen-All shipments will be delivered after 8 p.m. This change to nighttime drop-off is still within your delivery requirements and will increase our efficiency by allowing our drivers to avoid rush-hour traffic.

This change in hours will not affect our overall time from order to delivery; you can expect the same quick turnaround on your orders—the shipment will simply arrive later in the day.

As always, our driver will contact your warehouse regarding estimated arrival time.

If you have any questions or concerns regarding this change, please feel free to contact me.

Sincerely,

J.T. Drummond
Director, Customer Service & Operations

If you are asking the customer's permission to make a change:

Here at Kleen-All Products, we are always looking for ways to work more efficiently and save time and money so that we can pass those savings on to our customers. Recently, my department came up with an idea that would streamline our deliveries ... but I need your buy-in for this to work.

Beginning with your recent order (purchase order #KAP2390, dated January 15, 2008), we would like to deliver all shipments after 8 p.m. This change to nighttime drop-off is still within your delivery requirements and will increase our efficiency by allowing our drivers to avoid rush-hour traffic.

If you are alerting customers to a temporary change in delivery procedures:

This letter is to alert you to a change in delivery hours for Kleen-All shipments until April 2008.

Please note that, beginning with your recent order (purchase order #KAP2390, dated January 15, 2008) and lasting until April 1, Kleen-All shipments will be delivered after 8 p.m. This change to nighttime drop-off is still within your delivery requirements ...

If you are conforming to the customer's delivery specifications:

This letter is to acknowledge receipt of the revised delivery specifications for Frank's Finer Food Stores and to inform you that we are prepared to adhere to those specifications.

Beginning with your recent order (purchase order #KAP2390, dated January 15, 2008), all Kleen-All shipments will be delivered after 8 p.m.

Dear Mr. Morelli:

This message is to alert you to a change in all future deliveries of Kleen-All shipments.

Please note that, beginning with your recent order (purchase order #KAP2390, dated January 15, 2008), all Kleen-All shipments will be delivered after 8 p.m.

This change to nighttime drop-off is still within your delivery requirements and will increase our efficiency by allowing our drivers to avoid rush-hour traffic.

This change in hours will not affect our overall time from order to delivery; you can expect the same quick turnaround on your orders—the shipment will simply arrive later in the day.

As always, our driver will contact your warehouse regarding estimated arrival time.

Sincerely,

<e-mail signature, including name, title, company and contact information>

Letter Announcing Pricing Change

Purpose

- To formally alert customers of a change in product pricing

Alternative Purposes

- To alert customers of a decrease in pricing
- To alert customers of a pricing change for a specific product
- To alert a customer to a pricing change on his or her order

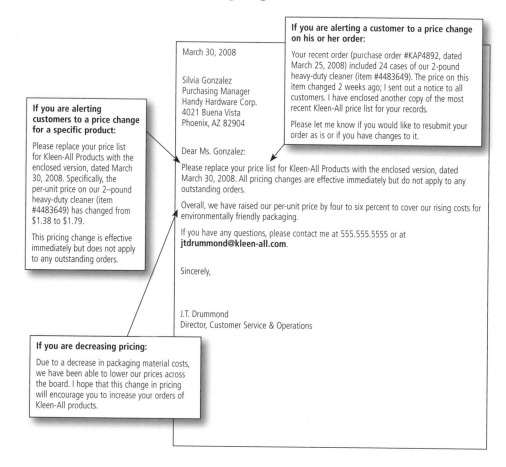

If you are alerting a customer to a price change on his or her order:

Your recent order (purchase order #KAP4892, dated March 25, 2008) included 24 cases of our 2-pound heavy-duty cleaner (item #4483649). The price on this item changed 2 weeks ago; I sent out a notice to all customers. I have enclosed another copy of the most recent Kleen-All price list for your records.

Please let me know if you would like to resubmit your order as is or if you have changes to it.

If you are alerting customers to a price change for a specific product:

Please replace your price list for Kleen-All Products with the enclosed version, dated March 30, 2008. Specifically, the per-unit price on our 2–pound heavy-duty cleaner (item #4483649) has changed from $1.38 to $1.79.

This pricing change is effective immediately but does not apply to any outstanding orders.

If you are decreasing pricing:

Due to a decrease in packaging material costs, we have been able to lower our prices across the board. I hope that this change in pricing will encourage you to increase your orders of Kleen-All products.

March 30, 2008

Silvia Gonzalez
Purchasing Manager
Handy Hardware Corp.
4021 Buena Vista
Phoenix, AZ 82904

Dear Ms. Gonzalez:

Please replace your price list for Kleen-All Products with the enclosed version, dated March 30, 2008. All pricing changes are effective immediately but do not apply to any outstanding orders.

Overall, we have raised our per-unit price by four to six percent to cover our rising costs for environmentally friendly packaging.

If you have any questions, please contact me at 555.555.5555 or at **jtdrummond@kleen-all.com**.

Sincerely,

J.T. Drummond
Director, Customer Service & Operations

E-Mail

Dear Ms. Gonzalez:

Please replace your price list for Kleen-All Products with the attached PDF version, dated March 30, 2008.

All pricing changes are effective immediately but do not apply to any outstanding orders.

Overall, we have raised our per-unit price by four to six percent to cover our rising costs for environmentally friendly packaging.

If you have any questions, please contact me.

Sincerely,

<e-mail signature, including name, title, company and contact information>

Letter Announcing Change of Customer Contact

Purpose

- To formally introduce customers to a new individual contact within your company

Alternative Purposes

- To introduce customers to your replacement
- To introduce customers to your superior
- To introduce customers to yourself as their new contact

February 26, 2008

David Morelli
Purchasing Agent
Frank's Finer Food Stores Warehouse
49002 Commercial Drive
Pittsburgh, PA 49284

Dear Mr. Morelli:

Beginning today, your contact for shipping and ordering questions here at Kleen-All is Yolanda Maldona. Yolanda was just promoted to operations manager and will assume responsibility for the day-to-day functions of the operations department, including tracking orders and overseeing shipments to Frank's Finer Food Stores.

Yolanda has more than 6 years of experience working in Kleen-All's operations department and will now manage a staff of 24, including our warehouse employees. She will report directly to me.

Please direct all orders, questions and customer service-related issues to Yolanda. Her direct number is 555.555.5555, and her e-mail address is **ymaldona@kleen-all.com**.

I am confident that this transition will be a smooth one. However, if you have any concerns, please feel free to contact me directly.

Sincerely,

J.T. Drummond
Director, Customer Service & Operations

If you are introducing your replacement:

Beginning today, your contact for shipping and ordering questions here at Kleen-All is Yolanda Maldona. Yolanda is replacing me as operations manager, as I was promoted to director this week.

If you are introducing a new superior:

Beginning today, your contact for shipping and ordering questions here at Kleen-All is Yolanda Maldona. Yolanda was recently hired as our vice president of operations and will assume responsibility for the day-to-day functions of the operations department, including tracking orders and overseeing shipments to Frank's Finer Food Stores.

Yolanda has more than 15 years of experience in operations and will now manage our group, including our warehouse employees. We are all excited to have someone with her experience and expertise in charge.

If you are introducing yourself:

Let me introduce myself. I am the new director of customer service and operations at Kleen-All and will be your new contact for shipping and ordering questions. I will assume responsibility for the day-to-day functions of the operations department, including tracking orders and overseeing shipments to Frank's Finer Food Stores.

Beginning immediately, please direct all orders, questions and customer service-related issues to me.

E-Mail

Dear Mr. Morelli:

Beginning today, your contact for shipping and ordering questions here at Kleen-All is Yolanda Maldona. Yolanda was just promoted to operations manager and will assume responsibility for the day-to-day functions of the operations department, including tracking orders and overseeing shipments to Frank's Finer Food Stores.

Yolanda has more than 6 years of experience working in Kleen-All's operations department and will now manage a staff of 24, including our warehouse employees. She will report directly to me.

Please direct all orders, questions and customer service-related issues to Yolanda via e-mail at **ymaldona@kleen-all.com** or by phone at 555.555.5555.

I am confident that this transition will be a smooth one. However, if you have any concerns, please feel free to contact me directly.

Sincerely,

<e-mail signature, including name, title, company and contact information>

Letter Announcing Discontinued Product

Purpose

- To formally alert customers of a discontinued product

Alternative Purposes

- To give customers advance notice that a product will be discontinued
- To alert customers that an entire group or line of products is discontinued
- To alert a customer to a discontinued product on his or her order

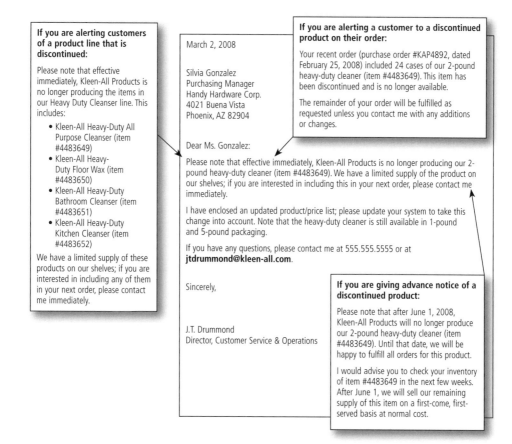

If you are alerting customers of a product line that is discontinued:

Please note that effective immediately, Kleen-All Products is no longer producing the items in our Heavy Duty Cleanser line. This includes:

- Kleen-All Heavy-Duty All Purpose Cleanser (item #4483649)
- Kleen-All Heavy-Duty Floor Wax (item #4483650)
- Kleen-All Heavy-Duty Bathroom Cleanser (item #4483651)
- Kleen-All Heavy-Duty Kitchen Cleanser (item #4483652)

We have a limited supply of these products on our shelves; if you are interested in including any of them in your next order, please contact me immediately.

If you are alerting a customer to a discontinued product on their order:

Your recent order (purchase order #KAP4892, dated February 25, 2008) included 24 cases of our 2-pound heavy-duty cleaner (item #4483649). This item has been discontinued and is no longer available.

The remainder of your order will be fulfilled as requested unless you contact me with any additions or changes.

March 2, 2008

Silvia Gonzalez
Purchasing Manager
Handy Hardware Corp.
4021 Buena Vista
Phoenix, AZ 82904

Dear Ms. Gonzalez:

Please note that effective immediately, Kleen-All Products is no longer producing our 2-pound heavy-duty cleaner (item #4483649). We have a limited supply of the product on our shelves; if you are interested in including this in your next order, please contact me immediately.

I have enclosed an updated product/price list; please update your system to take this change into account. Note that the heavy-duty cleaner is still available in 1-pound and 5-pound packaging.

If you have any questions, please contact me at 555.555.5555 or at **jtdrummond@kleen-all.com**.

Sincerely,

J.T. Drummond
Director, Customer Service & Operations

If you are giving advance notice of a discontinued product:

Please note that after June 1, 2008, Kleen-All Products will no longer produce our 2-pound heavy-duty cleaner (item #4483649). Until that date, we will be happy to fulfill all orders for this product.

I would advise you to check your inventory of item #4483649 in the next few weeks. After June 1, we will sell our remaining supply of this item on a first-come, first-served basis at normal cost.

E-Mail

Dear Ms. Gonzalez:

Please note that effective immediately, Kleen-All Products is no longer producing our 2-pound heavy-duty cleaner (item #4483649).

We have a limited supply of the product on our shelves; if you are interested in including this in your next order, please contact me immediately. Otherwise, please consider purchasing the same heavy-duty cleaner in our more popular amounts of 1 pound or 5 pounds.

I have attached a PDF of an updated product/price list; please update your system to take this change into account.

If you have any questions, please feel free to contact me.

Sincerely,

<e-mail signature, including name, title, company and contact information>

Letter with Product Change Notice

Purpose

- To provide all relevant customers with an official product change notice (PCN)

Alternative Purposes

- To send a revised PCN
- To alert customers that a PCN is coming
- To respond to an order that does not take into account a PCN

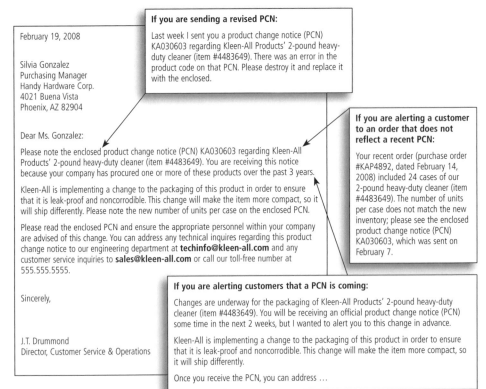

If you are sending a revised PCN:

Last week I sent you a product change notice (PCN) KA030603 regarding Kleen-All Products' 2-pound heavy-duty cleaner (item #4483649). There was an error in the product code on that PCN. Please destroy it and replace it with the enclosed.

February 19, 2008

Silvia Gonzalez
Purchasing Manager
Handy Hardware Corp.
4021 Buena Vista
Phoenix, AZ 82904

Dear Ms. Gonzalez:

Please note the enclosed product change notice (PCN) KA030603 regarding Kleen-All Products' 2-pound heavy-duty cleaner (item #4483649). You are receiving this notice because your company has procured one or more of these products over the past 3 years.

Kleen-All is implementing a change to the packaging of this product in order to ensure that it is leak-proof and noncorrodible. This change will make the item more compact, so it will ship differently. Please note the new number of units per case on the enclosed PCN.

Please read the enclosed PCN and ensure the appropriate personnel within your company are advised of this change. You can address any technical inquires regarding this product change notice to our engineering department at **techinfo@kleen-all.com** and any customer service inquiries to **sales@kleen-all.com** or call our toll-free number at 555.555.5555.

Sincerely,

J.T. Drummond
Director, Customer Service & Operations

If you are alerting a customer to an order that does not reflect a recent PCN:

Your recent order (purchase order #KAP4892, dated February 14, 2008) included 24 cases of our 2-pound heavy-duty cleaner (item #4483649). The number of units per case does not match the new inventory; please see the enclosed product change notice (PCN) KA030603, which was sent on February 7.

If you are alerting customers that a PCN is coming:

Changes are underway for the packaging of Kleen-All Products' 2-pound heavy-duty cleaner (item #4483649). You will be receiving an official product change notice (PCN) some time in the next 2 weeks, but I wanted to alert you to this change in advance.

Kleen-All is implementing a change to the packaging of this product in order to ensure that it is leak-proof and noncorrodible. This change will make the item more compact, so it will ship differently.

Once you receive the PCN, you can address ...

E-Mail

Dear Ms. Gonzalez:

Please note the attached PDF of a product change notice (PCN) KA030603 regarding Kleen-All Products' 2-pound heavy-duty cleaner (item #4483649).

You are receiving this notice because your company has procured one or more of these products over the past 3 years.

Kleen-All is implementing a change to the packaging of this product in order to ensure that it is leak-proof and noncorrodible. This change will make the item more compact, so it will ship differently.

Please note the new number of units per case on the enclosed PCN.

Please read the attached PCN and ensure the appropriate personnel within your company are advised of this change.

You can address any technical inquires regarding this product change notice to our engineering department at **techinfo@kleen-all.com** and any customer service inquiries to **sales@kleen-all.com** or call our toll-free number at 555.555.5555.

Sincerely,

<e-mail signature, including name, title, company and contact information>

Return Materials Authorization Letter

Purpose

- To provide a customer with specific information on the return materials authorization (RMA) process

Alternative Purposes

- To provide the customer with an RMA number
- To follow up on an incorrect RMA
- To send an RMA form along with the order

If you are sending an RMA form with the initial order:

This letter accompanies a shipment of Frank's most recent order from Kleen-All Products. The shipment is based on your purchase order #KAP2390, dated January 15, 2008. Enclosed please find a return materials authorization (RMA) form; use this form in case you need to return part or all of this shipment.

If you return any materials, please note that you must have an RMA number for each case you are returning; you can obtain an RMA number by contacting our customer service department immediately at 555.555.5555.

If you are providing an RMA number with the form:

Enclosed please find a return materials authorization (RMA) form for the products you received with our order #KAP8329. Please note the following RMA numbers, which you will need to include on the form:

- 1 case of Kleen-All all-purpose cleaner (item #448359) – RMA #JR2-5903852
- 3 cases of Kleen-All laundry detergent (item #448343) – RMA #JR2-5903853
- 4 cases of Kleen-All dish soap (item #4483632) – RMA #JR2-5903854

If you are following up on an incorrect RMA:

As you recall, the last time you returned materials to Kleen-All, the RMA form was incorrect. Please pay careful attention to the instructions on the form this time and note that you must have an RMA ...

January 14, 2008

Silvia Gonzalez
Purchasing Manager
Handy Hardware Corp.
4021 Buena Vista
Phoenix, AZ 82904

Dear Ms. Gonzalez:

Enclosed please find a return materials authorization (RMA) form for the products you received with our order #KAP8329. Please note that you must have an RMA number for each case you are returning; if you have not obtained an RMA number, please contact our customer service department immediately at 555.555.5555.

Specific instructions for our return process are included on the form.

Please attach a copy of your completed RMA form to the outside of your box or pallet and return to the address on the form. All RMA numbers are valid for 30 days from date of issue.

If you have any questions, please contact our customer service department at **sales@kleen-all.com** or at 555.555.5555.

Sincerely,

J.T. Drummond
Director, Customer Service & Operations

P.S. Note that opened products are nonreturnable unless defective or due to sales error on behalf of Kleen-All Products.

E-Mail

Dear Ms. Gonzalez:

Attached please find a PDF of a return materials authorization (RMA) form for the products you received with our order #KAP8329.

Please note that you must have an RMA number for each case you are returning; if you have not obtained an RMA number, please contact our customer service department immediately at 555.555.5555.

Specific instructions for our return process are included on the form.

Please attach a copy of your completed RMA form to the outside of your box or pallet and return to the address on the form. All RMA numbers are valid for 30 days from date of issue.

If you have any questions, please contact our customer service department at 555.555.5555.

Sincerely,

<e-mail signature, including name, title, company and contact information>

Letter Requesting Inventory Update

Purpose

- To formally request that a customer provide an inventory count on one or more of your products

Alternative Purposes

- To replace a defective or out-of-date product
- To follow up with a request to return a particular product
- To request return on behalf of your supplier

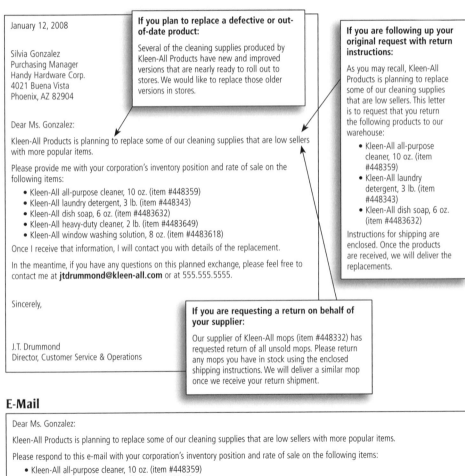

January 12, 2008

Silvia Gonzalez
Purchasing Manager
Handy Hardware Corp.
4021 Buena Vista
Phoenix, AZ 82904

Dear Ms. Gonzalez:

Kleen-All Products is planning to replace some of our cleaning supplies that are low sellers with more popular items.

Please provide me with your corporation's inventory position and rate of sale on the following items:

- Kleen-All all-purpose cleaner, 10 oz. (item #448359)
- Kleen-All laundry detergent, 3 lb. (item #448343)
- Kleen-All dish soap, 6 oz. (item #4483632)
- Kleen-All heavy-duty cleaner, 2 lb. (item #4483649)
- Kleen-All window washing solution, 8 oz. (item #4483618)

Once I receive that information, I will contact you with details of the replacement.

In the meantime, if you have any questions on this planned exchange, please feel free to contact me at **jtdrummond@kleen-all.com** or at 555.555.5555.

Sincerely,

J.T. Drummond
Director, Customer Service & Operations

If you plan to replace a defective or out-of-date product:

Several of the cleaning supplies produced by Kleen-All Products have new and improved versions that are nearly ready to roll out to stores. We would like to replace those older versions in stores.

If you are following up your original request with return instructions:

As you may recall, Kleen-All Products is planning to replace some of our cleaning supplies that are low sellers. This letter is to request that you return the following products to our warehouse:

- Kleen-All all-purpose cleaner, 10 oz. (item #448359)
- Kleen-All laundry detergent, 3 lb. (item #448343)
- Kleen-All dish soap, 6 oz. (item #4483632)

Instructions for shipping are enclosed. Once the products are received, we will deliver the replacements.

If you are requesting a return on behalf of your supplier:

Our supplier of Kleen-All mops (item #448332) has requested return of all unsold mops. Please return any mops you have in stock using the enclosed shipping instructions. We will deliver a similar mop once we receive your return shipment.

E-Mail

Dear Ms. Gonzalez:

Kleen-All Products is planning to replace some of our cleaning supplies that are low sellers with more popular items.

Please respond to this e-mail with your corporation's inventory position and rate of sale on the following items:

- Kleen-All all-purpose cleaner, 10 oz. (item #448359)
- Kleen-All laundry detergent, 3 lb. (item #448343)
- Kleen-All dish soap, 6 oz. (item #4483632)
- Kleen-All heavy-duty cleaner, 2 lb. (item #4483649)
- Kleen-All window washing solution, 8 oz. (item #4483618)

Once I receive that information, I will contact you with details of the replacement. In the meantime, if you have any questions on this planned exchange, please feel free to contact me.

Sincerely,

<e-mail signature, including name, title, company and contact information>

Letter Accompanying Credit Application for New Customer

Purpose

- To outline your requirements for becoming a customer

Alternative Purposes

- To send a credit application after receiving an order
- To ask for business references
- To send a second request for a completed credit application

If you are asking for business references:

When a customer cannot provide adequate information on his or her credit application, we request three business references. Please provide contact information for three of your vendors, including names and phone numbers of individuals within the company.

We will contact your references within 3 days of receiving their contact information, and I will contact you ...

If you are sending a second request for a completed application:

Enclosed please find a second copy of our credit application. Please complete it and return to the address or fax number above so that we can begin doing business. If you have any questions regarding this application, please do not hesitate to call me.

February 18, 2008

William J. Perrin
Director of Operations
Eljay Food Corp.
8328 W. Augusta St.
Atlantic City, NJ 02849

Dear Mr. Perrin:

Thank you for your interest in purchasing Kleen-All Products cleaning supplies for your stores.

We request that all new customers provide some basic financial information. Please complete and fax back the enclosed credit application so that we can begin doing business. I have also enclosed a copy of our latest price list for your records.

We will process your credit application within 3 days of receiving it, and I will contact you to let you know that you can place your first order. Note that Kleen-All Products requires a minimum order of $1,000.

Thank you, and I look forward to working with you.

Sincerely,

J.T. Drummond
Director, Customer Service & Operations

If you have already received an order:

We received your order for Kleen-All Products, but we cannot process it until we get some basic financial information from you. We ask this of all new customers. Please complete ...

E-Mail

Dear Mr. Perrin:

Thank you for your interest in purchasing Kleen-All Products cleaning supplies for your stores.

We request that all new customers provide some basic financial information. Please complete and return the attached PDF of our credit application so that we can begin doing business. I have also attached a PDF of our latest price list.

We will process your credit application within 3 days of receiving it, and I will contact you to let you know that you can place your first order.

Note that Kleen-All Products requires a minimum order of $1,000.

Thank you, and I look forward to working with you.

Sincerely,

<e-mail signature, including name, title, company and contact information>

Letter Requesting Shipping Guidelines

Purpose

- To request a customer's requirements for delivery of merchandise

Alternative Purposes

- To request shipping guidelines after an order has been received
- To request shipping guidelines after an order has been delivered
- To suggest shipping guidelines if the customer has none

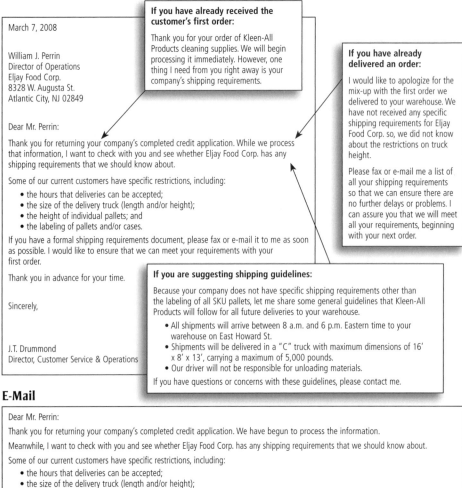

March 7, 2008

William J. Perrin
Director of Operations
Eljay Food Corp.
8328 W. Augusta St.
Atlantic City, NJ 02849

Dear Mr. Perrin:

Thank you for returning your company's completed credit application. While we process that information, I want to check with you and see whether Eljay Food Corp. has any shipping requirements that we should know about.

Some of our current customers have specific restrictions, including:

- the hours that deliveries can be accepted;
- the size of the delivery truck (length and/or height);
- the height of individual pallets; and
- the labeling of pallets and/or cases.

If you have a formal shipping requirements document, please fax or e-mail it to me as soon as possible. I would like to ensure that we can meet your requirements with your first order.

Thank you in advance for your time.

Sincerely,

J.T. Drummond
Director, Customer Service & Operations

If you have already received the customer's first order:

Thank you for your order of Kleen-All Products cleaning supplies. We will begin processing it immediately. However, one thing I need from you right away is your company's shipping requirements.

If you have already delivered an order:

I would like to apologize for the mix-up with the first order we delivered to your warehouse. We have not received any specific shipping requirements for Eljay Food Corp. so, we did not know about the restrictions on truck height.

Please fax or e-mail me a list of all your shipping requirements so that we can ensure there are no further delays or problems. I can assure you that we will meet all your requirements, beginning with your next order.

If you are suggesting shipping guidelines:

Because your company does not have specific shipping requirements other than the labeling of all SKU pallets, let me share some general guidelines that Kleen-All Products will follow for all future deliveries to your warehouse.

- All shipments will arrive between 8 a.m. and 6 p.m. Eastern time to your warehouse on East Howard St.
- Shipments will be delivered in a "C" truck with maximum dimensions of 16' x 8' x 13', carrying a maximum of 5,000 pounds.
- Our driver will not be responsible for unloading materials.

If you have questions or concerns with these guidelines, please contact me.

E-Mail

Dear Mr. Perrin:

Thank you for returning your company's completed credit application. We have begun to process the information.

Meanwhile, I want to check with you and see whether Eljay Food Corp. has any shipping requirements that we should know about.

Some of our current customers have specific restrictions, including:

- the hours that deliveries can be accepted;
- the size of the delivery truck (length and/or height);
- the height of individual pallets; and
- the labeling of pallets and/or cases.

If you have a formal shipping requirements document, please fax or e-mail it to me as soon as possible. I would like to ensure that we can meet your requirements with your first order.

Thank you in advance for your time.

Sincerely,

<e-mail signature, including name, title, company and contact information>

Letter Requesting Proposal/Bid from Vendor

Purpose

- To formally request a proposal on a project from a business or individual

Alternative Purposes

- To request a proposal from a known vendor
- To request a bid or price quote from a vendor
- To request more information and references from a vendor

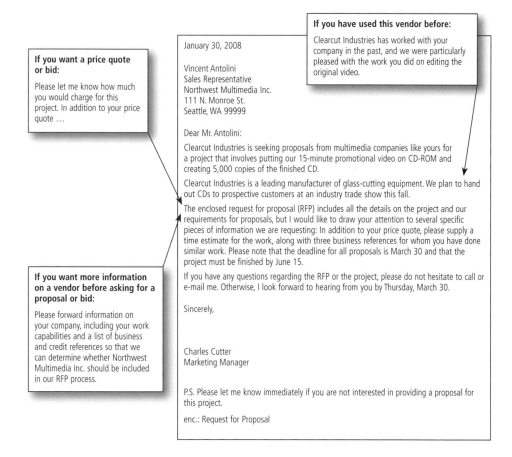

If you have used this vendor before:

Clearcut Industries has worked with your company in the past, and we were particularly pleased with the work you did on editing the original video.

If you want a price quote or bid:

Please let me know how much you would charge for this project. In addition to your price quote …

If you want more information on a vendor before asking for a proposal or bid:

Please forward information on your company, including your work capabilities and a list of business and credit references so that we can determine whether Northwest Multimedia Inc. should be included in our RFP process.

January 30, 2008

Vincent Antolini
Sales Representative
Northwest Multimedia Inc.
111 N. Monroe St.
Seattle, WA 99999

Dear Mr. Antolini:

Clearcut Industries is seeking proposals from multimedia companies like yours for a project that involves putting our 15-minute promotional video on CD-ROM and creating 5,000 copies of the finished CD.

Clearcut Industries is a leading manufacturer of glass-cutting equipment. We plan to hand out CDs to prospective customers at an industry trade show this fall.

The enclosed request for proposal (RFP) includes all the details on the project and our requirements for proposals, but I would like to draw your attention to several specific pieces of information we are requesting: In addition to your price quote, please supply a time estimate for the work, along with three business references for whom you have done similar work. Please note that the deadline for all proposals is March 30 and that the project must be finished by June 15.

If you have any questions regarding the RFP or the project, please do not hesitate to call or e-mail me. Otherwise, I look forward to hearing from you by Thursday, March 30.

Sincerely,

Charles Cutter
Marketing Manager

P.S. Please let me know immediately if you are not interested in providing a proposal for this project.

enc.: Request for Proposal

E-Mail

Dear Mr. Antolini:

Clearcut Industries is seeking proposals for a project that involves putting our 15-minute promotional video on CD-ROM and creating 5,000 copies of the finished CD.

The attached request for proposal (RFP) includes all the details on the project and our requirements for proposals. If you have any questions regarding the RFP or the project, please do not hesitate to contact me. Otherwise, I look forward to hearing from you by Thursday, March 30.

<e-mail signature, including name, title, company and contact information>

Letter Accepting Proposal/Bid from Vendor

Purpose

- To formally accept a proposal from a vendor

Alternative Purposes

- To accept a pricing bid from a vendor
- To introduce a change in the project
- To acknowledge receipt of a proposal

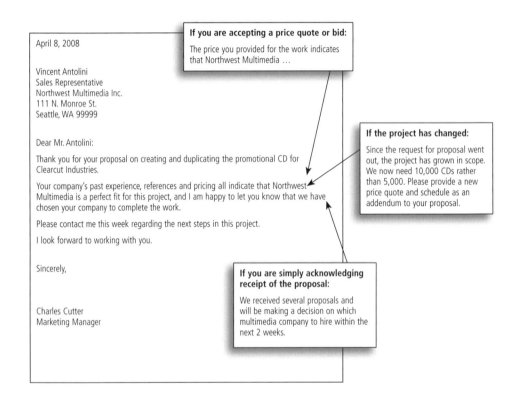

April 8, 2008

Vincent Antolini
Sales Representative
Northwest Multimedia Inc.
111 N. Monroe St.
Seattle, WA 99999

Dear Mr. Antolini:

Thank you for your proposal on creating and duplicating the promotional CD for Clearcut Industries.

Your company's past experience, references and pricing all indicate that Northwest Multimedia is a perfect fit for this project, and I am happy to let you know that we have chosen your company to complete the work.

Please contact me this week regarding the next steps in this project.

I look forward to working with you.

Sincerely,

Charles Cutter
Marketing Manager

If you are accepting a price quote or bid:
The price you provided for the work indicates that Northwest Multimedia …

If the project has changed:
Since the request for proposal went out, the project has grown in scope. We now need 10,000 CDs rather than 5,000. Please provide a new price quote and schedule as an addendum to your proposal.

If you are simply acknowledging receipt of the proposal:
We received several proposals and will be making a decision on which multimedia company to hire within the next 2 weeks.

E-Mail

Dear Mr. Antolini:

Thank you for your proposal on creating and duplicating the promotional CD for Clearcut Industries.

I am happy to let you know that we have chosen your company to complete the work. Please contact me this week regarding the next steps in this project.

I look forward to working with you.

<e-mail signature, including name, title, company and contact information>

Letter Rejecting Proposal/Bid from Vendor

Purpose

- To formally reject a proposal from a vendor

Alternative Purposes

- To reject a pricing bid from a vendor
- To request more information on a proposal
- To announce the termination or postponement of the project

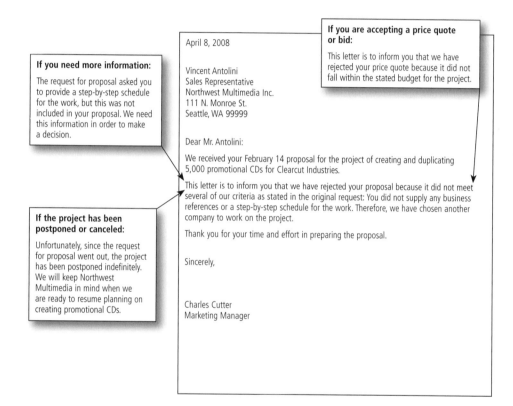

If you need more information:

The request for proposal asked you to provide a step-by-step schedule for the work, but this was not included in your proposal. We need this information in order to make a decision.

If the project has been postponed or canceled:

Unfortunately, since the request for proposal went out, the project has been postponed indefinitely. We will keep Northwest Multimedia in mind when we are ready to resume planning on creating promotional CDs.

If you are accepting a price quote or bid:

This letter is to inform you that we have rejected your price quote because it did not fall within the stated budget for the project.

April 8, 2008

Vincent Antolini
Sales Representative
Northwest Multimedia Inc.
111 N. Monroe St.
Seattle, WA 99999

Dear Mr. Antolini:

We received your February 14 proposal for the project of creating and duplicating 5,000 promotional CDs for Clearcut Industries.

This letter is to inform you that we have rejected your proposal because it did not meet several of our criteria as stated in the original request: You did not supply any business references or a step-by-step schedule for the work. Therefore, we have chosen another company to work on the project.

Thank you for your time and effort in preparing the proposal.

Sincerely,

Charles Cutter
Marketing Manager

E-Mail

Dear Mr. Antolini:

We received your proposal for creating and duplicating 5,000 promotional CDs for Clearcut Industries.

We have rejected your proposal because it did not meet several of our criteria as stated in the original request: You did not supply any business references or a step-by-step schedule for the work.

Thank you for your time and effort in preparing the proposal.

<e-mail signature including name, title, company and contact information>

Friendly Letter Discontinuing Business with Vendor

Purpose

- To formally announce that you are halting business relations with a vendor

Alternative Purposes

- To suspend relations for an indefinite period
- To suggest improvements to a vendor's business
- To offer your name as a reference

March 23, 2008

James T. Grundy
Sales Manager
Corrugated Cardboard Inc.
2950 N. Halsted St.
San Antonio, TX 69219

Dear Mr. Grundy:

As you may have guessed, RF Kind & Sons has been looking for ways to cut costs. One of the areas we have researched is the packaging for our shipments, including the various boxes you supply for us. We have found that we can save considerable money by switching to a new type of bagged packaging, which is available from Taiwan.

We plan to change over to this new packaging as soon as possible. We will order one or two more shipments of your boxes to ensure that our needs are covered until we can make the change, but after that, I regret to say that we will no longer need any of your products.

We have enjoyed a long and satisfactory relationship with Corrugated Cardboard, and I would like to thank you and everyone who has worked on our account for your excellent work. I wish you luck in the future.

Sincerely,

Hannah Evans
Director of Operations

If you are suspending relations for an indefinite period:

We plan to try out this new packaging as soon as possible. We will order one or two more shipments of your boxes to ensure that our needs are covered until we can make the change, and after that, we will perform a test of the new packaging. We will probably end up using a mix of the two; I will contact you when we are ready to begin ordering boxes from you again.

We have enjoyed a long and satisfactory relationship with Corrugated Cardboard, and I would like to thank you and everyone who has worked on our account for your excellent service. Please contact me if you have any questions about this transition.

If you are suggesting improvements:

We plan to change over to this new packaging as soon as possible. However, if you can match the price of the bags on some of your smaller boxes, we might consider using a mix of your boxes and the new packaging. Please contact me if you are interested in discussing this possibility.

If you are offering to serve as a reference:

We have enjoyed a long and satisfactory relationship with Corrugated Cardboard, and I would be happy to give you an excellent reference if you would like. Just let me know if you provide someone with my name so that I can expect his or her call.

Thank you, James, and please thank everyone who has worked on our account for their excellent service. I wish you luck in the future.

E-Mail

Dear Mr. Grundy:

As you may have guessed, RF Kind & Sons has been looking for ways to cut costs. One of the areas we have researched is the packaging for our shipments, including the various boxes you supply for us.

We have found that we can save considerable money by switching to a new type of bagged packaging, which is available from Taiwan.

We plan to change over to this new packaging as soon as possible. We will order one or two more shipments of your boxes to ensure that our needs are covered until we can make the change, but after that, I regret to say that we will no longer need any of your products.

We have enjoyed a long and satisfactory relationship with Corrugated Cardboard, and I would like to thank you and everyone who has worked on our account for your excellent service.

I wish you luck in the future.

Sincerely,

<e-mail signature, including name, title, company and contact information>

Stern Letter Discontinuing Business with Vendor

Purpose

• To formally announce that you are halting business relations with a vendor

Alternative Purposes

• To suspend relations for an indefinite period
• To suggest improvements to a vendor's business
• To threaten to report a vendor to a professional association
  or the Better Business Bureau

If you are suspending relations for an indefinite period:

We were willing to overlook a few errors, but now these errors are beginning to have a negative impact on our business. Therefore, I have decided to find another box supplier for the immediate future.

Please refund the cost of the A boxes that we did not receive and then put our account on hold. Once your warehouse has sorted out this problem, give me a call and we can discuss whether RF Kind & Sons is ready to give your company another chance.

If you are threatening to report the vendor to a professional association:

I have registered an official complaint against Corrugated Cardboard, Inc. with the National Association of Manufacturers and with the National Paperbox Association. I feel strongly that your warehouse cannot continue to miss the obligations set forth in our contract, and I want to make sure that other companies do not suffer from these shipping errors.

March 23, 2008

James T. Grundy
Sales Manager
Corrugated Cardboard Inc.
2950 N. Halsted St.
San Antonio, TX 69219

Dear Mr. Grundy:

As you are aware, I have registered several complaints about incomplete shipments from Corrugated Cardboard in the past 4 months.

Our latest shipment (order #59238502) arrived at our warehouse yesterday and it too was incomplete. We received only the size B boxes and now have to postpone several shipments of our own due to the missing A boxes.

We were willing to overlook a few errors, but now these errors are beginning to have a negative impact on our business. Therefore, I have decided to find another box supplier. We will not be ordering from Corrugated Cardboard again, effective today.

Please refund the cost of the A boxes that we did not receive and then close our account.

Sincerely,

Hannah Evans
Director of Operations

If you are suggesting improvements:

Based on my own experience as a director of operations, I would like to recommend that your warehouse hire a quality-improvement consultant to help find a solution for this ongoing problem.

Meanwhile, because your company's shipping errors are beginning to have a negative impact on our business, I have decided to find another box supplier. We will not be ordering from Corrugated Cardboard again, effective today. Please refund the cost of the A boxes that we did not receive and then close our account.

E-Mail

Dear Mr. Grundy:

As you are aware, I have registered several complaints about incomplete shipments from Corrugated Cardboard in the past 4 months.

Our latest shipment (order #59238502) arrived at our warehouse yesterday, and it too was incomplete. We received only the size B boxes and now have to postpone several shipments of our own due to the missing A boxes.

We were willing to overlook a few errors, but now these errors are beginning to have a negative impact on our business.

Therefore, I have decided to find another box supplier. We will not be ordering from Corrugated Cardboard again, effective immediately.

Please refund the cost of the A boxes that we did not receive and then close our account.

Sincerely,

<e-mail signature, including name, title, company and contact information>

Letter Accompanying Contract for Vendor

Purpose

- To emphasize and outline information in a new vendor contract

Alternative Purposes

- To introduce a replacement for an expired contract
- To introduce a revised contract
- To request more information before signing a contract

If you are introducing a replacement for an expired contract:

Our contract for receiving your products will expire next month. Enclosed please find a new contract for 2008-2009 that continues the terms of our agreement for LKW Plastics to supply assorted products, including valves, hoses and other parts, to Granger Assembly National.

This is the same basic contract that currently exists between our companies. Please review the contract, sign both copies and return one to me at the above address.

January 19, 2008

Barbara L. Lincoln
Director of Operations
LKW Plastics Inc.
6213 W. 18th St.
Duluth, MN 69210

Dear Mrs. Lincoln:

Enclosed please find a contract that outlines the terms of our agreement for LKW Plastics to supply assorted products, including valves, hoses and other parts, to Granger Assembly National.

This is our standard contract for all regular vendors and includes our guidelines for delivery, payment terms and contingency plans for special orders. Please review the contract, sign both copies and return one to me at the above address.

If you have any questions on the information contained in the contract, please contact me and I will do my best to answer them.

I look forward to doing business with you.

Sincerely,

Ed Lee
Manager of Midwest Customer Service & Operations

If you are introducing a revised contract:

Please replace the contract I sent previously with the one enclosed. The original contract did not include the payment terms we discussed over the phone; this draft is identical to the first except for those terms, which are outlined in section III.

Please review the contract, sign both copies and return one to me at the above address.

If you are requesting more information:

This is our standard contract for all regular vendors and includes our guidelines for delivery, payment terms and contingency plans for special orders. Please review the contract, sign both copies and return both to me at the above address.

Before I sign this contract, I need a completed copy of the credit application, that I sent you earlier this month. Please return that form with the contracts, and after we review your information, I will send a signed contract back to you.

E-Mail

Dear Mrs. Lincoln:

Attached please find a PDF of a contract that outlines the terms of our agreement for LKW Plastics to supply assorted products, including valves, hoses and other parts, to Granger Assembly National.

This is our standard contract for all regular vendors and includes our guidelines for delivery, payment terms and contingency plans for special orders. Please print out and review the contract, sign both copies and mail one to me at the address below.

If you have any questions on the information contained in the contract, please contact me and I will do my best to answer them.

I look forward to doing business with you.

Sincerely,

<e-mail signature, including name, title, company and contact information>

Letter Announcing Change in Shipping Address

Purpose

- To let vendors know of a change in your shipping address

Alternative Purposes

- To let vendors know of a change in your front office address
- To announce the opening of an additional warehouse
- To schedule deliveries that fall during a warehouse move

If you are announcing an additional new warehouse:

As of May 1, 2008, Granger Assembly National is adding a new warehouse space to our Midwest region. We ask that, beginning with that date, LKW Plastics deliver all shipments to:

<insert address and second paragraph>

Please make sure that all your drivers, delivery companies and other relevant personnel and vendors are aware of this change of address.

If you are requesting the scheduling of deliveries on or around your warehouse move:

If you have any long-distance deliveries that are estimated to arrive between April 25 and May 1, I ask that you contact me directly to schedule a specific date and location for the delivery.

If you are announcing a change in your front office address:

As of May 1, 2008, the headquarters of Granger Assembly National will move to:

Granger Assembly National
762 Harlem Ave.
Kansas City, MO 48210

Our warehouse location will not change, nor will any telephone numbers or e-mail addresses.

March 2, 2008

Barbara L. Lincoln
Director of Operations
LKW Plastics Inc.
6213 W. 18th St.
Duluth, MN 69210

Dear Mrs. Lincoln:

As of May 1, 2008, Granger Assembly National will move its warehouse facilities to a new address. As of that date, please deliver all shipments to:

Granger Assembly National
Docks 1 – 5
55902 Commercial Drive
Kansas City, MO 48210

Our shipping guidelines will remain the same except for this address change, and our telephone numbers and e-mail addresses will not change. Also, please note that our main office address and contact information will stay the same; you can continue to send your bills and other office correspondence as usual.

Please make sure that all your drivers, delivery companies and other relevant personnel and vendors are aware of this change of address. We will vacate the current warehouse over the weekend of April 30-May 1, and no Granger shipments will be received there after close of business on Saturday, April 30.

Thank you.

Sincerely,

Ed Lee
Manager of Midwest Customer Service & Operations

E-Mail

Dear Mrs. Lincoln:

As of May 1, 2008, Granger Assembly National will move its warehouse facilities to a new address. As of that date, please deliver all shipments to:

Granger Assembly National Warehouse
55902 Commercial Drive
Kansas City, MO 48210

Our shipping guidelines will remain the same except for this address change, and our telephone numbers and e-mail addresses will not change.

Also, please note that our main office address and contact information will stay the same; you can continue to send your bills and other office correspondence as usual.

Please make sure that all your drivers, delivery companies and other relevant personnel and vendors are aware of this change of address. We will vacate the current warehouse over the weekend of April 30-May 1, and no Granger shipments will be received there after close of business on Saturday, April 30.

Thank you.

Sincerely,

<e-mail signature, including name, title, company and contact information>

Letter Announcing Change of Contact for Accounting Department

Purpose

- To formally introduce vendors to a new contact for billing and accounting

Alternative Purposes

- To introduce vendors to a new warehouse manager
- To announce a new lockbox address for invoices and billing
- To announce new payment terms for vendors

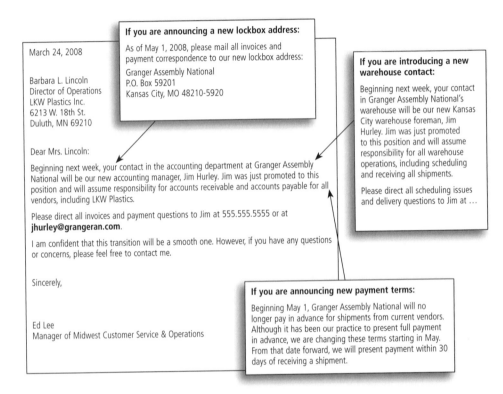

If you are announcing a new lockbox address:

As of May 1, 2008, please mail all invoices and payment correspondence to our new lockbox address:

Granger Assembly National
P.O. Box 59201
Kansas City, MO 48210-5920

If you are introducing a new warehouse contact:

Beginning next week, your contact in Granger Assembly National's warehouse will be our new Kansas City warehouse foreman, Jim Hurley. Jim was just promoted to this position and will assume responsibility for all warehouse operations, including scheduling and receiving all shipments.

Please direct all scheduling issues and delivery questions to Jim at …

March 24, 2008

Barbara L. Lincoln
Director of Operations
LKW Plastics Inc.
6213 W. 18th St.
Duluth, MN 69210

Dear Mrs. Lincoln:

Beginning next week, your contact in the accounting department at Granger Assembly National will be our new accounting manager, Jim Hurley. Jim was just promoted to this position and will assume responsibility for accounts receivable and accounts payable for all vendors, including LKW Plastics.

Please direct all invoices and payment questions to Jim at 555.555.5555 or at **jhurley@grangeran.com**.

I am confident that this transition will be a smooth one. However, if you have any questions or concerns, please feel free to contact me.

Sincerely,

Ed Lee
Manager of Midwest Customer Service & Operations

If you are announcing new payment terms:

Beginning May 1, Granger Assembly National will no longer pay in advance for shipments from current vendors. Although it has been our practice to present full payment in advance, we are changing these terms starting in May. From that date forward, we will present payment within 30 days of receiving a shipment.

E-Mail

Dear Mrs. Lincoln:

Beginning next week, your contact in the accounting department at Granger Assembly National will be our new accounting manager, Jim Hurley.

Jim was just promoted to this position and will assume responsibility for accounts receivable and accounts payable for all vendors, including LKW Plastics.

Please direct all invoices and payment questions to Jim at 555.555.5555 or at **jhurley@grangeran.com**.

I am confident that this transition will be a smooth one. However, if you have any questions or concerns, please feel free to contact me.

Sincerely,

<e-mail signature, including name, title, company and contact information>

Letter Announcing Temporary Closing of Warehouse Due to Inventory

Purpose

- To inform vendors that your warehouse will be temporarily closed for inventory

Alternative Purposes

- To note that you will be returning merchandise by a specific date
- To request confirmation of merchandise received
- To request confirmation of a product count

If you are returning merchandise before inventory:

In the next 2 weeks, we will be examining all SKUs currently in the warehouse and will return any unopened merchandise that we deem unusable or unnecessary, using the process set forth by each vendor. I may be contacting you for an RMA number in the next few days.

If you are requesting confirmation of a specific shipment or product line:

To help us arrive at an accurate count during inventory, please confirm that your upcoming shipment that fulfills our order #93458 contains 12 pallets of 12-gauge hose and three pallets of 0.125-millimeter valves. I have entered these amounts into our computer system and need confirmation within the next week.

February 19, 2008

Barbara L. Lincoln
Director of Operations
LKW Plastics Inc.
6213 W. 18th St.
Duluth, MN 69210

Dear Mrs. Lincoln:

Every spring, Granger Assembly National closes its warehouses for a complete inventory of its stock.

This year, we will close our Kansas City warehouse beginning Wednesday, April 13 and reopen our doors on Monday, April 18. Please note that we will not accept any deliveries during this time.

As we get closer to this inventory period, I will contact you directly regarding any shipments that may be scheduled to arrive between these dates to discuss alternatives.

Please note that I will be checking voice mail and e-mail during inventory but may not be immediately available.

Sincerely,

Ed Lee
Manager of Midwest Customer Service & Operations

If you are requesting confirmation of a product count:

I have found a discrepancy between your order form and your catalog.

To help us arrive at an accurate count during inventory, please confirm that one pallet of your 12-gauge hose contains 2,500 individual hoses.

E-Mail

Dear Mrs. Lincoln:

Every spring, Granger Assembly National closes its warehouses for a complete inventory of its stock.

This year, we will close our Kansas City warehouse beginning Wednesday, April 13 and reopen our doors on Monday, April 18.

Please note that we will not accept any deliveries during this time.

I will contact you directly regarding any shipments that may be scheduled to arrive between these dates to discuss alternatives.

Please note that I will check voice mail and e-mail during inventory, but may not be immediately available.

Sincerely,

<e-mail signature, including name, title, company and contact information>

Letter Requesting Information from Vendor on Back Order

Purpose

- To formally request an update on an order that is on hold or incomplete

Alternative Purposes

- To follow up on a continued back order
- To follow up on a partial shipment
- To cancel an order due to a back order

If you are following up on a partial shipment:

The last shipment that Granger Assembly National received from your company (order #93458) did not include three pallets of 0.125-millimeter valves, which have apparently been placed on indefinite back order. I am concerned about the lack of specific information on when we will receive these products and need more information.

March 22, 2008

Barbara L. Lincoln
Director of Operations
LKW Plastics Inc.
6213 W. 18th St.
Duluth, MN 69210

Dear Mrs. Lincoln:

I received notification that Granger Assembly National's order #93458 for 12 pallets of 12-gauge hose and three pallets of 0.125-millimeter valves has been placed on indefinite back order. I am concerned about the lack of specific information on when we will receive these products and need more information.

Please complete the enclosed Vendor Back Order Form, supplying all information on expected delivery of the products. Also, please note that as spelled out in our contract, Granger Assembly National has the right to cancel this order at any time if the information you provide is not acceptable to our delivery needs.

Thank you in advance for your prompt reply.

Sincerely,

Ed Lee
Manager of Midwest Customer Service & Operations

If you are following up on a continued back order:

Thank you for your prompt response to my questions regarding the back order of items on our order #93458. I sincerely hope that you can expedite this order to your best abilities. Please contact me as soon as you have an estimated delivery date for all items ordered.

I will call you directly if I have not heard from you by March 31.

If you are canceling an order due to a back order:

I received notification that Granger Assembly National's order #93458 for 12 pallets of 12-gauge hose and three pallets of 0.125-millimeter valves has been placed on indefinite back order. If you cannot personally guarantee that these items will be delivered and in our possession by the end of this month, I would like to cancel this order and receive a full refund.

E-Mail

Dear Mrs. Lincoln:

I received your notification that Granger Assembly National's order #93458 has been placed on indefinite back order.

I am concerned about the lack of specific information on when we will receive these products and need more information.

Please complete and return the attached PDF of our Vendor Back Order Form, supplying all information on expected delivery of the products.

Also, please note that as spelled out in our contract, Granger Assembly National has the right to cancel this order at any time if the information you provide is not acceptable to our delivery needs.

Thank you in advance for your prompt reply.

Sincerely,

<e-mail signature, including name, title, company and contact information>

Friendly Letter Questioning a Charge

Purpose

- To question a vendor about an unwarranted bill or charge

Alternative Purposes

- To request detailed information on billing history
- To request a credit on an overpayment
- To check the status of an order

If you are checking the status of an order:

This week, I received an All-Coil bill for an order of 3-inch coils that totals $2,460. I cannot find our corresponding purchase order for these materials and have no record of receiving them.

We did, however, order 2,000 5-inch coils (item #KR-4585), which we have not yet received. If this charge is, in fact, for our outstanding order, please check your records and let me know when we can expect delivery.

If you are requesting a credit on an overpayment:

Our accounting department paid a recent bill for an order of 3-inch coils that totals $2,460. I cannot find our corresponding purchase order for these materials and have no record of receiving them. Please credit our account for this amount and send me an updated statement.

If you have any question or concern regarding this overpayment, please let me know.

January 7, 2008

Manuel Matamoros
Operations Manager
All-Coil
6401 Damen Ave.
Omaha, NE 49204

Dear Mr. Matamoros:

I am writing to ask you to help me sort out some confusion over payments due to your company.

This week, I received an All-Coil bill for an order of 3-inch coils that totals $2,460. I cannot find our corresponding purchase order for these materials and have no record of receiving them. It is possible that these items were back ordered and were part of a larger order, but I cannot find any evidence that we owe you payment on shipments received last year.

Please check your records of this payment and let me know if this invoice is viable. If so, I will need copies of the appropriate purchase order or order form and the packing slip.

Thank you in advance for your help.

Sincerely,

Ed Lee
Manager of Midwest Customer Service & Operations

If you are requesting more information on billing history:

I would appreciate it if you would retrieve copies of all of our purchase orders and payment history for the last half of 2007 and forward those to me. I would like to make sure that we are in agreement regarding payments due from this point forward.

E-Mail

Dear Mr. Matamoros:

Regarding your message with the attached bill, I cannot find our corresponding purchase order for these materials and have no record of receiving them.

It is possible that these items were back ordered, and were part of a larger order, but I cannot find any evidence that we owe you payment on shipments received last year.

Please check your records of this payment and let me know if this invoice is viable. If so, I will need copies of the appropriate purchase order or order form and the packing slip.

Thank you in advance for your help.

Sincerely,

<e-mail signature, including name, title, company and contact information>

Stern Letter Disputing a Charge

Purpose

- To alert a vendor to an unwarranted bill or charge and demand resolution

Alternative Purposes

- To request detailed information on billing history
- To request a credit on an overpayment
- To cancel business relations

January 7, 2008

Manuel Matamoros
Operations Manager
All-Coil
6401 Damen Ave.
Omaha, NE 49204

Dear Mr. Matamoros:

There is a serious problem with your invoice system that needs to be addressed immediately.

This week I received an All-Coil bill for an order of 3-inch coils that totals $2,460. We never issued a purchase order for these materials and have no record of receiving them.

I have no intention of paying this bill, which was issued by your accounting department on January 5. In fact, I plan to pull your previous invoices to make sure that we received everything that we have paid for to date.

Please rectify the situation with this unwarranted invoice immediately. I will watch for your reply with your assurance that this invoice has been voided and that this will not happen again.

Sincerely,

Ed Lee
Manager of Midwest Customer Service & Operations

If you are requesting a credit on an overpayment:

Our accounting department paid a recent bill for an order of 3-inch coils that totals $2,460. However, we never issued a purchase order for these materials and have no record of receiving them.

I am requesting an immediate full credit to our account. I will watch for your reply with your assurance that this credit has been applied and that this will not happen again.

If you are requesting more information on billing history:

… everything that we have paid for to date. Please forward copies of all our purchase orders and payment history for the last half of 2007 so that I can compare our records with yours.

If you are canceling business relations:

As of today, I am dropping All-Coil from our list of approved vendors, and we will terminate all business with you. We simply cannot check every invoice for accuracy.

E-Mail

Dear Mr. Matamoros:

The bill that you attached in your message reveals a serious problem with your invoice system that needs to be addressed immediately.

We never issued a purchase order for the materials billed and have no record of receiving them.

I have no intention of paying this bill. In fact, I plan to pull your previous invoices to make sure that we received everything that we have paid for to date.

Please rectify the situation with this unwarranted invoice immediately.

I will watch for your reply with your assurance that this invoice has been voided and that this will not happen again.

Sincerely,

<e-mail signature, including name, title, company and contact information>

Notification of Upcoming Large or Special Order

Purpose

- To warn a vendor that you will be placing an unusually large or otherwise special order

Alternative Purposes

- To ask a vendor whether it can handle a special order
- To ask a vendor for expedited shipping
- To ask a vendor for special payment terms

If you are asking a vendor if it can handle a special order:

We need a vendor who can supply us with a valve identical to the 0.125-millimeter valve that LKW Plastics manufactures, but we need it in an unusual size: 0.133 millimeters. If your company has the capability to produce these valves, we can guarantee an order of at least five gross of them. Perhaps you can discuss this with your engineers and find out whether your shop can create this size valve.

If you are asking a vendor for special payment terms:

We would like to rely on LKW Plastics to provide all our hoses and valves for this contract, which will total nearly $80,000 of business this year. I believe that this increased volume will make Granger Assembly National one of your largest customers; therefore, I propose that we begin paying by an invoice system, rather than paying 100 percent in advance, beginning with our first order.

January 13, 2008

Barbara L. Lincoln
Director of Operations
LKW Plastics Inc.
6213 W. 18th St.
Duluth, MN 69210

Dear Mrs. Lincoln:

Granger Assembly National just received a large contract, and we will be increasing our production output as soon as we can procure the staff and other necessary resources.

As soon as I obtain approval from our vice president of operations, I will be placing an order for five gross of your 12-gauge hose pieces and seven gross of your 0.125-millimeter valves. I realize that this order is substantially larger than our usual requests, and, therefore, would like to ensure that LKW Plastics can supply these quantities.

Please contact me as soon as you have the necessary information so that we can discuss the logistics of this upcoming order.

Thank you in advance for your prompt reply.

Sincerely,

Ed Lee
Manager of Midwest Customer Service & Operations

If you are asking a vendor if it can handle expedited shipping:

As soon as I obtain approval, I will forward a purchase order for 12 pallets of 12-gauge hose and three pallets of 0.125-millimeter valves. However, we must receive delivery of these items by the end of this month. I am giving you this advance warning in the hope that you can reserve these items for us and ship them as soon as you receive the purchase order, which I expect to provide you with next week.

E-Mail

Dear Mrs. Lincoln:

Granger Assembly National just received a large contract, and we will be increasing our production output as soon as we can procure the staff and other necessary resources.

As soon as I obtain approval from our vice president of operations, I will be placing an order for five gross of your 12-gauge hose pieces and seven gross of your 0.125-millimeter valves.

I realize that this order is substantially larger than our usual requests, and, therefore, would like to ensure that LKW Plastics can supply these quantities.

Please contact me as soon as you have the necessary information so that we can discuss the logistics of this upcoming order.

Thank you in advance for your prompt reply.

Sincerely,

<e-mail signature, including name, title, company and contact information>

Letter Outlining Delivery Specifications

Purpose

- To inform a new vendor of your company's guidelines or specifications for delivery of shipments

Alternative Purposes

- To alert a vendor of a change or update to existing delivery specifications
- To let a vendor know that it has not followed your delivery specifications
- To warn a vendor that it will be fined for noncompliance with your specifications

January 13, 2008

Barbara L. Lincoln
Director of Operations
LKW Plastics Inc.
6213 W. 18th St.
Duluth, MN 69210

Dear Mrs. Lincoln:

I will be your contact for matters related to the delivery of goods to Granger Assembly National and my department here in Kansas City will handle all your shipments.

I have enclosed a copy of our delivery specifications, which are also available in the vendor section of our Web site at **www.grangeran.com/vendors.html**. We ask that all vendors adhere to each stated requirement in the document, paying particular attention to our requirements for pallet height and noncompliance fees, which are found in Section Two.

Also, please note that we have listed three preferred carriers for deliveries. If you choose to use a carrier that is not listed here, you may do so, but Granger Assembly National will not pay for the use of an outside carrier. We also do not accept cash on delivery (c.o.d.).

Please review all the delivery specifications and let me know if you have any questions or concerns.

Sincerely,

Ed Lee
Manager of Midwest Customer
Service & Operations

If you are addressing a vendor who has not followed your delivery specifications:

My warehouse manager reported that the LKW Plastics shipment we received on January 10 did not meet our delivery specifications. These specifications include guidelines for the type and size of pallets, which your delivery did not follow.

I have enclosed a copy of our delivery specifications for your review. We ask that all vendors ...

If you are alerting a vendor to a change in your delivery specifications:

Please note that Granger Assembly National has updated its delivery specifications for vendors. These changes are effective immediately.

I have enclosed a copy of the new delivery specifications, which are also available in the vendor section of our Web site at **www.grangeran.com/vendors.html**. We ask that all vendors adhere to each stated requirement in the document, paying particular attention to our new requirements for pallet height, which are found in Section Two. Pallet height limits were previously 53 inches for single-SKU pallets, and 72 inches for mixed-SKU pallets. As of January 5, the height limit for all pallets is 84 inches.

If you are warning a vendor that it will be fined for noncompliance:

My warehouse manager reported that the LKW Plastics shipment we received on January 10 did not meet our delivery specifications. These specifications include guidelines for the type and size of pallets, which your delivery did not follow. This noncompliance resulted in extra time and effort in unloading and storing your pallets; therefore, the standard noncompliance fee of $400 per pallet, or a total of $6,000, will be billed to your company.

I have enclosed a copy of our delivery specifications for your review. We ask that all vendors ...

E-Mail

Dear Mrs. Lincoln:

Let me introduce myself: I will be your contact for matters related to the delivery of goods to Granger Assembly National, and my department here in Kansas City will handle all your shipments.

I have attached a PDF of our delivery specifications, which are also available at **www.grangeran.com/vendors.html**.

We ask that all vendors adhere to each stated requirement in the document, paying particular attention to our requirements for pallet height and noncompliance fees, which are found in Section Two.

Also, please note that we have listed three preferred carriers for deliveries. If you choose to use a carrier that is not listed here, you may do so, but Granger Assembly National will not pay for the use of an outside carrier. We also do not accept cash on delivery (c.o.d.) deliveries.

Please review all the delivery specifications and respond to this e-mail if you have any questions or concerns.

Sincerely,

<e-mail signature, including name, title, company and contact information>

Letter Notifying Vendor of Partial Shipment Received

Purpose

- To inform a vendor that an order was only partially filled

Alternative Purposes

- To demand an explanation for the missing materials
- To request more information on a back order
- To request a credit for the missing materials

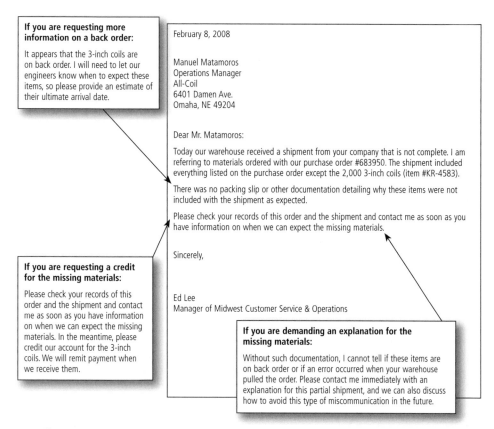

If you are requesting more information on a back order:

It appears that the 3-inch coils are on back order. I will need to let our engineers know when to expect these items, so please provide an estimate of their ultimate arrival date.

February 8, 2008

Manuel Matamoros
Operations Manager
All-Coil
6401 Damen Ave.
Omaha, NE 49204

Dear Mr. Matamoros:

Today our warehouse received a shipment from your company that is not complete. I am referring to materials ordered with our purchase order #683950. The shipment included everything listed on the purchase order except the 2,000 3-inch coils (item #KR-4583).

There was no packing slip or other documentation detailing why these items were not included with the shipment as expected.

Please check your records of this order and the shipment and contact me as soon as you have information on when we can expect the missing materials.

Sincerely,

Ed Lee
Manager of Midwest Customer Service & Operations

If you are requesting a credit for the missing materials:

Please check your records of this order and the shipment and contact me as soon as you have information on when we can expect the missing materials. In the meantime, please credit our account for the 3-inch coils. We will remit payment when we receive them.

If you are demanding an explanation for the missing materials:

Without such documentation, I cannot tell if these items are on back order or if an error occurred when your warehouse pulled the order. Please contact me immediately with an explanation for this partial shipment, and we can also discuss how to avoid this type of miscommunication in the future.

E-Mail

Dear Mr. Matamoros:

Today our warehouse received a shipment from your company that is not complete.

I am referring to materials ordered with our purchase order #683950. The shipment included everything listed on the purchase order except the 2,000 3-inch coils (item #KR-4583).

There was no packing slip or other documentation detailing why these items were not included with the shipment as expected.

Please check your records of this order and the shipment and reply to this e-mail as soon as you have information on when we can expect the missing materials.

Sincerely,

<e-mail signature, including name, title, company and contact information>

Letter Notifying Vendor of a Wrong Shipment Received

Purpose

- To inform a vendor that a shipment was received in error

Alternative Purposes

- To demand an explanation for the shipment
- To request more information on the correct shipment
- To insist on keeping the shipment until the correct goods are received

February 8, 2008

Manuel Matamoros
Operations Manager
All-Coil
6401 Damen Ave.
Omaha, NE 49204

Dear Mr. Matamoros:

We have received a shipment from your company that does not correlate with our last order.

I have enclosed a copy of our latest purchase order (#683950). Shipment of this order should have been due this week. However, the delivery we received does not match the list of items on the purchase order; in fact, it is so different from our order that I wonder whether we received the wrong shipment altogether.

Please compare the purchase order with the packing slip, which I have also enclosed. Then, when you have traced the problem, please contact me and let me know when we can expect our correct shipment, and when and how you would like to retrieve the materials currently in our possession.

Sincerely,

Ed Lee
Manager of Midwest Customer Service & Operations

If you are demanding an explanation for the wrong shipment:

Please compare the purchase order with the packing slip, which I have also enclosed. Then, when you have traced the problem, please contact me and let me know how this error occurred. I am concerned about the mix-up and specifically would like to know what has happened to the delivery of our ordered materials.

If you are requesting more information on the shipment:

Please compare the purchase order with the packing slip, which I have also enclosed. Is this supposed to have been our shipment of materials? Should we keep those items that match our current order? I will do whatever it takes to get the correct items in-house as quickly as possible, but I would like your advice on this.

If you are insisting on keeping the shipment until the correct goods are received:

I will keep this entire shipment in my possession until the correct materials are delivered and checked. Once we have received our complete order, we can make arrangements for your carrier to pick up the materials we received this week.

E-Mail

Dear Mr. Matamoros:

We have received a shipment from your company that does not correlate with our last order.

I have attached a PDF of our latest purchase order (#683950). Shipment of this order should have been due this week. However, the delivery we received does not match the list of items on the purchase order; in fact, it is so different from our order that I wonder whether we received the wrong shipment altogether.

Please compare the purchase order with the packing slip, which I have also attached.

Then, when you have traced the problem, please contact me and let me know when we can expect our correct shipment, and when and how you would like to retrieve the materials currently in our possession.

Sincerely,

<e-mail signature, including name, title, company and contact information>

Letter Notifying Vendor of a Shipment Not Received

Purpose

- To inform a vendor that you have not received a scheduled shipment

Alternative Purposes

- To demand an explanation for the missed shipment
- To request a delay of payment for the materials in the missed shipment
- To cancel the original order

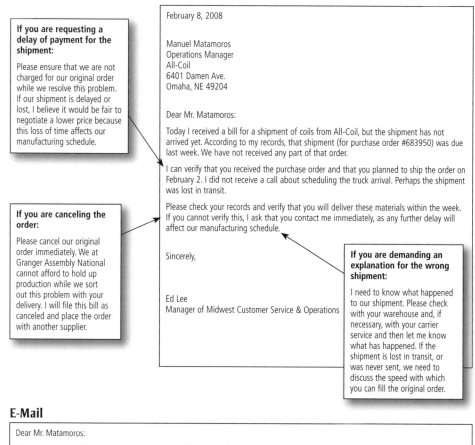

If you are requesting a delay of payment for the shipment:

Please ensure that we are not charged for our original order while we resolve this problem. If our shipment is delayed or lost, I believe it would be fair to negotiate a lower price because this loss of time affects our manufacturing schedule.

If you are canceling the order:

Please cancel our original order immediately. We at Granger Assembly National cannot afford to hold up production while we sort out this problem with your delivery. I will file this bill as canceled and place the order with another supplier.

February 8, 2008

Manuel Matamoros
Operations Manager
All-Coil
6401 Damen Ave.
Omaha, NE 49204

Dear Mr. Matamoros:

Today I received a bill for a shipment of coils from All-Coil, but the shipment has not arrived yet. According to my records, that shipment (for purchase order #683950) was due last week. We have not received any part of that order.

I can verify that you received the purchase order and that you planned to ship the order on February 2. I did not receive a call about scheduling the truck arrival. Perhaps the shipment was lost in transit.

Please check your records and verify that you will deliver these materials within the week. If you cannot verify this, I ask that you contact me immediately, as any further delay will affect our manufacturing schedule.

Sincerely,

Ed Lee
Manager of Midwest Customer Service & Operations

If you are demanding an explanation for the wrong shipment:

I need to know what happened to our shipment. Please check with your warehouse and, if necessary, with your carrier service and then let me know what has happened. If the shipment is lost in transit, or was never sent, we need to discuss the speed with which you can fill the original order.

E-Mail

Dear Mr. Matamoros:

Today I received a bill for a shipment of coils from All-Coil, but the shipment has not arrived yet.

According to my records, that shipment (for purchase order #683950) was due last week. We have not received any part of that order.

This e-mail chain verifies that you received the purchase order and that you planned to ship the order on February 2. However, I did not receive a call about scheduling the truck arrival. Perhaps the shipment was lost in transit.

Please check your records and verify that you will deliver these materials within the week.

If you cannot verify this, I ask that you contact me immediately, as any further delay will affect our manufacturing schedule.

Sincerely,

<e-mail signature, including name, title, company and contact information>

Letter Accompanying Requirements for Child Labor/Illegal Alien Documentation

Purpose

- To formally request documentation from a vendor that is necessary to the legality or bylaws of your company

Alternative Purposes

- To request documentation assuring that the vendor does not employ illegal aliens
- To request affirmation of compliance with specific guidelines
- To follow up on an unanswered request for documentation

February 25, 2008

Manuel Matamoros
Operations Manager
All-Coil
6401 Damen Ave.
Omaha, NE 49204

Dear Mr. Matamoros:

Enclosed please find a copy of our "Global Market Employment Practices." We send this to all of our vendors to ascertain that each company is in compliance with our mission statement, which supports the rights of all workers and other individuals to a safe workplace, fair wages and respectful treatment. This includes compliance with child labor laws and ensuring a diversified work force.

Please review the document and, when you are ready, sign it and return the original to me. We need to receive this by March 15 in order to continue to do business with All-Coil. If you cannot personally verify that your company's various locations meet these legal and ethical standards, perhaps you can forward this document on to the appropriate person.

Thank you in advance for your time in providing this verification.

Sincerely,

Ed Lee
Manager of Midwest Customer Service & Operations

If you are requesting affirmation of compliance with specific guidelines:

Enclosed please find a copy of our "Employment Practices Guidelines," which outlines the hiring and work practices that our vendors must follow in order to support our eligibility for federal funds. We send this to all of our vendors to ascertain that each company is in compliance with our mission statement, which supports the rights of all workers and other individuals to a safe workplace, fair wages and respectful treatment.

If you are following up on your initial request for documentation:

Last month I sent you our "Global Market Employment Practices" and requested the return of a signed copy. I have not heard from you and am concerned that your lack of response may affect my company's ability to order from All-Coil.

I have enclosed another copy of the document. Please review it and, when you are ready …

If you are seeking assurance that the vendor does not employ illegal aliens:

Enclosed please find a copy of our "Employment Practices Verification" guidelines. We send this to all of our vendors to ascertain that each company is in compliance with U.S. law regarding the employment of illegal aliens.

Please review the document and, when you are ready, sign it and return the original to me. We need to receive this by March 15 in order to continue to do business with All-Coil. If you cannot personally verify that your company does not employ illegal workers, perhaps you can forward this document on to the appropriate person.

E-Mail

Dear Mr. Matamoros:

Attached please find a PDF of our "Global Market Employment Practices." We send this to all of our vendors to ascertain that each company is in compliance with our mission statement, which supports the rights of all workers and other individuals to a safe workplace, fair wages and respectful treatment. This includes compliance with child labor laws and ensuring a diversified work force.

Please review the document and, when you are ready, sign it and mail the original to me.

We need to receive this by March 15 in order to continue to do business with All-Coil.

If you cannot personally verify that your company's various locations meet these legal and ethical standards, perhaps you can forward this document on to the appropriate person.

Thank you in advance for your time in providing this verification.

Sincerely,

<e-mail signature, including name, title, company and contact information>

Letter Responding to Customer Complaint about Product

Purpose

- To formally respond to a customer complaint about one or more products

Alternative Purposes

- To explain why the complaint was unwarranted
- To take the blame for a faulty product
- To outline what action is being taken to address the complaint

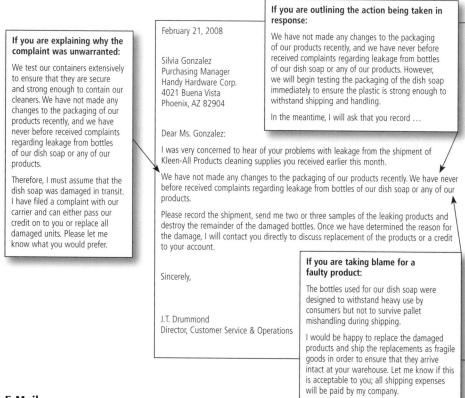

If you are explaining why the complaint was unwarranted:

We test our containers extensively to ensure that they are secure and strong enough to contain our cleaners. We have not made any changes to the packaging of our products recently, and we have never before received complaints regarding leakage from bottles of our dish soap or any of our products.

Therefore, I must assume that the dish soap was damaged in transit. I have filed a complaint with our carrier and can either pass our credit on to you or replace all damaged units. Please let me know what you would prefer.

If you are outlining the action being taken in response:

We have not made any changes to the packaging of our products recently, and we have never before received complaints regarding leakage from bottles of our dish soap or any of our products. However, we will begin testing the packaging of the dish soap immediately to ensure the plastic is strong enough to withstand shipping and handling.

In the meantime, I will ask that you record …

February 21, 2008

Silvia Gonzalez
Purchasing Manager
Handy Hardware Corp.
4021 Buena Vista
Phoenix, AZ 82904

Dear Ms. Gonzalez:

I was very concerned to hear of your problems with leakage from the shipment of Kleen-All Products cleaning supplies you received earlier this month.

We have not made any changes to the packaging of our products recently. We have never before received complaints regarding leakage from bottles of our dish soap or any of our products.

Please record the shipment, send me two or three samples of the leaking products and destroy the remainder of the damaged bottles. Once we have determined the reason for the damage, I will contact you directly to discuss replacement of the products or a credit to your account.

Sincerely,

J.T. Drummond
Director, Customer Service & Operations

If you are taking blame for a faulty product:

The bottles used for our dish soap were designed to withstand heavy use by consumers but not to survive pallet mishandling during shipping.

I would be happy to replace the damaged products and ship the replacements as fragile goods in order to ensure that they arrive intact at your warehouse. Let me know if this is acceptable to you; all shipping expenses will be paid by my company.

E-Mail

Dear Ms. Gonzalez:

I am very concerned about your problems with leakage from the Kleen-All Products cleaning supplies you received.

We have not made any changes to the packaging of our products recently, and we have never before received complaints regarding leakage from bottles of our dish soap or any of our products.

Please take the following three steps to help us resolve this problem:

1. Record the shipment
2. Send me two or three samples of the leaking products
3. Destroy the remainder of the damaged bottles

Once we have determined the reason for the damage, I will contact you directly to discuss replacement of the products or a credit to your account.

Sincerely,

<e-mail signature, including name, title, company and contact information>